Sicario

Succubus

Sicario and Succubus Two Book Set
Copyright ©2023 Regis P Sheehan

ISBN 978-1506-900-37-7 PBK

August 2023

Published and Distributed by
First Edition Design Publishing, Inc.
P.O. Box 17646, Sarasota, FL 34276-3217
www.firsteditiondesignpublishing.com

"Of blood and fire..."

Sicario

Regis P. Sheehan

SICARIO

A novella by
REGIS P. SHEEHAN

This is a work of fiction in its entirety.

The opinions and characterizations in this book are those of the author, and do not necessarily represent official positions of the United States Government.

Dedicated to the memory of Colombia's faceless judges

"All empires are created of blood and fire."

~Pablo Emilio Escobar-Gaviria

= ONE: SNAJPER =

Mostar, Bosnia
May 1992

The mortar round popped out of its steel tube with a dull *plonk* and soared up into the chilly Spring air.

A few long seconds the projectile reached the apex of its trajectory. Its initial energy expended, the round nosed over and silently plummeted back toward earth. Upon impact the shell exploded with a bright flash and a shroud of dirty gray smoke. The blast threw metal shards and rocky debris out in all directions.

Zlatko Piric sheltered under the rubble of a brick wall as he waited for all of the flying material to settle down. When he was satisfied that it had done so, he continued to scrabble forward slowly along the wall on his hands and knees.

A rattle of gunfire sounded in the distance. Heedless of the danger, Zlatko carefully pushed forward on his own for another half block. His progress was slow and painful but caution and survival truly were handmaidens in this environment.

Finally he came to a rise overlooking the narrow Neretva River that bisected the city of Mostar. As he burrowed into his new position, he realized that he was looking down at the *Stari Most*, a national treasure.

The *Stari Most*, or Old Bridge, was an arched stone pedestrian structure that dated back many centuries to the year 1566. In happier days it had been a magnet for foreign tourists. Now it was merely a checkpoint – one of many – in a fiercely contested urban battlefield.

Zlatko had been in the Mostar area for more than a month now as part of the BiH 4th Corps. As a member of the *Armija BiH*, or the Army of Bosnia-Herzegovina, he was immersed in an alphabet soup of warring factions that had been spawned by the break-up of the Yugoslav nation state, which had begun in the previous year.

The politics of the struggle – which literally often did pit neighbor against neighbor, and former schoolmate against former schoolmate - no longer interested him so much. In any event, he was from the Sarajevo area. He knew not a soul from Mostar.

The evening was approaching, but there was still enough ambient light for him to see a handful of his enemies on the other side of the bridge. They were clearly Bosnian Serbs who retained the name of the JNA, or Yugoslav National Army, for their formations.

For the moment at least, the *Armija* was allied with the Croatian HVO against the Serb forces, although that condition would also change in the not too distant future.

A Bosniak, Zlatko was - like most of his fellow BiH soldiers – at least a nominal Muslim. Having grown up under the somewhat benevolent style of Communism fostered by Josip Broz Tito, for him being a Muslim was more of an ethnic than a religious identity. Such a lack of religious fervor was not unusual for members of his generation.

As he maintained watch on the Serbs at the other end of the *Stari Most*, Zlatko slowly unzipped a long carry bag and withdrew a bolt-action rifle. The weapon was a Zastava M48 rifle. It was a Yugoslav copy of the German Mauser. With its scarred wooden stock, it was his prized possession. Fixed atop the receiver of the gun was a Zrak ON-76 telescopic sight.

Somewhat ironically, it was Serbian manufactured.

As a boy at primary school, Zlatko had been a member of the Union of Pioneers. This was not unusual, as participation in the UP was mandatory at the time.

His Pioneer membership also facilitated his place on his school's shooting team. He soon found that the marksmanship events, at which he excelled, were more enjoyable than the political meetings, which he dreaded.

2

When he was scooped up into the *Armija* upon the outbreak of the war, his precision shooting background quickly became evident to his superiors. Almost immediately they selected him to be a *snajper* – a sniper - so as not to waste his talents with the other common soldiers on the line. There he excelled.

The Serbs were huddled behind a collection of overturned cars on the far side of the Neretva. Although this provided them with a degree of both cover and concealment, the men were a bit too nonchalant, given their lethal surroundings.

Watching intently, he could see that one of the JNA soldiers was deferring to a tall, slender figure. The latter was an officer perhaps? That was most likely the case, he decided.

Zlatko slipped the bolt of the M48 to the rear and locked it open. Next he took a five-shot stripper clip from a pouch and inserted the five 8mm bullets, each stacked one atop the other along the clip, into the magazine of the weapon. Lastly, he closed the bolt, chambering one of the rounds, and sighted in on his targets through the Zrak scope.

Although he was right eye dominant, Zlatko kept both eyes open, as he had long ago been taught to do. Carefully, he focused on the head of the probable officer. Thankfully the man was fairly stationary.

Zlatko relaxed. He allowed his breath to leak out. And then he eased the trigger back, firing the weapon.

His aim was accurate. The presumed officer abruptly careened backward and dropped out of sight as the report of the shot echoed off of the surrounding masonry.

Zlatko quickly worked the bolt. He moved his point of aim ever so slightly to the left and fired again. A second man fell.

Zlatko placed a third shot. While the third man toppled to the ground as well, he could see that the Serb was still moving, anxiously scuttling into better cover underneath one of the wrecked vehicles.

There was no return fire, as the stunned remaining Serbs were more intent on keeping their heads down than in shooting back at an unseen foe.

Zlatko slipped the rifle back into its bag, zipped it tight, and started crawling back out of his hide.

That was enough for today.

= TWO: LA CATEDRAL =

Medellin, Colombia
July 1992

It was an enterprise that essentially began with one of the more banal of crimes - a pedestrian kidnapping.

By the early 1980's an amalgamation of cocaine traffickers centered in the Antioquia department of northeastern Colombia had been enjoying an amazing degree of success - and unbelievable wealth - as a result of their illegal endeavors. At that time, profits of nearly a million U.S. dollars per day were achievable. Judged by future gains still to be realized, these sums would later appear to be puny.

Their unprecedented level of financial success attracted the attention not only of law enforcement officials, but of other political factions as well.

On November 12, 1981, leftist guerrillas of the M-19 movement acted. Performing the unthinkable, they kidnapped a twenty-six year old woman named Marta Nieves-Ochoa from the campus of the University of Antioquia. Marta was the daughter of Fabio Ochoa and the sister of Jorge – both significant players in the drug mafia. In a dangerous display of impudence, the M-19 was demanding more than the equivalent of twelve million U.S. dollars for her release.

Aside from the direct threat to the Ochoa family, the emerging drug lords immediately recognized a more pervasive threat to themselves on a distinctly personal basis. If a member of the well-positioned Ochoas could be held for ransom, then did not each of their families represent a lucrative target for more of the same?

If so, where would it stop?

They decided, forcefully, that it would stop right there and then.

A month after Marta's abduction more than two hundred of the traffickers met at a restaurant outside of the city of Medellin. During the course of that assembly they agreed to pool their financial and direct action resources to combat the incipient problem. Concurrently, they planned to teach the M-19 and their pretenders an unforgettable lesson in Machiavellian politics, Colombian style.

The traffickers formed an ad hoc organization, to which they gave the fairly unambiguous name of *Muerte a los Secuestradores* – or Death to Kidnappers – MAS.

MAS had the advantage of enormous financial resources and extensive human capital in the form of cadres of experienced killers. Both of these were thrown into the battle against the M-19 with ruthless abandon.

Over the next six weeks MAS actively waged unrestrained war, killing M-19 guerrillas, as well as kidnapping members of their families and holding them hostage. The violence extended from Colombia to Miami and New York. Bona fide members of the M-19 were not alone in the unwanted spotlight. Competing traffickers, law enforcement officers, judges and journalists found themselves targeted by the unforgiving attention of MAS as well.

By mid-February of 1982 the M-19 relented under the pressure. Marta was released to her family unharmed. MAS had won the conflict.

As an outgrowth of their success, several of the more prominent traffickers decided that they might be able to continue to combine their expertise in order to bring their illicit product to market in a more orderly, efficient and effective manner. They would form an alliance – a Cartel if you will.

The grouping solidified the structure that was already known to many as the Medellin Cartel. Pablo Emilio Escobar-Gaviria, a one time petty thief, served as its chief executive officer.

Escobar's star was on the rise. Later that same year *Don Pablo*, as the recipients of his largesse in the Medellin slums knew him, was elected to a seat in the Colombian Congress. His organization continued to dominate the coke trade. It effectively controlled the conversion and processing of the *la cocaina*, as well as its packaging, and transportation into the United States for distribution.

By 1989 Forbes had listed Escobar as the seventh richest man in the world. His greatest fear however, was not from competitors, such as the Rodriguez-Orejuela bothers of the Cali Cartel. No, the greatest threat came from the United States judiciary system, specifically the threat of extradition to an American prison.

Escobar had more than good reason to worry. In 1987 one of his close associates, Carlos Lehder-Rivas, had been arrested and sent to Jacksonville, Florida for a federal trial. The proceedings ended with a sentence of life in prison for the brazen trafficker.

That this was a central concern to Escobar was evident by the words from his own mouth. More that once he had remarked to loyal hangers-on that, given the choice, he would much prefer to occupy a grave in Colombia rather than a prison cell in the United States.

Following a variety of coercive measures applied by the Cartel however, the Colombian government decided in July of 1991 to end the practice of extradition of Colombian nationals to America. Henceforth, justice would be restricted to the borders of Colombia itself – where the influence of the Cartels could make itself felt.

Freed of the possibility of an unwanted trip to the U.S., yet under the ever-present threat of assassination from his domestic enemies, Escobar devised an ingenious personal security strategy. In the summer of 1991, he surrendered himself to Colombian authorities and submitted to a period of imprisonment.

There was a catch however. Escobar consented only to be sent to a prison that he himself designed, and one that was operated by the staff that he himself selected.

Called the Envigado, or more colloquially, *La Catedral,* the facility was more of a resort than a prison. It boasted such non-traditional amenities as a bar, a gym, a disco, a soccer field, a lavish master bedroom, color television, Jacuzzis, and of course frequent alcohol and drug-fueled co-ed parties.

It was from *La Catedral* that Escobar continued to run his drug smuggling empire and - protected by his own handpicked men – often meted out Cartel justice to rivals and those of his own circle whom he suspected of disaffection. Envigado justice often resulted in torture and death for selected opponents.

Such a solution did not sit well with the authorities in the United States. Through its ambassador in Bogota, Washington made its displeasure loudly and frequently known.

Finally embarrassed by the situation of its own devising, the Colombian government agreed to transfer Escobar to a real prison; one operated by the military.

Escobar would have none of it. On July 22d, 1992 Escobar and a number of his henchmen simply walked out of Envigado - which was surrounded by Colombian forces at the time – and went into hiding.

Among those who went with him that night was a trusted henchman, bodyguard and killer named Alvaro de Jesus-Agudelo, who was known to the group simply as *El Limon.*

For Washington, it was the last of very many straws.

= THREE: ZLATKO =

Vicinity of Gornji Vakuf, Bosnia
August 1992

The humidity clung heavily to the trees that day, even at that high elevation. Zlatko Piric and four other members of the *BiH Armija* patrol were operating in a mountainous region about a hundred kilometers west of the capital of Sarajevo.

Maintaining good tactical awareness, the patrol had been moving along in a single file through the trees. They were especially careful to remain north of the single lane dirt roadway off to their right. They were scouting for contact with a contingent of HVO Croats who were also reported to be in the area.

The BiH patrol had been about to stop for a lunch break when they heard a sharp and shattering blast of automatic weapons in the near distance ahead of their position. The shooting was immediately followed by the discordant sounds of a vehicle leaving the roadway and crashing into the trees. The vehicle apparently came to rest as the sonorous drone of a horn began to echo across the slope.

Moving forward, the patrol quickly encountered a handful of men in the mottled green camouflage patterned uniforms of the HVO. A brief exchange of gunfire took the Croats by surprise and persuaded them to pull back higher into the slope of the mountain, abandoning their ambush position.

As his partners provided cover, Zlatko moved down and into the crash site to investigate.

Fifty meters down the hillside, Zlatko found an up-ended Toyota Land Cruiser settled against a broken tree. Moving closer, he saw that the driver was still inertly jammed behind the steering wheel. From the positioning of the body, it was apparent that the driver had suffered from a broken neck.

Off to the right was another man. He was lying a short distance away from the passenger's side of the Land Cruiser, his face smeared with blood. This second man was still quite alive. Furiously alive, in fact.

Both of the men were dressed in casual civilian clothing and appeared to be unarmed.

As the survivor saw Zlatko's approach, he held up a cautioning arm. "*Ja sam Amerikanac*," he called in heavily accented Serbo-Croatian. I'm an American.

"*Ja sam iz Americke Ambassade*," he quickly added. I'm from the American Embassy.

Except, Zlatko knew, there was no American Embassy. Not in Bosnia.

On the other hand, like most Bosniaks, he was highly aware of the fact that the U.S. Government had just formally recognized Bosnia as an independent country in April. Further, Washington had established diplomatic relations with the Bosnian government, just that month. The embassy to Bosnia however was physically located in Vienna, Austria – not in Sarajevo.

Zlatko moved forward, keeping the muzzle of his weapon aimed at the figure on the ground. "*Americki?*" he asked uncertainly.

"*Da*," the man replied painfully. "*Da. Da. Americki!*"

"I speak English," Zlatko told him. "Some."

The injured man propped himself up on one elbow and extracted an I.D. card from his wallet. "My name's Ostermann," he said. "I think my leg's broken."

Zlatko squinted at the laminated green and white card. "*Vojnik?*" he asked tentatively. "You are... soldier?"

"*Vojnik, da*," the other rasped. "I'm a U.S. Army officer - a major. I'm with the Defense Attaché Office at the American Embassy in Vienna."

"Yes. And you are now here why?"

"*Istrazivanje*," Ostermann said, gritting his teeth in pain. "Survey... I guess you could call it a survey."

"And this one?" Zlatko motioned to the dead man who was still trapped in the Toyota.

"Sergeant First Class Grendahl. Also from the embassy... How is he?"

"Dead," Zlatko said flatly. "Looks like... Sorry."

Ostermann grimaced as he shook his head in silent reply.

Zlatko was unaware of any American military presence in the country. Nevertheless, he quickly decided, any on the ground representation of NATO was all to the good.

He quickly organized the returning members of his patrol to construct a makeshift litter. With that, they clumsily transported Ostermann back up to the dirt roadway. Gaining better footing on the ground, they then moved the American officer rearward toward their unit's encampment.

Zlatko's commander, a former attorney in Tuzla, had a shrewd eye for public relations. After seeing to Ostermann's medical care for several days, he authorized Zlatko to escort the injured military intelligence officer back to an UNPROFOR base. There the United Nations authorities arranged for the major to be evacuated to a U.S. air base in Italy for further medical attention.

***

Highly impressed with Zlatko's resourcefulness and command of English - and more than grateful for his rescue - Major Ostermann did not forget Zlatko. During his period of recuperation, he made a formal referral to the attaché section at the Defense Intelligence Agency. In it he strongly recommended that they consider recruiting the Bosniak combatant as a confidential asset for the U.S. Government.

While the suggestion did not excite the interest of the decision making chain at DIA, it did catch the attention of another covert office in the Washington suburbs.

= FOUR: JALISCO =

Guadalajara, Mexico
Early September 1992

The two men met at a dusty roadside stand near the Laguna de Chapala, some twenty-five miles south of the city. Sunlight gleamed off of the water's surface as they clinked a pair of frosted bottles of Bohemia beer together and up-ended them for a swig.

The purpose of the semi-clandestine meeting was to assess the results of the massive on-going sweep.

The lightly complected black man, Jesus Arnold by name, was a DEA agent attached to the consulate in Guadalajara. He savored a rinse of cold beer running down his gullet and then plopped the bottle back onto the wooden surface of the outdoor table. "And you are who again?"

"Nestor Vasalikis," Chalice lied easily, opening a set of leather encased credentials. "ONI."

Another lie.

Arnold squinted at the expressionless photo in the creds. Unusual name. But the man with the closely cropped gunmetal gray hair sitting across from him did have a certain Mediterranean look to him. He was but one of a number of the sudden influx of arrivals from Washington.

Not that Arnold could be faulted. The cable that he had previously received from DEA Headquarters advised him that a certain Vasalikis of ONI would be turning up to help monitor the search efforts.

The presence of Naval Intelligence was a bit odd, but not all that far out of the ballpark. The fact was that the U.S. Government viewed the Mexican Navy as being a considerably more reliable institution than either the Police or the Army. It wouldn't be the first strange development to crop up in the midst of a narco investigation.

There had been some recent hot intel – part American, part Mexican, part Interpol - to the effect that the fugitive Pablo Escobar had crossed into Mexico following his escape from Envigado. Specifically, he was said to be in the west central *estado* of Jalisco.

Escobar immediately went into hiding, so the story went, in one of the more upscale sectors of Guadalajara.

A massive manhunt quickly ensued, comprised of officers of the Mexican federal Police, Jalisco State Judicial Police, the military, and others. For several days scores of private residences and high-end hotels were carefully searched for Escobar.

But.

"Nothing," Chalice/Vasalikis confirmed. "They're coming up empty ... Negative on the locals' searches. Technical takes on our side likewise are all coming up zero. Looks like we have some bad info."

"Nothing coming in from any of our informants either," Arnold replied with a faint drawl. "We ain't got shit. So to speak."

Chalice took another swop of beer. "I'm sure Escobar is somewhere," he said. "But he isn't here. Not in Guadalajara."

"Lot'a folks in Washington going to be sorry to hear this," Arnold mused.

Chalice was sure that the DEA agent was correct. Washington was eagerly hopeful for a quick snatch following Escobar's *escape* from his designer prison. The unspoken game plan called for the Cartel leader to be grabbed, boxed up and then shipped directly north. To be delivered into the waiting arms of the United States Government.

Not going to happen though.

"Asshole's a ghost," Arnold mused, turning his attention to the lake. "Stone ghost."

"But we'll get him," Chalice said.

"Yeah we will", the DEA agent confirmed. "Surely we will."

= FIVE: MYRIAM =

Medellin, Colombia
September 18, 1992

In 1986 Guillermo Cano-Isaza, the long-time editor and publisher of the Bogotá daily newspaper *El Espectador*, won Colombia's National Journalism Award. His journalistic colleagues throughout the world agreed that the award was supremely well merited.

Throughout the remainder of the year Cano intensified his public criticism of the undue influence that drug mafia traffickers wielded in the political life of the nation. Among his strongly held positions was his support for the their extradition to the United States for criminal prosecution and long term incarceration.

His constant drumbeat against the influence of the Cartels did not go unnoticed.

A week before Christmas of 1986, Cano exited the *Espectador* building and climbed into his car. As he did so, a motorcycle bearing two men roared up next to his vehicle and skidded to a halt.

The man on the back of the bike hopped off and immediately began firing into Cano's vehicle with a submachine gun, in full view of horrified passers-by.

Leaving Cano's bleeding body slumped behind the wheel of his car, the shooter jumped back onto the rear of the motorcycle and disappeared into the early evening Bogota traffic.

It did not take long for the news of Cano's murder to make it back to Medellin. When it did arrive, Escobar and his close associates reportedly threw a small but festive party to celebrate the happy event.

***

Six years later, on the morning of September 18, 1992, a thirty-eight year old Colombian judge named Myriam Rocio-Velez exited her residence in the southern suburbs of Medellin.

As is the case with many countries in South America, Colombia has a Napoleonic system of justice. Among other things, this involves judges who function as both investigators and prosecutors. One of the more significant matters that Rocio was investigating was the murder of Guillermo Cano-Isaza. More particularly, she was looking into the pivotal role that had been played in the crime by Pablo Escobar.

In order to safeguard Rocio and her compatriots, she was part of group that had been designated as the "faceless judges" in order to provide them with a degree of anonymity. To enhance her security, the Colombian Government also supplied her with a small protective detail from the PNC, or the National Police. The goal was to free such judges from public pressure and threats of violence, enabling them to carry out their duties with greater freedom of action.

That was the theory, in any event.

Soon after her vehicle started off in traffic that morning, she and her police escorts were cut off by a pursuing white sedan. Four gunmen, known in the Colombian killing trade as *sicarios*, piled out of the sedan and started shooting.

After a brief but violent gunfight Myriam Rocio-Velez, along with three of her police bodyguards, lay dead in the street. The four *sicarios* threw themselves back into their vehicle and made good their escape.

Shortly thereafter the President of Colombia, Cesar Gaviria-Trujillo, issued the following statement:

> *"Colombia is the victim of the uncontrollable appetite for drugs affecting the world. The bullets that killed the brave judge Myriam Rocio-Velez just*

three days ago were bought with money paid for by consumers of cocaine."

At the time of her death, Rocio-Velez was just one of eighty-two Colombian judges who had been murdered in the past thirteen years.

= SIX: CAZADOR =

Out of Dulles
Early April 1993

The Delta flight was about ten minutes out of IAD – Dulles International – when it cut through the cloudy sky and pulled up into the sunshine. As the Boeing's engines throttled back, and the plane settled into a straight and level altitude, a voice echoed from the overhead speakers.

"This is the First Officer speaking. Like to welcome y'all aboard today," he said in a chatty tone with a slightly southern accent. "Sorry for the choppy weather coming out Dulles, but it was either a little weather or a late wheels up. And we know you folks want to get to where you're going on time today."

After a pause, the voice continued its practiced banter. "Ah, Air Traffic Control is promising us a smooth ride all the way down to Miami, so the worst of it should be behind us... We're turning off the seatbelt sign now," a bell chimed throughout the cabin, "and we invite you to sit back and enjoy the ride with your seatbelts loosely fastened if you're not moving around the cabin...

"Flight time to Miami is, ah... two hours and fifteen minutes. Let us know if we can do anything for you. Enjoy the flight and thanks for choosing Delta."

The man in 10C allowed himself a thin smile as he adjusted the eyeglasses perched on the bridge of his nose. Glancing out of the window, he cracked opened his paperback copy of John LeCarre's *The Russia House*.

The worst of it should be behind us, he reflected disdainfully. *Buddy, you just don't know.*

He was nearly three chapters into the spy novel when the drink cart came clattering down the narrow aisle. "Something to drink sir?" the middle-aged flight attendant asked over the high-pitched whine of the engines.

"I'd like to get a double Scotch, just one chunk of ice. If I can," 10C said, slipping a bookmark between the pages of his book.

"You certainly may," the attendant agreed, peering into a metal drawer full of tiny liquor bottles. "Glenlivet okay?

"Just fine, thanks."

The attendant smilingly passed the drink, collected the payment, and continued on her way down the aisle.

10C dumped both bottles into his plastic cup, and swirled it over the broken sliver of ice. He took a sip and returned his attention to the paperback novel in front of him.

He was very aware of the fact that it had been more than eight months since Pablo Escobar and his associates walked out of his Envigado prison unopposed. After his departure, the U.S. Government had quickly shifted into high gear.

Within a day of Escobar's *escape*, a senior level strategy session of the Deputies' Committee had been convened in the surprisingly cramped Situation Room of the White House.

The modest dimensions of the fabled *Sit Room* always surprised newcomers. Such was the case of the junior NSC staffers. Despite momentarily star struck reactions, the gravity of the moment quickly brought them back to earth as they focused on their note-taking responsibilities.

After reviewing a number of possible options, the D-Committee members unanimously agreed that the most appropriate response would be to significantly ratchet up the level of U.S. military assistance provided to the Colombian authorities. Much of this assistance would be funneled to the Colombian National Police.

The Deputies also agreed to recommend to their Principals a further set of covert action options. Some of these would most certainly not be shared with the Colombian authorities.

Shortly after the meeting adjourned an Assistant Secretary of State placed a telephone call to the U.S. Ambassador to Colombia. As it happened, the Ambo was in town for consultations and was staying at the home of friends in the nearby Maryland suburb of Chevy Chase.

In guarded terms, the caller advised the Ambassador of the day's events and recommended that he return to post at the earliest possible opportunity. Immediately, if at all possible.

At the same time, a senior member of the National Security Council staff placed a secure call to the Northern Virginia offices of something called "JICSA". The call placed them officially on alert status as well.

JICSA – the somewhat inelegantly named *Joint Inter-Departmental Committee on Special Activities* – was more commonly known to government insiders simply as the Org. Comprised of a small cadre of professional staff and a wider selection of skilled contractors, the Org was itself a covert special activity whose exact structure constantly morphed, depending upon the missions at hand.

JICSA had a physical presence housed in a gathering of low, sand-colored buildings located off of Route 123 in the Tysons/McLean area, just inside the Beltway. It operated under the cover of a private research group – one that actually made a profit. The cover name was *Global Threat Analysis.*

The JICSA director had been waging a non-stop bureaucratic struggle to get the Org into the hunt for Escobar long before the date of the D-Committee meeting. Short of sending a case officer to Guadalajara for situational awareness purposes however, JICSA had been confined to an analytical standby role.

Now, close to a year after Escobar's disappearance, the NSC gave in to the persistence of the Director. JICSA was authorized to go operational.

His Org colleagues knew the man in seat 10C simply as Aachen. He was a pale skinned figure with thinning blond hair, sporting a bushy mustache. Both were now running to gray. Thanks to his Bavarian roots and his Guatemalan wife, he was competent with both German and Spanish.

A former special agent/criminal investigator with the Air Force Office of Special Investigations, Aachen was a senior Org case officer. The JICSA interim director had designated him as the senior controller for Org assets on the ground in Colombia. The case, it was decreed, would be known as Operation ARDENT CAZADOR.

Although Aachen had driven past the JICSA headquarters many times, he had never been inside the building. It was unlikely that he ever would be.

For Aachen, this was to be the first of many trips into Colombia in support of the search for Escobar. Somewhat incongruously, at least initially to him, Aachen's cover would be that of a flower broker. In fact he had spent a few days in preparation for the assignment learning enough to be somewhat conversant with the mechanics of the floral business.

As he discovered, Colombia was a major source of flowers for the United States. Given its fairly ideal soil and growing climate – as well as its three-hour flight time from Miami – it was well positioned to be a major supplier of floral products for the eastern half of the U.S. In fact, Colombia was the second largest supplier of cut flowers to America – behind the Netherlands.

To assist him in his cover identity, associates of the Org had arranged for Aachen to serve as a legitimate representative of a modest floral distributorship in the northeast. His trips to Colombia would therefore also serve to develop legitimate contracts for distributors at home.

A prime source of fresh flowers for the American floriculture sector was the Colombian province of Antioquia – and the city of Medellin.

= SEVEN: SHOOT HOUSE =

"Wally World", North Carolina
May 1993

The five-man entry team was stacked on the door. All five soldiers were supremely confident of their tactical abilities, yet all were ever so slightly feeling the tension of wanting to do a superior job. *Needing* to do a superior job.

The air conditioning system had been purposely shut down some time ago. The air in the darkened hallway was therefore now thick with humidity and dank with the acrid smell of freshly cut plywood.

Each man wore an olive green flight suit and a scuffed pair of blackened leather boots. They were equipped with double hearing protection – consisting of soft foam earplugs clamped under a pair of plastic and rubber earmuffs. They observed the world through a pair of tightly fitting shooting goggles.

In their gloved hands, each man carried the relatively new M4 carbine, which was basically a more compact version of the venerable Colt M16 family of weapons. They were intensely aware of the fact that their M4's were loaded with live 5.56mm ammunition. Each M4 had a lethal round in the chamber, safeties off, ready to fire.

Strapped against each of their legs, sitting at mid-thigh in rugged nylon drop holsters, was a similarly loaded 9mm Sig-Sauer P226 semi-automatic pistol.

There was no daylight between the five men. Indeed, all were in close physical contact. Their bodies were jammed together chest to back as a single, briefly intimate organism.

The team leader was the Number Three Man, located in the center of the stack. He knew – or rather felt - that they were ready to go, but movement wasn't his call just now.

That call actually belonged to the Number Five Man, at the tail end of the stack.

Tail End Charlie, a.k.a. Number Five, glanced across the stack and saw that they were properly arrayed and ready to move. Happy with that, he settled into his assault position and forcefully squeezed the shoulder of the man in front of him with his left hand, indicating that he was ready to move.

Number Four repeated the movement, sending the squeeze quickly up the line.

When Number One received the squeeze on his shoulder, he placed his left hand on the doorknob and gently flexed his torso on his knees once, twice and three times.

On the third bounce he flung open the door and quickly stepped into the room. Immediately seeing a target to his front, he engaged it with two quick rounds from his M4 and continued moving to his right to cover his area of responsibility.

Number Two at once flowed in behind him, moving oppositely to the left and catching sight of a target in the far corner of the room. *BOOM-BOOM.*

Numbers Three, Four and Five flowed in as well, placing shots into the other targets that had been situated behind the hostages in the room.

BOOM-BOOM.

BOOM-BOOM.

BOOM-BOOM.

"Clear right!" Number One shouted, holding his corner and continuing to scan the room through the front sights of his M4.

Burnt gunpowder wafted sourly though the air in the tight confines of the room.

"Clear left!" Number Two called from the opposite corner.

"All clear!" Number Three sounded.

A horn buzzed from a speaker over their heads. "End-Ex. End-Ex," the electronic voice droned. "Make your weapons safe!"

All five men thumbed the selector switches of their weapons onto the safe setting. Next they pulled the depleted mags out of the magazine wells, and each ejected a live round from the chamber of their weapons. As they did so, a Safety NCO entered the room and physically verified the empty M4 chambers one by one.

While the Safety NCO was doing this, another man strode in to eyeball the accuracy of the shot placement in the three painted styrofoam targets.

"Good shooting," the latter proclaimed flatly, not at all surprised by his findings. "Ten good hits. No misses. No friendly casualties."

Number Three, the team leader was an E-8, or a Delta master sergeant. He pulled the goggles off of his face and mopped the perspiration away with the sleeve of his flight suit. He gave the Training NCO a perfunctory nod of acknowledgement. Expected performance. No more, no less.

"Feeling game Toby?" came a voice to his rear.

Toby turned to see a familiar face – a chief warrant officer from the Operations and Intelligence section.

"You know it Chief," he said absently. "What's up?"

"Alpha Squadron is on deck starting next week," the square jawed CWO announced, somewhat unnecessarily.

"Yep," Toby agreed. "And?"

"Ever thought about a trip to Colombia?" the CWO asked, grinning slightly.

"All right guys," the electronic voice interrupted, crackling from the speaker overhead. "Lets gaggle up on room six and do it again."

Toby nodded to the camera in the ceiling. He gave it a thumb's up and motioned for his men to follow him back out into the hallway.

Colombia, he reflected. Sweet.

= EIGHT: BLACK TEAM–GREEN TEAM =

Bogota, Colombia
May 1993

It was just past midnight when a taxi rolled to a stop in front of a garishly lit downtown Bogota establishment. Although it had the air of a nightclub, the place was known to anyone who cared to know to be a brothel with a lengthy and popular history.

It was called *Carlita Bonita's.*

The taxi's sole passenger was clearly a middle aged Gringo who sported close cropped graying hair and an olive complexion. He paid his fare, tipped the driver, and climbed out of the vehicle.

The air was still fresh and damp with the recent sprinkling of Andean rain. The street was fully alive with swarms of people – mostly men – sauntering along the sidewalks.

Peering about somewhat self-consciously, the passenger pushed through the front door of *Carlita Bonita's* and wandered into the so-called clubroom.

The smoky bar was fairly well crowded with customers and workers alike, the majority of whom appeared to be locals. Some sort of music – merengue, he assumed – blared in the background as a series of colored lights flashed overhead. The effect was a bit more jarring to the senses than erotic, he decided.

Ironically, there was no "Carlita" connected with the establishment. The owner was actually diminutive fellow who went by the street name of Chicoco. Chicoco was paid to be a good friend of the United States, as the occasion arose. This was just such an occasion.

The visitor weaved through a throng of jostling bodies, finally wedging into a place at the edge of the small bar. He caught the attention of the bartender after a few moments of waiting.

"*Si jefe?*"

"I'm looking for a girl," the Gringo said, a bit more loudly than he would have preferred.

"Then you have come to the right place *jefe*," the bartender replied with a weary smile.

"Yeah. A girl named Paloma."

"Paloma?" the bartender repeated. He gestured toward a woman with brightly dyed red hair who was sitting a few stools away. Tapping loudly on the bar, he nodded toward the Gringo. "*El te quiere*," he said, matter of factly, then turned back to his business.

The redhead, a thin thirty-ish woman wearing a sequined bra and a tight leather miniskirt, immediately brightened up and moved over next to the newcomer.

"*Ay chico ... Hablas Espanol?*" she asked with a practiced smile.

"Not really, no."

"No? Okay. It's okay. I am Paloma," she said, quickly getting to the point. "You want me?"

"Yes, I do. Very much," the man admitted. "A friend recommended you to me."

"Oh yes?"

"Yes. A friend named Boris. From Kiev."

"Ah," she said, slowing the pace of the approach as she turned the data over in her mind. "Okay. Then buy me a drink."

The man followed her to a small circular table by the far wall. As they settled into the rickety wooden chairs, the waiter began to fill a pair of oversized shot glasses with pours of *aguardiente*, the popular anise flavored Colombian liquor.

"How do you know this *Boris*?" Paloma asked, accenting the second syllable of the name.

Her new client smiled as a waitress delivered the two shots of clear fluid to the table. "Boris sees you almost every weekend," he said. "On Sundays ... He says that you are *muy fantastico.*"

Paloma silently indicated her recognition and tossed back the glass of *aguardiente* in a single gulp. Rising, she caught hold of the Gringo's hand. "Come to the back with me," she said.

She led her client back through the crowded dance floor and into a hallway that sported a series of scarred wooden doors. She pushed open one of the doors at the end of the hall and unceremoniously stepped into the tiny room.

Sitting in a chair next to the single, rumpled bed was a burly Caucasian man with long yellow hair and a neatly trimmed beard. He looked up expectantly from the bottle of *Aguila* beer that he was nursing. A couple of empties were scattered on a side table.

"Alright," the Gringo said, locking eyes with the other man.

Paloma accepted a handful of folded peso notes from her client and left the room without a further word.

The Gringo paused for a few seconds as Paloma's footsteps retreated down the hallway.

After another long moment, he pulled a brass MACV-SOG challenge coin from his pocket. On the front of the coin was the somewhat cartoonish depiction of a human skull wearing a jaunty military beret. On the reverse side was the arrow-shaped blue shoulder patch of the U.S. Army Special Forces.

With a flip of his thumb, he tossed the coin across the room and onto the bed next to the blond man.

The latter picked up the coin and examined it carefully, both front and back. It represented the Military Assistance Command Vietnam – Studies and Observations Group. Back in the day, MACV-SOG had been a highly classified unit that conducted sensitive reconnaissance and recovery missions into denied areas during the war in Southeast Asia. It had a high rate of success – as well as a high rate of casualties among its operators.

"You must be Chalice," the blond man said at long last.

"And you're Medved." The Gringo recognized his asset from the briefing photos he had seen at a safe house in the Fort Lauderdale area the previous week.

"Um-humm. You can just call me Bear though," the other said. "Easier that way. The *chica* there called me *El Oso.*"

"I guess she would," Chalice agreed, glancing back at the closed door. "When did you get in?"

"Couple of days ago," Bear said. "Okay to talk here?"

"Good enough," Chalice said. "You were SOG?"

"Yep," Bear said. "A tour or two. Or three. Ran missions across the fence in Laos ... But I guess you already know that though..." He glanced up from the coin in his hand. "What's *your* background?"

"Mine?" Chalice reflected, easing himself into the other remaining chair in the room. "Don't have one."

Bear pursed his lips. "Yeah, got it. A ghost. Living in the moment and all that. Right?"

"Pretty much – yes."

In truth, Chalice was a former Green Beret combat veteran himself. However, after having suffered a back injury in a night training jump, he left SF to become a HUMINT agent handler within the ranks of Military Intelligence. After twenty plus years of service, he retired from the Army and was soon thereafter recruited to be a case officer with JICSA - the Org.

In addition to being a MACV-SOG veteran in a previous life Medved – or Bear - had been a locally renowned deep cover narc with the Allegheny County Police Department in Pittsburgh. In fact, he had been so successful that more than one of his superiors had expressed doubts as to whether he could ever return to the fold as a *normal* police officer. They were aptly correct in that observation.

Bear had been part of a turbulent undercover investigation while on loan from the ACPD to the DEA in Haiti. Unbeknownst to the DEA however, the Org clandestinely intruded itself into the case, focusing on the terrorist aspects at hand. At the conclusion of the investigation, Bear parted ways with both the ACPD and his family, becoming a full-time Org contract asset.

"So what are we doing here?" Bear asked.

"What was your brief?"

Bear took another swop of beer and wiped his lips. "Come here. Meet you. Be available to do the necessary."

"So far so good then," Chalice replied. "You know what's going on in-country now. We are here to support the main op... The Org has at least two cells in country. That I know of. A Black Team and a Green Team."

"Right. Black and Green," Bear said. "I'm with you so far. And?"

"You and I – well, we're the Green Team," Chalice continued in a soft tone of voice. "We are here to conduct liaison with U.S. military elements, of which there are several. And to support the main push by the locals."

Bear nodded. "And this Black Team?"

Chalice shook his head. "Unknown. Complete OpSec on this one. We don't know who is on the Black Team and we never will. We're to have no contact with them whatsoever."

Bear rolled the Aguila bottle between his large hands. "So how do we coordinate with them?"

"There's a senior Org controller down here as well. All info will channel through him."

Bear took a moment to digest that. "Then I'm assuming that there's to be no contact with the Embassy on this?"

"Not from us. Why?"

"I just guess that the Embassy down here is packed full with DEA," Bear said. "At the moment, I don't see any need to interact with them."

"No issue there," Chalice said.

Bear tipped the bottle upward to catch the last swallow. "Great," he said. "Let's kick it then."

= NINE: TARGETING =

Fort Lauderdale, Florida
May 1993

In more normal times, Aachen would have been conducting his briefing at the secure facilities offered by Homestead Air Force Base, located south of Miami and north of the Keys. These were not normal times however.

Thanks to Hurricane Andrew, having flattened Homestead that past August, those facilities were no longer available. For this particular case, the Org was making do with an impromptu safe house in central Fort Lauderdale. It was an area of Broward County that had been largely spared the violence of the hurricane.

The three men in the leased apartment were sitting at a table in the kitchen area. Rich smells of dark, percolating coffee wafted across the room as the pot burbled on the counter top. All three were studying copies of the ARDENT CAZADOR case file that lay on the table in front of them.

Seeing that the others had finished their review, Aachen reached back into a ballistic nylon courier bag and withdrew a packet of surveillance photographs. The first print was an 8x10 black and white close-up shot. It was clearly an intensified long distance shot of a female subject.

The subject of the shot was an alluring young Hispanic woman. She had pale, delicate features that were framed by long glossy black hair. Apparently having been caught sharing in a moment of laughter with friends, her head was tilted back in reaction to what someone was saying.

Rogelio Lopez took the photo in his hands, openly admiring the image of the young woman. "*O-kay*," he said. "What's this? Someone from Hollywood?"

"No, not from Hollywood," Aachen murmured. "Manati. It's a little 'ville just south of Barranquilla. Ever heard of it?"

"Never," Lopez admitted. He glanced at the sallow figure seated next to him. "You?"

Zlatko Piric was a new addition to the Org. He was fresh from the chaotic struggles of the Balkans, thanks to the eye of an alert talent spotter from the Org headquarters in Northern Virginia.

Zlatko grimaced sardonically. "You're kidding me – yes?"

"Guess not then," Lopez said, returning his attention to the photo. "If Zee doesn't know... Who is she?"

"Someone *you* need to know," Aachen said, getting up to retrieve the coffee pot from the brewer. He brought it back to the table, filled their empty mugs and took his seat again.

"Happy to do so," Lopez said. He and Zlatko Piric comprised the core of the Org's Black Team, destined for the CAZADOR op in Colombia.

Rogelio Lopez had been born in Camaguey, Cuba. As a child, he accompanied his mother and sister when they fled the Castro regime. His situation, as a male and therefore a probable future recruit for Castro's revolutionary legions, was more problematic than that of his sister's.

The Lopez family succeeded in bribing their way out, which included cash payments - and other matters that his mother would never discuss. Upon arrival in the United States, they settled just outside of Wilmington, Delaware. There they integrated themselves into area's small Cuban community.

Lopez's father, who had been a policeman with the Batista regime, remained behind in Cuba. Given his background, he would have been highly unpopular with the Castroites if detected. The senior Lopez declined the risk inherent in the escape attempt, opting instead to maintain a low profile in the countryside. Rogelio never saw the man again after leaving the island.

Following an indolent year of college, Lopez found a sales job with a local realty firm. Successful in the business, yet bored with the tedium, he invested his spare time in earning a private pilot's license and looking for adventure.

With his Cuban émigré contacts and nascent aviation skills, Lopez soon drew attention from certain anti-Castro factions in South Florida. Admittedly, he was attracted to the romance of their cause.

After nearly two years of clandestine activity, Lopez found himself locked up in the Metropolitan Correctional Center/Miami on federal weapons and conspiracy charges.

As it so often happens on the inside, while sitting in MCC Lopez talked to a guy. The latter, in turn, talked to another guy. Who then talked to a guy on the outside.

After a several more months of incarceration, Lopez was released from custody and was met by some influential personages. In due course his federal charges were dropped and his criminal record was expunged. And shortly thereafter, he became a paid asset of the Org.

At this point however, all of that was more than ancient history.

Aachen pushed another pair of photos across the table. They were clearly additional shots of the same woman. The images were rushed and somewhat blurred shots of her exiting a taxicab in some urban area. Probably taken in Latin America.

"Her name is Daria Arango. Arango-Urribe, to be exact," Aachen said. "Twenty-six years old. Born in the village of Manati. Moved to Cartagena after high school. Went from farm girl to party girl. Part-time bookkeeper. Part-time model."

"Yes?"

"Better for us though, she has since become the main squeeze of a fellow named Ivan Mondragon-Ortega."

"Who is...?"

Aachen paused for dramatic effect as he blew on the hot coffee and then treated himself to a brief sip. "Another local boy made good," he said. "Born in the town of Pereira.

Attended the University of Antioquia... He's now one of Pablo Escobar's staff accountants."

"Really?" Lopez said, passing the photos of Daria Arango over to Zlatko.

"Not exactly a member of the inner circle," Aachen cautioned. "But close enough... He's on speaking terms with Don Pablo, in any event."

"So that's our in?"

"Could be."

Lopez absently scanned through the remainder of more prosaic surveillance shots. "What's our angle with this girl?" he asked.

Aachen produced another memo from the courier bag, this one of a biographic nature on what was known to date about Arango, and passed it to Lopez. "Up to you to figure that out," he said. "But she's a bit of a wild child, so she could be vulnerable on a number of fronts."

Lopez latched onto a commercial, full-face shot of the girl. Evidently part of her aspiring model portfolio. "Yeah, he murmured. "But which one of the mice is she susceptible to?"

"Mice?" Zlatko started. "We using rats to catch her?"

"Not those kind of mice Zee," Aachen said, picking up on Lopez' expression. "It's a shorthand memory device. MICE stands for Money, Ideology, Compromise, and Ego."

"Usually a vulnerable target can be reached in one of those four areas," Lopez added.

"But which one for her?" Zlatko asked.

Aachen shook his head. "With her having a Cartel boyfriend and all, I don't see any great need for money from us."

"Maybe not," Lopez said. "Ideology. Not in play... Ego – maybe."

"And compromise is what?" Zlatko pressed.

"Blackmail. Exposing a personal secret."

"Ah, *kompromis...*" Zlatko appreciated. "So compromise her then."

Lopez nodded, passing the memo over to Zlatko for his review. "Okay. Maybe so."

He turned his attention to the boss. "When do we go in?"

"Soon," Aachen said. "Real soon." He produced a Spanish language newspaper. Earlier in the month a bomb had exploded in a Medellin parking lot. The lot was attached to a building that houses several judges. Two people were killed. Thirty-nine wounded.

"Clock's running."

= TEN: PARAGUAYOS =

Cartagena, Colombia
June 1993

Rogelio Lopez was standing outside of the customs/immigration area at Rafael Nunez International. He had been there for the better part of an hour, waiting for the Paraguayos. The mid-day Copa flight from Panama had landed a short while ago. According to Aachen's information, the three men should have been on it.

Lopez peered at his watch impatiently. The clearance procedures for an airport as small as this shouldn't be as slow as this.

But then again, he thought ruefully, we're on *Latin Time*. Allowances.

As he pondered that thought, he saw the doors to the secure area open. A collection of weary travelers began to file out. After a few minutes the Paraguayos came into view. They were near the middle of the pack, dutifully pulling their luggage along behind them.

Together, the three men were fairly easy to spot. All of them were Guarani Indians, members of the indigenous population from the Paraguayan-Bolivian border region. Short, thickly muscled and bronze-skinned, each had blue-black hair, sharp noses and wide mouths. All in all, they were not an unattractive assemblage.

But all of them, Lopez knew, were Org contract assets. Taken together, they formed a JICSA direct action team. This particular trio came highly recommended. Lopez knew that they had repeatedly proven themselves on an operational basis elsewhere in Central and South America over a number of years.

Stepping forward, he extended a hand to the largest of the group. The latter was a man with a closely trimmed haircut that would have done a Marine proud. *"Disculpa, Señor,"* he said. "You are here for the COPEX seminar?"

"Yes," the other replied, taking the hand and shaking it vigorously. "We'll be here till the fifteenth. Or longer."

Lopez nodded, acknowledging the agreed upon exchange protocol. "You are Galeano?"

"Yes."

"We have a van outside."

The three men followed Lopez out to the sidewalk and over into the parking area. As they packed their belongings into the back of the van, Galeano introduced Lopez to his colleagues.

"This man," he said, motioning to a bearded man with a friendly, open face, "is called Ayala."

"And that," he said with reference to the smallest figure – a clean shaven man with a fiercely intense gaze, "... is Benetez."

"Mucho gusto," Lopez said, shaking their hands and knowing that none of the offered names were true. "From here, we go to a safe house. You can get comfortable there. And then it's off for some food and drinks."

***

Dinner was a casual affair at a Chinese restaurant. Afterwards the four men shared drinks while relaxing at the safe house. The small structure, facing onto an alleyway, would be both their residence as well as their base of operations for the duration.

Lopez read them into the project as he recharged their glasses.

"Initial target," he said, dropping the 8x10 photo of Daria Arango-Urribe onto the coffee table. He followed that one with several more.

"Tan bonita," Ayala observed.

"She is," Lopez agreed. "Which should make the job just a bit more pleasant for you."

He placed a map of Cartagena across the tabletop. "As far as we know, she lives along the *Calle* 29 in the Getsemani neighborhood," Lopez said. "We think she works as a bookkeeper somewhere around here." He rested a finger on the map. "In the *Bocagrande* area."

"*Bocagrande?*" Benetez repeated questioningly.

"We passed through it tonight," Lopez said. "It's the more modern section of the city. The business section."

"Why her?"

"*Novia del Cartel,*" Lopez said. Cartel girlfriend.

"*De quien?*" Benetez asked.

"Need to know," Lopez responded. "Right now – you don't."

Galeano stared at the map for several long moments. "You have nothing more than this for us?"

"Not at the moment," Lopez admitted. "You have a starting point though... Find her and confirm her patterns of movement. Then we go from there."

"You said *initial* target, Galeano noted. "There are more?"

"We are less interested in this girl than in who she can lead us to."

"And then?"

"And then we take the next step."

"*Entendido,*" Galeano confirmed.

= ELEVEN: BLOQUE DE BUSQUEDA =

Cundinamarca Department, Colombia
July 1993

A lone black and white petrel cried out shrilly as it cut through the sharp and cloudless blue sky overhead. Riding the air currents, it banked steeply over the collection of humans below, eyeing them carefully. Seeing nothing of interest, the bird rolled and cut back lazily toward the west.

Toby watched the bird clear the area as he wiped a streak of perspiration from his forehead. Squinting, he pulled the brim of his olive drab boonie hat lower over his eyes and readjusted the fit of his sunglasses.

The sunglasses, of course, were Oakley's. He would be seen in nothing else.

Carefully, he surveyed the row of military-aged men arrayed before him. Each was similarly dressed in sweat stained green utility uniforms. They had just come in from a quick series of wind sprints, interspersed with a dozen or so push-ups after each dash. The goal was less conditioning – though that was part of it – than the active inducement of physical stress.

Several of the men were now gasping for breath as they faced the bank of paper targets. Their fingertips tremored slightly at the nine-millimeter semi-automatic handguns holstered at their hips.

The group stood shoulder to shoulder, evenly spaced. The men were intent upon the line of paper silhouettes that were stationed before a high berm of thickly packed dirt.

Toby glanced over at Staff Sergeant Diaz. Of Mexican descent, Diaz was one of the few Alpha Squadron men who spoke any degree of Spanish. Catching his eye, Diaz nodded in return.

The Delta Master Sergeant raised the plastic whistle to his lips. "Ready?" he called.

"*Listo?*" Diaz shouted, emphasizing the last syllable.

The men nodded in unison, eyes fixated on the dark silhouettes before them. It was only training, but none of them wished to appear weak before his fellows. And especially not before *los expertos Americanos.*

"Two rounds, two seconds."

"*Dos tiros, dos segundos.*"

Toby paused, and then blew a short blast on the whistle.

Almost as one, the green clad men rapidly drew their pistols, and extended both arms in a two-handed grip – as they had been taught – and then fired a quick pair of shots into the targets down range.

Toby blew the whistle again. "Holster up!"

"*Regressa a la chapusa!*" Diaz called.

In response, the shooters re-holstered their pistols and lifted their hands into the ready position in front of their chests.

Toby paused for a few heartbeats and then blew on the whistle again. Once again the men on the line drew their pistols and banged out two more back-to-back rounds.

"*A la chapusa!*"

Now the guns were heating up as they slid them back into their ballistic nylon holsters.

Two of the other grim faced Delta troopers, functioning as safety NCO's, paraded behind the trainees. They eyeballed the men carefully as Toby repeated the drill four more times.

"Cease fire!" Toby called after the sixth iteration.

"*Para el fuego!*"

"Make your weapons safe!"

"*Asegure sus armas!*"

"Safety NCO's, give their weapons a secondary check," Toby ordered.

The two sergeants completed their individual inspections to ensure that all of the chambers were clear. After getting a thumbs-up from each of them, Toby told Diaz to have the students move up and check their targets. Diaz nodded and relayed the information.

The trainees who were examining the hits on their paper targets were all members of the *Bloque de Busqueda* – the Search

Bloc. All were carefully handpicked officers of the PNC, or the Colombian National Police force.

Every member of the Search Bloc had been screened in an effort to weed out those who appeared to be susceptible to corruption. Each had been carefully vetted with an eye toward a past history of accepting bribes, integrity issues, family members or associates with criminal contacts and so forth.

The selection process had been conducted with a deadly purpose. These were the men trusted by the Colombian government to be in the forefront of the hunt for Pablo Escobar.

The training was being conducted by Delta at a newly constructed Search Bloc encampment. They were in the Cundinamarca Department, a few dozen kilometers east of the capital of Bogota.

Toby ambled up to the berm to join the Bloc shooters as they evaluated their targets. The range instructor NCO's mingled with them as Diaz translated their comments.

The trainees had been told to aim for center of mass, armpit level, on the man-sized silhouettes. In other words, shoot for the area of the human heart.

Toby saw that at least *some* of the men had accomplished that.

He was appreciatively assessing a particularly tight shot group on one of the targets when the Alpha Squadron commander appeared at his shoulder. The officer was a burly lieutenant colonel with thirteen years of previous experience in the Infantry, Rangers and Special Forces.

"Toby?"

"Sir."

"How's it looking with 'em?" The Alpha commander was a native of upstate New York of Italian heritage. His nickname in the unit was Lupo.

"Yeah, well," Toby observed. "It's probably more dangerous to stand in front of them than behind them. I'll give them that right now... But they do need work." He gazed sadly at the targets to his right. "They surely do."

"They must be doing something right," Lupo observed. "This unit has hunted down and killed about a dozen of the Cartel movers and shakers since the project began."

"But not finding Mr. Big," Toby countered.

"No," his C.O. agreed. "Not that."

Alpha Squadron had been in Colombia for close to two months now. The vast majority of their time had been spent providing tactical training to the Search Bloc. All of this was done on a covert basis – or as nearly so as possible.

"Okay," Lupo said. "Regardless, these particular guys have a hit coming up soon."

"Oh yeah?" Toby said, interested now.

"Right. The PNC has an informant who has placed SPRINTER in a house on the northern outskirts of Medellin, as of yesterday."

SPRINTER was Delta's internal code name for Escobar.

Toby spat a stream of tobacco juice into the dust. "Really sir? And just how good is this informant?"

"*Cosi-cosi*," Lupo shrugged, waggling an open hand. "But if nothing else it'll be a good training event for the boys."

"And our role?"

"We'll be going along," the commander said. "But only in an advisory capacity. No hands on and no trigger pulling. This is strictly an indigenous op."

Toby nodded. "Got it."

"Run 'em again then," Lupo said. "Carry on."

***

Standing off in the background were two other men who were distinctly not Latinos. Nor were they Delta troopers.

One was a shorter figure with tight, iron gray hair. The other was a larger man with flowing blonde hair and a closely cropped beard.

"So this is them?" Bear asked dubiously.

"That's them," Chalice confirmed. "The National Police. The Search Bloc."

"And it's the best they have?"

Chalice gave him a sideways glance. "They may not be Seventh Group," he said, referring to the Special Forces command whose legacy encompassed service in the Vietnam War to advisory operations in Latin America. "But they're reliable... Down here honesty counts as much as proficiency... More so."

"Got it," Bear acquiesced with a whiff of sarcasm. "They are *our* guys."

"They are the weapon. We're just pointing them," Chalice commented.

"If you say so."

= TWELVE: VIGILANCIA =

Cartagena, Colombia
July 1993

Ayala saw her first.

While cruising the San Diego district of Cartagena, he caught sight of a dark-haired woman walking purposefully along the street. She could have very well been their target - Daria Arango-Urribe. Dropping in behind her at a discrete distance, he followed her through the lunchtime throng until she stopped and entered a popular coffee shop.

"*Finalmente*," the bearded figure breathed hopefully.

Following up on the initial intelligence provided by Rogelio Lopez, the *Paraguayos* had scoured the Bocagrande area for more than three weeks, six days per week, searching for her workplace. This they did over and over again. No joy.

Reversing the strategy, they switched their focus to the Getsemani neighborhood, where she was believed to be residing. For the most part, the effort had been equally unrewarding.

Then, one humid and sunny morning, they were rewarded with the appearance of a young woman who strongly resembled Daria. She was coming out of the Getsemani area. Eschewing private transport, the subject had boarded a westbound public bus along Calle 29. Trailing along in their individual vehicles, two of the *Paraguayos* watched as she disembarked in the busy San Diego district.

And then they lost her.

Gaining confidence from that point, they decided upon a new surveillance plan. They agreed to concentrate their attention on the San Diego area from the morning to mid-afternoon, and then watch Getsemani in the late afternoon and early evening.

They were fairly confident that they were operating within the correct geographic area. In keeping with their focus, they had diligently logged the locations of each and every bookkeeping, tax advisory service and accounting firm within the general area.

And then there she was. Maybe.

Ayala ducked into a bookstore across the street from the coffee shop to cover himself. Palming his cellphone, he notified first Galeano and then Benetez of his find.

"*Cuidado*," he warned them. "Stay where you are."

Both acknowledged receipt of the message. Reacting automatically, they proceeded to take up secluded places at opposite ends of the block.

Snatching up a random book from the shelf, he positioned himself by the front window. He feigned interest in the volume of poetry as he waited for developments.

Within moments he was rewarded with the sight of the woman emerging from the shadows of the doorway. She came out of the coffee shop with a cup in hand and took a seat at a sidewalk table.

The young woman settled into her chair and crossed her legs attractively under her short skirt. She pushed her wide sunglasses up on her forehead, exposing her eyes. Taking a delicate sip from her drink through a straw, she pulled a folded magazine from her bag and opened it.

She *is* beautiful, Ayala thought. Strikingly so. Lopez was right about that.

Ay, Colombianas.

Ayala withdrew a photograph of Daria Arango from an internal jacket pocket. Shielding it from his fellow customers, he carefully compared the image on the photo with the face of the woman across the street.

It was the same woman, he concluded. Daria. Definitely her.

After some ten minutes or so of idle relaxation, the woman finished her drink and began to gather up her belongings.

Ayala called Benetez once again. "Beginning to move," he told his colleague. "Coming in your direction."

"*Lo tengo*," Benetez responded.

She was moving. Relaxed. Unhurried. Apparently killing time during her lunch break.

Ayala waited for a few cautious beats. Sensing the moment, he casually filed out of the bookshop and began to stroll along the sidewalk in the same direction that she was heading. He was traveling along the walkway opposite of her and several lengths behind.

Turning the corner with her, he noted the slight figure of Benetez. He had just finished his purchase from a newsstand and loosely started in behind her as well.

Seeing that Benetez now had the eye, Ayala slowed his pace considerably, dropping further back from the target. He knew that Galeano would be somewhere further up the same street, waiting for Daria to come into view.

And come into view she did.

The muscular team leader was sitting on a bench at the edge of a small city park when he saw he coming up the street. Upon hearing of her direction of travel, he had hustled to double back and get in front of her.

As she turned yet another corner, Galeano clambered out of his perch and followed her until she reached the end of the block. There she scampered up a short flight of steps and entered a red brick building.

Galeano continued on as if oblivious of her actions. As he passed the red brick doorway however, he took note of the classical gold stenciling across the ground floor bay window. The signage boasted that it was the premises of "*Mendoza e Hijos – Contadores Certificados*".

They had her.

= THIRTEEN: FERIA =

Santa Elena, Colombia
August 7, 1993

The blonde *Norteamericano* nodded appreciatively to his host as he absently wiped back a thin strand of wind-blown hair. He was truly enjoying the afternoon. As one of the guests of honor, how could he not?

Keeping his attention on the activities in the street, the honored guest dug a round tin of tobacco from the rear pocket of his jeans. As the music blared around him, he tapped the lid with a pair of fingers, extracted a pinch of tobacco from the tin and wedged it into the side of his cheek.

The elderly white haired gentleman standing next to him on the reviewing stand – Elfago Moreno-Muniz – happily returned the smile and turned his eyes back to the loosely orchestrated assemblage. As the Norteamericano well knew, Señor Moreno was the doyen of the provincial floricultural industry. Clearly, he was a good man to know.

Of less importance to him was the ruddy-faced *alcalde* of Santa Elena. The politician beamed happily to the guest and thenceforth ignored his presence on the reviewing stand.

As they watched, a stream of colorful *silleteros* – or flower farmers – marched along the narrow boulevard, filling it with posters and hand-made floats. A conglomeration of bands and solo guitar players accompanied the silleteros. All merrily added to the festivities.

Aachen was in the highlands of Santa Elena, among the *veredas,* the series of villages overlooking the city of Medellin, which was ensconced in the valley below.

"I am so sorry that Mister Tom could not visit with us this year," Moreno said, straining to raise his voice over the cacophony. "I always enjoy his company. He is a true gentleman... But you picked a very opportune time to make your first visit to us," he continued, "this being the *Feria de las Flores.*"

"Of course," Aachen agreed. He discretely extruded a bit of tobacco juice into a paper cup. "Tom was looking forward to being here today," he added. "But with the illness in his family and all..."

"I understand completely," Moreno interrupted with a raised hand. "Family is everything. Everything."

Both men fell silent to enjoy the *cabalgata*. One of the highpoints of the *feria*, was a display of horsemen – interspersed with a large number of comely female riders - who paraded before them. The riders trotted along the street, half a dozen abreast, smiling and grandly doffing their wide-brimmed cowboy style hats to the onlookers and official alike.

Aachen joined in the enthusiastic applause as the riders passed by. In return, one of the females smiled coyly and grandly blew him a kiss.

Not a bad TDY, he reflected.

In truth, all was quite well with Mister Tom O'Keefe and his family. His absence from the annual trip to Colombia was due not to illness but rather his willingness to provide operational cover for the Org.

The owner of TomaFlores, a flower brokerage firm in Lynn, Massachusetts, O'Keefe was a former U.S. Air Force logistics officer. Given his background, he had been assessed as someone likely to be favorably disposed toward assisting the Government in national security issues.

That assessment had been correct.

O'Keefe had been dully approached months ago by a pair of Special Agents from the FBI's Boston Field Office. In response to the pitch - to provide a covered position for an anonymous intelligence operative – he would receive a bit of free labor and the good will of a grateful Government. From the perspective of the Air Force veteran, it was a no-brainer.

In due course, O'Keefe was obliged to sign an NDA, or non-disclosure agreement. In so doing, he offered the cover of his business and guaranteed his confidentiality under the friendly threat of federal prosecution should he violate the agreement. In O'Keefe's case, the NDA was a mere procedural requirement that was hardly needed to ensure his cooperation.

In return, the Org ensured that Aachen would devote a portion of his time in Colombia to securing this year's shipment of flowers and plants to the TomaFlores concern.

"You are new to our business?" Moreno asked over the din.

"For the floriculture sector, pretty much," Aachen admitted. "My background is in marketing and sales."

"So. We are honored to have you with us today," Moreno said. "As you must know by now, Colombia is the second largest producer of cut flowers in the world. Here in Antioquia, we have over two thousand acres under production."

"Impressive," Aachen agreed.

"Yes. These *silleteros,* they work the fields for us. They are hard workers and they are very efficient," Moreno explained. "They have to be. The flowers themselves have maybe a twelve-week life cycle. After they are cut, we are able to ship them to Miami within twenty-four hours. And then they travel up to Mister Tom's distributorship for sale."

"Very efficient," Aachen observed, feigning a lively interest in the production of floral products. "And much appreciated on our end of the process."

In truth, his mind was focused less on the botanical cover activity and more the clandestine meeting that he planned later that evening in Medellin with a Cartel source. Nevertheless, he would spend the next few days in the area contracting for the upcoming product shipment to TomaFlores.

He smiled widely once again as the final riders of the *cabalgata* trotted past them.

***

The sun had long disappeared by the time that Aachen appeared below on the streets of Medellin. For the past forty-five minutes or so, he had been randomly cruising the area with an eye to his rearview mirrors. Now satisfied that he was free of surveillance, he was moving in for the meet.

Aachen was in the *Candelaria* section of the city, and was driving an SUV in a northerly direction along Carrera 50. The elegant *Basilica de la Candelaria* was coming up on his right.

And there he was, right on schedule. A lone male figure was standing near the corner in front of the church.

Aachen briefly flashed his headlights and continued moving. Following the agreed procedure, he made a right turn, then slowly squared the block and came back north onto Carrera 50 once again. He glided to a stop one block further than the site of the basilica.

As soon as the SUV pulled to the curb a man climbed into the passenger seat and slammed the door behind him. Wordlessly, Aachen pulled back into traffic and accelerated.

"*Hola Caiman,*" he said.

"*Hola jefe,*" the passenger replied. *Caiman*, his nickname, referred to his toothy, alligator-like smile. Or perhaps it was due to his reputation for native cunning among his peers. Maybe both.

Aachen kept his eyes on the road. "What do you have?"

"A name," Caiman said. "A senior man in the Cartels for you."

He would know. A former Colombian Army officer, Caiman's wife was connected by family to the warring Cartel factions. When that familial connection became common knowledge, his popularity with the Army High Command began to diminish. Eventually he was encouraged to leave the military and seek employment elsewhere.

Drawing upon his connections via his wife and others, he became, in effect, a free-lance information vendor.

Caiman slipped an index card out of his shirt pocket and elaborately placed it upon the dashboard. "So. He is called Gandalfo. He is with Los PEPEs. You know them?"

"I know them."

"His contact information is there. He is prepared to meet within the week."

Aachen stole a glimpse at his passenger. "Where is he? Where can we find him?"

"In Cali." He pursed his lips in the direction of the card. "It is all there."

Aachen made another right hand turn and started back toward the basilica. "*En la caja*," he said.

Caiman opened the glove compartment and withdrew and envelope that was thick with Colombian peso notes.

Murmuring his appreciation, the former officer secured the envelope inside his jacket. "*Gracias jefe.*"

"*De nada.*"

Nothing further was said as they made their way south again through the evening traffic. Caiman kept his eyes straight ahead, content with his role in the game.

Within a few moments Aachen eased the SUV to the sidewalk a few blocks short of the basilica. He nodded respectfully to his agent and offered his hand.

"*Proxima vez*," he said.

"*Si*," Caiman agreed. He hopped out of the SUV, lowered his head and started down a side street.

Aachen watched for a brief moment. Satisfied with Caiman's relative safety, he then re-entered traffic and disappeared.

= FOURTEEN: VACIO =

Suba District
Bogota, Colombia
August 8, 1993

"Three, two, one... And... Go!"

The sudden crack of a high explosive charge ripped through the calm of the Sunday evening. As the front door of the red brick structure splintered, the Search Bloc assault team poured through the gap.

Just as the last man in the stack disappeared though the portal, a second team of regular PNC officers scampered in behind them. High pitched calls of *"Policia! Policia! Manos arriba!"* echoed in their wake.

Chalice peered through the eyepiece of a night vision device. From his perspective, the scene on the other side of the broad *calle* was bathed in a sickly green glow of illumination.

Perched next to him and kneeling on the floor at the storefront window, Bear was monitoring the radio traffic with a hand-held set. Unable to decipher the rapid chatter of excited Spanish, he was waiting for an English speaking voice to come up on the air.

From both the radio speaker and from reverberations across the street they could hear an eruption of shouting and rapid heavy footfalls. A series of thumping noises emanated from the target house. Then – silence.

After some twenty minutes of muted activity, several of the Search Bloc members emerged from the doorway. Between the first two of PNC officers was a pair of scruffy, longhaired males dressed in jeans and t-shirts. Both men had their hands zip tied behind their backs.

A recognizable figure garbed in a mottled camouflage uniform came out behind them and crossed the street to the storefront location. Chalice powered off the night vision device and waited for Toby to enter the room.

"No joy," Toby sighed. "According to Diaz, it's *vacio*. A dry hole."

"And so what's with these guys?" Bear asked, nodding toward the two captives who were being roughly loaded into the back of a police van.

"*Mayimberos*," Toby replied. "Cops found a few duffle bags full of marijuana in there... They're taking them in for that."

"So not hardly Cartel members," Chalice said.

"And no Escobar," Bear added.

"Nope," Toby agreed. "No signs of SPRINTER but the cops will be there for the next few hours turning the place inside out. Meanwhile we're taking the assault team home."

"Tomorrow is another day," Bear quipped.

"That it is," Toby answered. "That it is."

= FIFTEEN: LOS PEPES =

Cali, Colombia
September 10, 1993

Rogelio Lopez toyed with a chilled glass of chardonnay, absently twirling the wine as he awaited the arrival of his host. He was sitting alone in the courtyard of a spacious, ornately decorated walled villa. As was only to be expected, the villa was located in the wealthier southern fringe of Cali.

Lopez had come alone. Alone and unarmed. In terms of decision-making, it was simplicity itself. No number of associates could have ensured safety if the reception had been hostile.

Nevertheless, Zlatko and the Paraguayos waited in two SUVs a few blocks away, glued to their cell phones. They were there to attempt a rescue if the situation went to hell. Truthfully however, none were optimistic of their chances *in extremis.*

Taking a sip of the wine, Lopez could barely see the hills of *Los Crystales* over the brim of the glass to the west. Silhouetted upon the mountain's crest in the evening gloom was the imposing statue of *Christo Rey.* The *Christo* was a Jesus motif with outstretched arms, reminiscent of the more famous structure above the city of Rio.

It was a depiction of Christ extending his love to the city of Cali.

The man Lopez had come to meet was most likely not a devout follower of the teachings of Christ. In fact, he was a key member of an assemblage that bore the unequivocal name of Los PEPEs, or *Perseguidos por Pablo Escobar.* People Persecuted by Pablo Escobar. The group was rapidly making a name for itself in terms of violent actions against Medellin figures to include multiple kidnappings, assassinations and car bombings.

In truth, Los PEPEs was not a conglomeration of common folk suffering under the infamous drug kingpin, as their propaganda widely alleged. Rather they were primarily composed of - and funded by - rival drug factions. Ascendant among those factions was Escobar's mortal enemy - the Cali Cartel.

The men of Cali began in a similar fashion as those of Medellin, that of smuggling marijuana and later turning to cocaine due to its profitability and ease of transport. Nonetheless, they perceived themselves as superior in every way to their competitors in Antioquia. Worse, they made no secret of their opinion.

Contrary to the sole source managerial style of the Medellin Cartel, the Cali Cartel was led by a collective leadership comprised of the Rodriguez-Orejuela brothers – Gilberto and Miguel – and Jose Santacruz-Londono, also widely known as Don Chepe.

Lopez glanced up as the door to the main house suddenly swung open. A pair of swarthy figures stepped out into the courtyard, the larger one glaring at him with barely contained menace. From behind them emerged a tall thin figure with long white hair and a wispy beard.

His host actually *did* resemble the Tolkien figure, Lopez reflected with carefully concealed amusement.

Lopez rose to shake the older man's hand. "I am honored to meet you *Señor...*"

"Gandalfo. That is enough," the other said, taking his seat. "And you are?"

"Rogelio."

"Rogelio. Yes."

Gandalfo motioned toward the wineglass and turned his full attention onto his guest as the smaller of the two bodyguards retreated back to the house.

The two men made small talk while awaiting the arrival of fresh drinks.

"What is your family background, if I may ask?"

"Cuban," Rogelio answered. "But mainly in the U.S."

"Yes," Gandalfo agreed. "The accent."

"Your home here," Lopez continued. "It is very impressive."

"Not my residence," Gandalfo corrected with a smile. "Just a place of convenience. *Nada mas.*"

A diminutive woman with distinctly Indio features emerged from the house with a tray of drinks. Wordlessly, she deposited a tumbler of iced vodka in front of Gandalfo and another glass of chardonnay before Lopez.

"*Gracias* Santos," Gandalfo murmured as she backed away, nodding respectfully.

He hoisted the vodka graciously. "*Saludos.*"

"*Saludos.*"

Gandalfo savored the initial bite of the vodka and then cradled the glass in his lap with both hands. "To business then... Which is?"

"Pablo Escobar," Lopez said. "And his location."

"Ah."

"You represent Los PEPEs, no?"

"Los PEPEs," Gandalfo repeated. "Yes, but one of many. I am one of many."

"With respect," Lopez offered, "you are much more than that, or I would not be here this evening."

"Ah," Gandalfo said again. "And who do *you* represent my friend?"

"*Los Americanos.*"

"The U.S. Government?" Gandalfo surmised.

Lopez nodded affirmatively. "You know that I do."

"And the American Government is very much interested in the location of Escobar?" he toyed.

"*Si.* It is very much interested in his location," Lopez replied.

Gandalfo took another sip of his vodka. "And what do you offer for our assistance in the search for this devil?"

"What do you want?"

"On behalf of the gentlemen of Cali," Gandalfo said, "primarily what we seek is exactly what every other citizen of Colombia seeks – the elimination of this Medellin bastard who has caused more than enough suffering of the innocents."

"And?"

Gandalfo hefted his glass as if to take another sip of his drink. "I have no inside knowledge, of course. But if the American Government were to take an... *elastic* position on future extradition requests with regards to Cali people, it might be well appreciated."

"Interesting. But I can make no guarantees," Lopez replied honestly.

"Of course."

"But I will convey your wishes to my people."

"It is appreciated," Gandalfo smiled.

Lopez pushed his wine glass aside. "And of Pablo Escobar," he said. "Tell me what do you know of his location? Now. Today."

"He is highly elusive," Gandalfo observed. "Although I think you already know that."

Lopez nodded silently.

"However," Gandalfo continued, "I can tell you three things. One – he has tried without success to move his family out of this country. Two – he is definitely still in Colombia. And three - he is most likely still in the Antioquia Department where he is the most comfortable."

"And?"

"And, certain people are seeking him aggressively. Most aggressively... If you wish, we will advise you as fresh information comes to our attention."

"That *is* my wish," Lopez replied.

"And ours," Gandalfo said, raising his glass to his guest. "To success then... With hopes for future considerations."

"To success," Lopez agreed. "And hope."

= SIXTEEN: GUAPO =

Cartagena Colombia
October 1993

The pale morning sunlight drifted though the half closed window blinds. Eventually the glow crept across the pillow and traced Daria Arango's face. Blinking sleepily, she turned away from the light and readjusted herself under the thin bed sheets.

After a few moments of silence, she sensed a slight bit of movement on the surface of the mattress. Reluctantly she opened her eyes and took in the form of the curly haired man lying inches away from her. She saw that he was sound asleep, and snoring softly.

Miguelito, she softly murmured. Unbidden, satisfying memories of the previous night flooded her consciousness.

Smiling, she resisted the urge to stroke the bare shoulder of the man, for fear of awakening him. Instead, she slowly eased herself out of the bed. Shrugging into a cotton robe, she padded out into the kitchen to make coffee.

***

The previous night, a Saturday, Daria had been in a quaint neighborhood wine bar with two of her girlfriends. The main topic of her conversation – as it had been for the past several weeks – was the absence of attention being shown to her by her boyfriend, Ivan.

Her ongoing complaint was that Ivan, though wealthy, generous and attractive, was frequently absent from her life. Over the past year he had been spending increasingly extended periods of time away from Cartagena, most often in Antioquia. Of late she began to suspect that there might be another woman involved in his absences. Or two.

Given that her companions had heard it multiple times all before, they were at a loss in terms of fresh advice. After an hour or so, they made their excuses and slipped away. But no sooner had they departed than a pair of sympathetic newcomers to the bar caught her eye and befriended her.

After making contact, the female of the pair, a fashionably dressed vivacious redhead, slipped across the barstools to sit next to Daria. The woman touched Daria's hand and quietly confided that she had overheard the story and was herself no stranger to the drama being described. For the very same reason, she said, she dumped her old *novio* and took up with the much more appreciative – and richer - gentleman who was with her that very evening.

Her slightly built male companion smiled pleasantly and raised his glass in her direction.

"I am called Paloma," the woman said.

"Daria."

Appreciative of their attention and understanding, Daria accepted another glass of wine in return for their conversation. And then another.

Eventually Paloma suggested that the three of them quit the stolid wine bar in search of a livelier place. She suggested a *discoteca* several blocks away with which they were familiar. As was Daria herself.

The *discoteca* was indeed more vibrant than the wine bar. As they entered it seemed to be in full swing. They were immediately hit with a blast of throbbing music. The bass beat was so intense that it reverberated against one's chest cavity. The dance floor was crowded with bodies that were bouncing and swaying, arms waving above their heads in the beams of the colored strobe lights.

The man, Chicoco, handed a few folded peso bills to one of the staff members. The latter nodded appreciatively and led the party to a corner table.

A little less than an hour later, Chicoco left the two women at the table as he went in search of another round of drinks.

Daria, feeling the effects of the alcohol, tried to focus on the conversation with Paloma. Concentration was proving all the more difficult over the noise of the music.

"Paloma," came Chicoco's reedy voice. "Look who I found at the bar." Standing next to Chicoco was a tall, muscular man with a shock of curly black hair and a closely trimmed beard.

"Miguelito!" Paloma exclaimed happily. "A surprise to see you!" Playing the gracious hostess, she put a hand on Daria's forearm. "Daria," she said, "this is Miguel Espino, an old friend of ours."

"Call me Mike," Espino said.

"*Muy guapo*," Daria breathed, in spite of herself.

"And a very sweet man as well," Paloma assured her.

Espino gave her a mock bow and extended a hand to the dance floor. "Care to?" he asked.

Daria accepted the encouragement from Paloma and took his hand in hers.

Much later Daria took her leave from her new friends. Arm in arm, she and Espino left the club and ambled down the sidewalk. Her apartment was not far away.

Slightly further down the street a motorized camera shutter clicked away as the Paraguayos recorded the pair with a telephoto lens. All according to plan.

= SEVENTEEN: COMPROMISO =

Cartagena, Colombia
October 1993

Daria worked late at the bookkeeping firm the following Monday. Given the lateness of the hour, she decided to treat herself to dinner at a Chinese restaurant in the neighborhood.

She consumed the meal at a leisurely pace. Sitting alone in a booth, she idly paged her way though a popular gossip *revista*, barely attending to the content. Finishing, she paid her bill and made her way back to the apartment.

Unlocking the door, she stepped into the interior hallway and flicked on the light. Immediately, she felt that something was amiss.

Warily, she turned the corner into the living room and lit one of the side table lamps. To her shock, a man was sitting on her couch, legs folded casually, staring at her.

Daria emitted the beginnings of a scream before a second man emerged from the bedroom and clamped a strong hand over her mouth.

"Quiet, *mi querida*," Rogelio Lopez said soothingly as she struggled against Benetez's clutches.

"Quiet," Lopez repeated. "We are not here to hurt you... Not to harm you... Only to talk."

Daria continued to squirm against Benetez, her surprise turning to panic. In response, Lopez rose from the couch to confront her.

"Of course, to be honest we *can* hurt you, if that is what it takes," he threatened. "Is that how it shall be?"

She paused and then shook her head in the negative.

"If my friend releases you, you must promise to be quiet. You understand me?"

She nodded in the affirmative.

Benetez slowly released his grip and took a step back.

Lopez grunted in approval. He motioned for her to sit at the small kitchen table, where a manila folder awaited her attention. Benetez took up a position behind her chair as she seated herself across from Lopez.

The Black Team leader waited as she began to calm down. "So," he said, "you are feeling a bit better?"

Daria nodded, unconvincingly.

"Good." Lopez opened the manila folder and pushed a black and white 8x10 photograph toward her. "Do you recognize this man?" he asked.

Daria gaped wide-eyed at the photograph before her. It was a copy of the official *cedula* – or national identification card – of Ivan Mondragon-Ortega.

"You know him?" Lopez prodded.

"Yes."

"He is?"

"Ivan," Daria sputtered. "My... My boyfriend."

"Not your fiancé?"

"No."

"But maybe?"

"... Maybe."

"Ah... What is his occupation?"

Daria soaked in the image, knowing that it must have been derived from official sources. "He is an accountant. Nothing more."

"For?"

She did not reply.

"For maybe Pablo Escobar," Lopez supplied. For reinforcement, Benetez placed a hand on her shoulder and squeezed tightly.

"Yes," she admitted, shrugging from the spark of pain.

"And these?" Lopez asked, producing another series of photos.

The sense of shock returning, Daria gazed at images of herself and Miguelito. The first was of the two of them walking down the street in front of the club, arm in arm.

Another depicted the pair stopping at a corner to embrace and kiss. A third was of them on the sidewalk at the entrance to her apartment building.

"He is a man," she said haltingly. "Just a man that I met."

"Clearly," Lopez agreed. "And his name?"

"Miguel."

Grunting in agreement, Lopez produced still another photograph from his folder. Daria gaped in amazement at the official photo of Miguelito. It appeared to have been a copy of American law enforcement credentials. Under the thumbnail photo were the words:

Michael G. Torres
Special Agent
Drug Enforcement Administration
United States Department of Justice

"You read English?" Lopez asked.

"Yes."

In response, he pushed yet another photocopy in front of her. It was the image of her Miguelito on a U.S. Embassy/Bogota identification badge in the name of Michael G. Torres. It indicated that Torres was a cleared American employee.

"Your new lover," Lopez said softly. "He appears to be an American DEA agent assigned to their embassy in Bogota... How interesting is that?"

In reality, the man they called "Torres" had no connection with the DEA. He was a contract Org asset who was, even then, back at his home in Tampa, having served his operational purpose.

"The beautiful *novia* of one of Don Pablo's financial people," Lopez mused. "Sleeping with an America narcotics agent... I wonder what the people in Medellin would think of that? ... I wonder what they would do to you."

Daria felt her lips growing cold and numb as the blood drained away from her face. She could only imagine too well how they might respond to such an accusation. "Who are you people?" she stammered.

Lopez paused for effect. "You know Los PEPEs?"

"You are with Los PEPEs?"

Lopez did not respond.

"What do you want from me?" she asked at last.

"Ivan Mondragon."

"Yes?"

"Where is he?"

= EIGHTEEN: SE BUSCA =

Bogota Colombia
October 1993

Aachen was sharing a pizza with the Green Team in Chalice's Bogota apartment. He ran a long, though insufficiently keen-edged, knife through the cheese and down into the crust of the pie to separate the slices. Bear meanwhile struggled with a corkscrew in the kitchen as he attempted to open a second bottle of cabernet.

"Jesus," Aachen groused. "You ever going to get that thing open?"

"Not something they taught at the police academy," Bear muttered.

Jerking back on the corkscrew, he finally extracted the cork with a sharply audible pop.

Aachen took a tentative bite of cheese and pepperoni. "Not bad," he commented, wiping his fingers on a paper towel.

"He's come out with an offer."

"An offer to...?" Chalice prompted.

"Surrender."

"Must be feeling the pressure," the Green Team leader observed, pulling a slice of the pizza onto his plate.

They paused while Bear sloshed a pour of red wine into all three of their waiting glasses. That done, he perched himself onto a chair and stretched his legs out.

"With conditions though," Aachen continued, eyeing the errant bits of shredded cork floating in his glass. "He said that he'd consider surrendering if the Colombian Government guaranteed his safety and ensured that – in his words – he'd only be housed in a 'humble, modest jail in Antioquia'."

"Good of him," Chalice commented. "That's it?"

"Not quite," Aachen said, raising his glass in a muted toast to his two associates. "He added that the government must agree to treat him as they would any other Colombian prisoner. And – most importantly, I'm sure - not to transfer him out of Antioquia for *any* reason."

"Extradition fears," Bear added. "Doesn't want to meet Uncle Sugar face to face... Not in a U.S. courtroom anyhow."

"And the Colombian response?" asked Chalice.

Aachen shook his head. "Negative. President Gaviria says any surrender has to be unconditional."

"Which means no surrender."

"Let's hope not."

Bear produced a wanted poster featuring Escobar's photograph and chucked it onto the table, next to the pizza box. "Came across this today," he said.

SE BUSCA
PABLO EMILIO ESCOBAR GAVIRIA
SOLICITADO POR LA JUSTICIA

$2.700'000.000.oo

DOS MIL SETECIENTOS
MILLIONES DE PESOS

"How much is that in real money?"

"More than a million, U.S." Chalice estimated.

"And Bush is chipping in another two million for him," Aachen said.

The number hung in the air.

"Man," Bear said at last, draining his wine glass. "We gotta find this guy!"

"Someone does," Aachen agreed.

= NINETEEN: SEQUESTRO =

Barranquilla, Colombia
October 1993

It had been quite a long and tiring day, the last of a three-day business trip to Barranquilla, Colombia's northernmost major city. Ivan Mondragon had worked though the dinner hour with the accountants for *Mercantil Cargo S.A*. He had been eager to finish with this project and head home the following morning.

Shortly after 8:00 p.m., he shook hands with *Mercantil's* lead accountant, closed his briefcase, and headed for the elevator. Satisfied with a job well done, he planned to go straight back to the hotel and have dinner alone in his room. Maybe with a bottle of Italian wine.

Like many entities and people alike in Colombia, *Mercantil* had a dual personality. On one hand, it was a legitimate cargo company, shipping Colombian products primarily to North America, but to Europe and Africa, though to a lesser degree. On the other hand, it was a major distributor for the Medellin Cartel, moving vast quantities of cocaine though its various modes of transportation.

Mondragon had been there to do an annual audit of their off the record books. Fortunately for all involved, the covert numbers of *Mercantil* tallied with those of Medellin.

When the elevator doors slid open, Mondragon stepped into the box. He was not alone. The other occupant was a bronze-skinned man with a short and tight military haircut.

Mondragon made to push the button for the parking garage level when he saw that it was already alit. "*Garaje*?" he said to other.

"*Si*," the man replied with a smile.

They rode in awkward silence as the elevator pinged down along the several levels to the ground. At last, the doors

65

yawned open at the empty lobby level, paused, and then closed once again.

Galeano waited until the doors had closed and the elevator was in motion before he took a half step forward and lashed an arm about Mondragon's neck. Moving quickly, he locked Mondragon into a classic police sleeper hold.

The bicep and forearm of his right arm were locked against his support hand, effectively closing off the arteries on both sides of Mondragon's neck. His left hand closed over his right, modulating the pressure against the neck. The crook of Galeano's elbow however cradled his victim's throat, allowing him the luxury of breathing.

Shocked, Mondragon dropped his briefcase and began to grapple futilely against the trapping arm of the Paraguayo. Within a dozen seconds however, the lack of blood flowing into his brain defeated him and he lapsed into unconsciousness.

Galeano dropped to a crouch to support Mondragon's suddenly limp body. He maintained the hold on the taller man as the elevator continued its descent.

When the door opened at the garage level, Ayala was waiting for them. Moving quickly, he uncapped a hypodermic needle and fed it into the arm of their prisoner. Allowing a few moments for the drug to take effect, Galeano released the sleeper hold and let him drop.

Ayala then assisted Galeano in pulling the slack body of Mondragon out of the elevator and hoisting it onto the back seat of a waiting sedan. They scrambled in behind, pulling the doors shut.

Satisfied, Galeano reached over to tap Benetez on the shoulder. Benetez nodded and drove the sedan out of the garage and into the Barranquilla night.

= TWENTY: INQUISICION =

**Barranquilla, Colombia
October 1993**

Ivan Mondragon-Ortega had regained consciousness some time ago. He had a severe headache. Beyond that, he was both hungry and thirsty.

Although uncertain of his present surroundings, he was acutely aware of the fact that a woolen sack had been draped over his head. The hood muffled both his hearing and his ability to breathe easily. Moreover, the sack assaulted his senses with a tang of moldiness. It frightened him, as it was intended to do.

He had initially tried to call out for help. His efforts earned no response from whoever was holding him. Maybe it was better to stay quiet and husband his resources, he decided.

Professionally connected to the Cartel though he may have been, Mondragon was not one of the hard men. He was certainly not a killer. His expertise was with numbers, bank accounts, and financial transfers – not with violence or physical action. He didn't even dabble in the product. The latter was a trait that his superiors especially appreciated in their money people.

By nature, the accountant was not inclined to resist whatever was coming. Nevertheless, he wanted to survive not only the moment, but any future repercussions from his employers as well. Quite possibly an attorney or an underling with a bag of money would soon appear to demand his freedom.

Mondragon knew that he was naked, save for his underpants, which his captors had allowed him to retain. For that small consideration at least he was grateful.

He tensed when he felt, or imagined that he felt, something rub against his bare foot. Rats? Worse?

He could sense that he was seated upright in a sturdy wooden chair. His arms and legs had been tightly secured to the arms and legs of the chair with generous applications of duct tape. Testing his bindings, he found no give in them whatsoever.

Without warning the woolen sack was unceremoniously torn from his head.

Blinking his eyes in the darkness, Mondragon tried to absorb his surroundings. The room was quiet but smelled damply of dirt and concrete. He wondered whether he was in cellar rather than a cell.

If it were the former, the situation could be much worse than he assumed.

A floodlight that had been emplaced a meter or so in front of him blazed to painfully white-hot life, temporarily blinding him. Clamping his eyes tightly shut, he could detect the movement of footsteps from behind the light source.

Suddenly a bucket of iced water was roughly thrown into his face and chest.

Yelping involuntarily, Mondragon shuddered and sputtered in the chill shock. "What?" he shouted. "Why am I here?"

Silence.

The sack went back on over his head and the light went off.

***

Some time later, maybe an hour, or perhaps only twenty minutes – Mondragon could not tell – the hood was pulled off of his head and the light came back on in all its brilliance.

"What is it?" Mondragon rasped, straining his parched throat. "What do you want from me?"

Heavy footsteps echoed in the darkness beyond the flare of light. There was the distinctive sound of a heavy galvanized metal bucket scraping against the cement floor.

He opened his mouth to speak when he was again drenched with another agonizing flood of frigid water.

The hood went on and the light went off.

***

It was much later, in Mondragon's flawed estimation, when the hood came off once again. As before, the blinding light painfully seared into his retinas of his eyes.

"No more," he begged. "Please."

Instead of a bucket-full of ice water however, a glass of cool juice was placed at his lips. Mondragon drank from it as deeply as could before it was taken away from him.

Opening his eyes, he saw that a man had positioned himself on a stool before him. The man was wearing a dark ski mask that covered his face completely, save for a pair of slanted eyelets.

A mask, Mondragon thought fitfully. *If I cannot see his face, maybe he will let me live through this hellacious nightmare.*

"How are you?" the masked man asked solicitously. His eyes, visible through the slits seemed to convey a sense of genuine concern.

"Better now," Mondragon gasped. He coughed noisily and spat a dollop of phlegm onto the floor. "But what is it that you want from me?"

"Not so much," the man in the ski mask said. "Just a bit of information... Are you hungry?"

Mondragon nodded affirmatively. Although his captor spoke Spanish fluently, he was clearly not a Colombian. In his current state, Mondragon could not quite place the accent.

"Then you must eat," the other said. "But first we have some questions for you."

"What are they?"

"Pablo Escobar," the man in the ski mask replied. "Where is he?"

"How would I know that?" Mondragon gasped, the edge in his voice betraying him.

"Ah," the man in the ski mask replied condescendingly. He nodded to a second man who placed a few bottles of fluid at his feet. The second man then stepped behind Mondragon.

"You know," the man in the ski mask said, "your boss has the famous question for people: *Plomo o plata?*"

By which he meant: lead or silver? Do you prefer a bullet or a bribe? Your choice.

In response to Mondragon's silence, the masked man continued, "We however have another question for you: Coke or Pepsi?"

Mondragon looked at his tormentor in honest confusion.

"No matter," the man said. "We have both."

As the second man seized Mondragon's head and pulled it backward, the first man popped open a bottle of Pepsi-Cola. He shook it vigorously with a thumb over its rim and then placed it under Mondragon's nose. Releasing his thumb, he fired the concoction up and into Mondragon's nasal cavity.

Ivan Mondragon shrieked with pain as the carbonated fluid shot through his nose and seemingly exploded into the frontal lobe of his brain. The pain to the very core of his being was indescribable.

"Another?" The man asked. "Of course, you must be very thirsty."

Before Mondragon could object, a second bottle of Pepsi rocketed through his nose and into his cranium.

"What?" Mondragon cried, breaking into a fit of coughing. Tears of pain ran down his cheeks. "What do you want?"

"As I told you", the man said. "Where is Escobar?"

Mondragon held his tongue, steeling himself for the agony that was surely to follow.

The hood came on and the light went off.

***

The man in the ski mask was staring at him again in the glare of the light. A six-pack of Pepsi rested ominously on the floor between them.

"No. Just stop. Wait," Mondragon protested. "I want to help you. I do."

His captor nodded understandingly. "Where is Escobar?"

Mondragon shook his head. "I told you honestly - I don't know. I swear to God!"

"Ah," the masked man said with a tone of regret. Reaching down, he popped the lid off of another bottle of Pepsi with a metal opener.

"No, wait!" Mondragon protested. "I tell you the truth. I don't know where Escobar is... But I know who is traveling with him."

The captor sat the bottle back on the floor. "Who?"

"El Limon. One of his bodyguards."

"El Limon?"

"His name is Alvaro de Jesus Agudelo."

"Yes?"

"And I know his cell number."

= TWENTY-ONE: SIGINT =

Over Caldas Department, Colombia
Late November 1993

Chalice adjusted the pale green David Clark headset for a more comfortable fit over his ears. Satisfied, he pushed the lip mike up and out of the way and reached for the plastic coffee cup in the holder before him. Squinting, he grimaced in the sunlight streaming in through the porthole shaped window to his right and took a sip of the hot brew.

The twin turboprop engines droned reliably as the Beechcraft Super King Air continued to bore its way through the bright blue sky toward the airspace over Medellin. Normally outfitted with eight rows of single seats separated by a narrow aisle, this particular ship was much more tightly configured.

This King Air, under the command of CW3 McAllister, also carried – in addition to Chalice - his co-pilot, three SIGINT operators and several racks of sophisticated electronics gear. The result was a bit off-putting, if one was given to touches of claustrophobia. Chalice was not.

Although the entire flight crew was composed of active duty members of the U.S. Army, all were wearing civilian clothing and none carried any military identification. They were members of the covert technical intelligence team that was flying in support of the Search Bloc, all in pursuit of Pablo Escobar.

Early on Chalice had decided that his favorite crewmember was a dark haired, thirtyish Latina named Esparza. He was happy to see her on board again today.

Esparza sat across the aisle from Chalice and was actively prepping a series of monitors situated in front of and above her seat. She studiously avoided eye contact with the Org passenger.

The Louisiana twang of McAllister's voice came over the headsets as they crossed over Caldas Department and into Antioquia. "Okay Maggie. We're operational. Go ahead and reel 'er out."

"Roger," Esparza replied. She glanced upward and flicked an olive drab toggle switch near her forehead.

Chalice heard a familiar humming sound in the body of the plane as a lengthy antenna began to unwind out of the belly of the plane.

Esparza watched one of her screens attentively until the humming stopped and the antenna was fully extended, trailing out behind the tail of the King Air.

"Antenna deployed Chief," she said into her lip mike. "All looks to be in the green."

"Thanks, Maggie," McAllister answered. "Go ahead and light it up then."

Intensely businesslike, Staff Sergeant Esparza began typing a series of numbers – targeting data for the cell number of Alvaro de Jesus Agudelo – into her keyboard and then turned to the business of fine-tuning the tracking software. She mumbled something indecipherable to Chalice into the mike. A male SIGINT operator who was sitting forward of her position nodded and gave a thumbs up signal.

This was Chalice's fourth liaison ride in the tech unit's King Air since the Org – in the person of Aachen – had passed along the intel derived from the questioning of Ivan Mondragon. Bear had been aboard during three other similar surveillance flights with McAllister.

To date, snippets of cell phone calls from the device alleged to be in the possession of Escobar had been sniffed out of the vapors, but nothing appeared that was related to his trusted bodyguard, known by his nickname of *El Limon*. No joy, in the terminology of the crew.

Bored, Chalice eased back in his seat and began to page through a newsweekly magazine. The article that caught his eye had nothing to do with his adventures in Latin America but much to do with the bitter, on-going war in the Balkans.

Recently, or at least at the time of the dated edition, Bosnian Croat forces had destroyed the historic *Stari Most* bridge in Mostar, Bosnia-Herzegovina. According to the reporter, the Croatians had blasted the old stone bridge with repeated high explosive rounds of tank fire, dropping the four hundred year old structure into the green waters of the river.

In keeping with the back and forth propaganda of the struggle however, the Croats countered by accusing the Bosniak Muslims of blowing up the historic bridge themselves and then pointing the finger of blame at their opponents.

Chalice shook his head, studying before and after photographs of the bridge.

"We have a contact," the male SIGINT operator quietly announced, intruding on Chalice's reflections. He sat the magazine down.

"Copy that," Esparza said crisply. She tweaked the settings on her equipment to verify the reading. Satisfied, she keyed her mike. "Chief, we have possible contact on Target SHIELD," she reported.

"*Possible* contact?" McAllister immediately responded.

Esparza hesitated. "Wait one..." She watched as the read back on the frequency strengthened. "Correction. Contact with SHIELD is now positive... Weak signal though. Very weak. And fading."

The craft's multiple recorders whirred to life, hungrily absorbing the cellular voice broadcast of Target SHIELD – El Limon.

"Shit," Esparza breathed to herself. Back on the intercom: "Lost the contact Chief. Need a three-sixty to reacquire target."

The voice recorders ceased their activity, calmly awaiting the chirp of a fresh signal from the ground.

"Yep," McAllister answered. He placed the King Air into a gentle left bank. He wanted to bring the plane back around and onto its original track without damaging – or worse, losing – the expensive antenna that flowed along behind them.

Chalice twisted in his seat to observe the SIGINT operators. They resembled nothing so much as a trio of thirty-something computer gamers, totally focused on their expensive gadgets.

The turn seemed to take forever but they eventually came around and were once again back on the same heading as before.

The King Air sailed quietly along until the male SIGINT operator came up on the air once again. "Contact. Target SHIELD. Confirmed... Still have a poor signal from target however."

"Good going," McAllister said.

Esparza acknowledged the transmission and peered at her screen until the contact faded out once again. She keyed her mike. "Chief. Contact lost but SHIELD definitely confirmed. The trace is right below us in the city of Medellin. I estimate location as being just west of the central city point."

"Okay Maggie, "McAllister said. "We'll repeat the three-sixty and try for another pick-up."

"Roger. Standing by."

Chalice smiled faintly as he jotted a note on an index card.

= TWENTY-TWO: ASYLUM? =

Frankfurt, Germany
November 1993

On the afternoon of Sunday, November 28th a Lufthansa airliner out of Bogota touched down on the cold runway of the *Flughaven Frankfurt am Main*. This alone was hardly notable, as the Frankfurt airport was one of the busiest destinations in Europe. What was notable was the fact that among the passengers of this flight was the Escobar party.

The senior member of this group was Maria Victoria Henao-Escobar, Pablo's wife. Now thirty-two years of age, Maria had married the aspiring drug kingpin when she was a mere fifteen years old.

Traveling with her was their daughter, Manuela, age nine, and their son Juan Pablo, age seventeen. With the teenaged Juan Pablo, and rounding out the party, was his twenty-one year old girlfriend.

Unbeknownst to the Escobars, as they flew through the night to Germany, they had been the focus of high-level international political attention. The President of the Republic of Colombia, Cesar Gaviria-Trujillo, had been on the phone with German authorities. Gaviria had personally requested that Berlin deny the expected request for asylum. In this effort he had the full support of the United States Government.

Not surprisingly, the flight's manifest included an undeclared American DEA agent. The latter was on board to track the movements of the family. He sat quietly apart from the clearly apprehensive family members as the Lufthansa jet was directed to taxi toward a remote portion of the field.

Alerted, uniformed members of the *Bundesgrenzschutz* – the Federal Border Guards – awaited their arrival at planeside.

This was not Escobar's first attempt to smuggle his family to safety that same year. In February the core family members, along with several extended relatives and several bodyguards, a group numbering fifteen in all, had attempted to fly out of Medellin for Miami. They were stopped on a procedural point of order. Colombian law required that both parents sign immigration papers authorizing children to leave the country. Pablo had failed to sign the documents.

A month later, Escobar offered to surrender himself if Washington were to guarantee protection of his family. In a statement from the U.S. Embassy Washington declined the offer, noting that the drug lord was unacceptably attempting to involve the United States in an internal Colombian matter.

Then in June the family attempted to slip across the border into Venezuela using sets of false documents. That effort too came to naught.

After the Escobars disembarked from the plane the officers of the *Bundesgrenzschutz* took charge of them and escorted them into a private set of offices for a meeting with other federal officials. There they discovered that Maria Victoria was carrying some $80,000 in cash, plus a quantity of gold and jewelry.

The Germans listened attentively to their story and provided the four of them with lodging for the night. The next day, on November 29th, they were placed on a flight back home to Colombia.

***

Upon arriving in Bogota, a Colombian police detail conveyed the Escobars from the airport and deposited them at the Tequendama Hotel in downtown Bogota. The police then withdrew, leaving them exposed to their fate.

Upon learning that they were sharing the facility with the infamous Escobars, staff members and guests alike began to flee the hotel in droves. In short order, the family had the spacious Tequendama largely to themselves.

At that precise point, Los PEPEs chose to release a statement to the media. Their message was that they had decided to resume their unrestricted actions against Pablo Escobar.

= TWENTY-THREE: EL LIMON =

Barrio Los Olivos
Medellin Colombia
Late November 1993

Propping his feet up on the scarred wooden coffee table, Alvaro – *Limon* to his diminishing number of friends - once again turned to the television for distraction. Unsurprisingly, the afternoon programming was flooded with so-called *novellas.* These were the sexually charged, yet essentially tame, soap operas that were so popular with the domestic female TV audience.

"*Cono carajo,*" he swore to himself, tossing the remote control onto the couch. This life on the run was driving him crazy.

More than crazy. He felt as though his skull was about to burst asunder with boredom.

It had been eight months since their departure from the prison at Envigado. During that period of time Alvaro had witnessed loyal supporters fall away, succumb to their enemies or become police informants. In contrast, their own position had degenerated from being the absolute masters of their environment to that of mere prey.

Escobar, although he never blessed with movie star good looks, had been a man of some vanity. Now however, he had abandoned even that. Wolfing down bowls of spaghetti in his self-imposed confinement, the boss was gaining weight and neglecting his appearance. How that might be connected to his thought processes also worried the bodyguard.

In the bedroom next to him Alvaro could hear his boss speaking to his son, Juan Pablo, on his cell phone. That also served to piss him off mightily.

Time and again Alvaro had cautioned Don Pablo to stay off of the cell phone. *A la mierda,* he thought with exasperation.

Just stay off of the damn thing! Most especially stay off the cell when it came to speaking with members of his own family. Those people were assuredly, he told the *Padron*, being watched by the government.

It was to no avail however. Don Pablo was keenly aware of the risk but felt that he was ever so much smarter than the forces of the government. Truth be told, he had proven that to be the case time and again in the recent past. So who was Alvaro to question him?

On another level however, Alvaro recognized Don Pablo's obsession. To come from such a position of recent power to... this.

Now the famous Padron could not even guarantee the safety of his own family. Before, such a matter would have been unimaginable. Beyond contemplation.

Not now however.

Now the Don and his family were closer to the condition of hunted animals in the forest. They were susceptible to the first man to catch them in the sights of his gun.

Alvaro recognized that Escobar needed to experience some degree of contact with his family. And apparently this could only take place though telephone calls to his son.

To hell with it, he sighed. He latched onto his own cell phone and dialed the number of his girlfriend.

A soft feminine voice answered after several rings. "Hello?"

"Lora. It's me," he said.

"Alvaro? Alvaro, I miss you," the woman cooed excitedly.

"I miss you too," he said in a near whisper. "Do you still love me?

"I love you much!" she gushed. "When can I see you?"

"Soon," he lied. "Soon I think."

***

High overhead, Esparza's face lit up as she clamped the pads of her headset tightly against her ears. She made a hurried note on a pad at her side and reached for her keyboard.

Bear was riding in the liaison seat when he noticed the abrupt change in her demeanor.

"Chief!" he heard her say over the intercom, her voice an octave or two above normal. "We have two simultaneous contacts. Targets SPRINTER and SHIELD are both up on the air!"

"Great, Maggie," McAllister immediately replied. "Can you posit them?"

Bear put through a call to Chalice who was back at the SIGINT base near Bogota. "The home team just scored," Bear told him. "Better get ready to move."

"Got it," Chalice said. "Will do."

"Both are weak and fading," Esparza continued. "But they are within a two or three block radius below. She called up a mapping image on her visual display. "Barrio Los Olivos."

"You're the best, Maggie," McAllister cracked, high fiving his co-pilot.

Esparza was beaming as she locked in the coordinates of the intercepts.

= TWENTY-FOUR: ZASTAVA =

Bucaramanga, Colombia
Late November 1993

The player in the gold jersey adroitly juked to the left and dodged a blue shirted defender. Seeing an opening, he gave the ball a solid kick. The black and white ball whirled across the grass and skipped neatly into the net.

"*GOL!*" someone nearby screamed happily.

The people around Zlatko leapt to their feet and shouted in jubilation. In spite of himself, Zlatko was swept up in their enthusiastic applause for the score.

Like most Europeans, Zlatko was an avid fan of football – or as his new American colleagues insisted on calling it - soccer. As much as he tried, he could not fathom their relative disinterest in the world's most popular sport. To his mind, football transcended both culture and language, unlike their own game of the same name.

The local fans were just settling back to their seats when Lopez appeared in the crowded aisle with two cans of beer. "He's here," he said, passing one of the beers to the Bosnian.

Zlatko assented wordlessly. In all of his life, he never imagined that he would wind up in a place with such an unpronounceable name as Bucaramanga. Taking a long gulp of the cold beer, he sat it aside and trailed Lopez out to the exit.

A city located to the northeast of Medellin, Bucaramanga is located in close proximity to the border with Venezuela. Both he and Lopez were there to meet with Aachen. The Org coordinator had traveled to the capital of the Santander department to pursue a fresh lead in the hunt.

During the course of the year, Escobar's henchmen had been responsible for at least five major bombing events throughout the country. The body count from those attacks left some fifty-five people dead and nearly three hundred maimed or otherwise injured.

In mid-summer however, a crime of an entirely different nature had taken place. The honorary consul of Italy in Bucaramanga – an otherwise anonymous sixty-eight year old man named Giuseppe Narducci – had been forcibly abducted. The kidnappers, who failed to identify themselves, demanded a ransom that was equivalent to $2,000,000 U.S. dollars for his release unharmed.

As it developed however, no ransom was ever paid. Narducci died four months later of an apparent heart attack while still being held in captivity.

Colombian authorities subsequently found his body. The honorary consul had been unceremoniously dumped in a remote area of the countryside.

Most recently – on November 20th to be exact – Colombian police officers in Bucaramanga found themselves engaged in a violent gunfight with two suspicious men. During the course of the encounter, the police succeeded in killing both of the suspects.

Acting on information from a clandestine source, Aachen accompanied a representative from the U.S. Embassy for a meeting with the police. The source had indicated his belief that the kidnappers had been members of the Cartel. Aachen had hoped that the incident might provide another piece of the puzzle in the search for Escobar.

The Black Team members found Aachen alone in his SUV, parked on the far edge of the stadium lot.

"How did it go?" Lopez asked, leaning into the driver's window.

Aachen shook his head with a frown. "Nothing for us," he said. "The case isn't related to our guy." He peered absently at the stadium beyond them. "The Police are saying that the two they killed were both FARC. Looks like what it was what always seemed to be – a crime committed to raise money. Nothing more than that."

FARC was the self-styled Revolutionary Armed Forces of Colombia. A Leftist guerrilla group, it had been at war with the government since the mid-sixties. While occasional cooperation with the Cartel

s was not unheard of, the FARC had its own highly political objectives.

"*Mala suerte* for *Senor* Narducci then," Lopez observed dispassionately.

"This man, ah, Narducci," Zlatko began. "He is *diplomata*?"

"No," Aachen replied, climbing out of the SUV. "Just what they call an honorary consul. Narducci was an upstanding private citizen, someone who volunteered to represent Italian interests in the area. No diplomatic status at all."

"So. A wasted trip," Zlatko observed.

"Not entirely a waste," Aachen countered, climbing out of his vehicle. "It gives me the chance to pass something along to you."

Aachen pulled open the rear hatch of the SUV and tossed aside a blanket, revealing a worn leather case. The container was some four feet in length, with a familiar shape. Reaching in, Aachen unzipped the full length of the case and then stood back to allow Zlatko a clear view of the contents.

It was an M48 Zastava. Wooden stock and all, it was nearly identical to the weapon that Zlatko had used during the war. Next to the gun was a separate, smaller bag holding a few boxes of 8mm ammunition and a Zrak ON-76 scope.

Zlatko looked over at Aachen questioningly. "And this is for why?" he asked.

"*Slucaj*," Aachen replied.

Zlatko returned his attention to the weapon and nodded his head in subdued silence.

"*Slucaj*?" Lopez queried Aachen. "What the hell is that?"

"Contingency."

= TWENTY-FIVE: CIERRE =

Bogota, Colombia
December 1, 1993

It was still early in the morning but Colonel Hugo Martinez was already at his desk, mulling over a report that had been freshly received from the Americans. He dropped the report folder on the desktop and plucked a steaming cup of coffee from its porcelain saucer.

Could it really be true, he wondered? Could they actually be close to finally getting the bastard?

Could this be *cierre*? Closure at long last?

The commander of the Search Bloc was under intense pressure and had been so for most of the year. He glanced up at a framed black and white photograph of himself and *Presidente* Gaviria. Happier times.

Although publicly it was all smiles and expressions of confidence, not a day went by that he did not hear from someone in the government asking for an update on the hunt for Escobar. How close are we to catching him? Where is he now? How much longer will this escapade take? Are you aware of the costs involved in this project?

And then there were the more lethal forms of pressure. Suggestions, not at all subtle, from anonymous contacts that he might be better served to abandon the hunt. Maybe quit the National Police altogether and retire to Miami. Enjoy life.

The nameless callers noted that Martinez had a lovely family – for the moment. Maybe he should give some thought to their welfare for a change. Maybe they enjoyed the experience of living.

Maybe not.

All of this was intensified by the fact that his son, also named Hugo, was a lieutenant in the National Police. The younger man was also a member of the Search Bloc.

The Colonel knew that Lieutenant Hugo Martinez was even then in Medellin with the Search Bloc. They were attempting to finalize the location of the Cartel leader.

If found, there was little doubt in the Colonel's mind that Escobar could be taken alive. Nor truthfully would they want him to be so taken. Better a corpse than a prisoner this time.

Colonel Martinez feared neither charges of nepotism nor those of his son's potential failure. Contrarily, he feared that his son might be successful in locating Escobar. Martinez knew that the senior police officer responsible for ending the run of Escobar could be a major target of retaliation by surviving Cartel killers.

The next few days would be even more stressful.

Martinez crossed himself absently and returned his attention to the American report.

= TWENTY-SIX: EL SICARIO =

Barrio Los Olivos
Medellin, Colombia
December 2, 1993

The beige brick residence sat peacefully on 79th Street in the upper middle class Medellin neighborhood of Barrio Los Olivos. The house was leased to an aunt of Pablo Escobar, but she was not there now. For the moment, at least, the neighborhood was almost preternaturally quiet.

For the past two months the sole continuous residents of the Los Olivos house were Pablo Escobar himself and his most trusted bodyguard, Alvaro de Jesus Agudelo – *El Limon*.

The Org was not unfamiliar with the location. Thanks to SIGINT coverage, it was one of four potential hide sites in the general neighborhood that they had surveilled, mapped and planned for over the past two weeks.

Late that morning, after breakfasting on a bowl of pasta, Escobar made a phone call to his son - Juan Pablo - in Bogota. He was sitting in a small bedroom on the third floor of the house. The room was some twelve feet square with a double bed. While comfortable, it was by no means up to his customarily luxurious standards.

Over the course of the lengthy call, Escobar gave his son detailed instructions for a message to be released to the public. The content of the message detailed his alleged harsh and unwarranted persecution at the hands of the Colombian authorities.

Unknown to Escobar as he carefully listed his grievances, the call was being monitored by the Colombian police – as well as the airborne tech unit. Both elements worked to triangulate the location of the telephone in Medellin.

A ground based SIGINT intercept operator immediately recognized the contact for what it was. Reacting quickly, he alerted both Aachen and the air assets.

At once, Aachen notified Chalice and Lopez, ordering them to cover the various possible exits adjoining the target house on 79th Street. Aachen himself moved to cover Site B a little more than a block away. The Paraguayans meanwhile were directed to a fourth potential location on the other end of the barrio.

For his part, CW3 McAllister scrambled his aircrew all of which were housed at a nearby airfield. Within minutes of the alert, their Beechcraft King Air was off the ground and into the clouds above Medellin, sniffing for signals. This time, however, McAllister wasn't concerned about simply burning avgas. As was the case with the intercept operators who were in the back with the racks, he knew that they were working a good contact today.

Once the American support units were notified and rolling, the SIGINT section gave a heads-up to the Colombian techs attached to the Search Bloc.

Moving from their separate sets of lodging, the Org teams eased into pre-selected positions within the target barrio. Chalice and Bear pulled into an area behind a row of houses with rear door exits – any of which could be concealing Escobar. Lopez and Zlatko meanwhile climbed the stairs into a vacant apartment that had been previously leased. The window of the apartment gave them a vantage point on both the side and front streets of the potential target house.

Gently, Zlatko placed the gun bag on an empty table and carefully withdrew the M48 Zastava. He had confidence in this particular gun, having zeroed it several days before. With long practiced hands he loaded the weapon and checked the scope settings.

Satisfied, he settled into a supported position a few feet back from the window. He was in the shadows and well out of view from the street.

And then they waited.

And waited.

***

A few hours later, shortly before 3:00 in the afternoon, Escobar dialed his son's cell number once again. As soon as the two phones connected, the sophisticated gear of the SIGINT and Search Bloc techs alike began to siphon up their electronic signatures.

SIGINT notified Aachen as the Search Bloc police began to swarm into the neighborhood. Aachen, in turn, advised Chalice and Lopez that they were going hot. Both teams immediately rogered up in response.

As Escobar was conversing with his son, he heard a noise from the first floor down below. Search Bloc officers were loudly banging on the door of the house. Almost at once they broke the door down and made forcible entry, screaming commands at the top of their lungs.

Alvaro – *Limon* – was quick to react. He loosed a volley of rounds down the steps at the police and dashed past Escobar toward the window. *"Vaya! Vaya!"* he yelled.

Alvaro went out the bedroom window first, dropping the three feet to the red tile roof of the adjacent building. At once he spotted the Search Bloc personnel on the street below. Resignedly, he opened fire on them with his pistol to provide cover for *Don Pablo's* escape.

The cops enthusiastically replied in kind.

Hit several times, Alvaro brazenly and futilely jumped another ten feet down to street level, gun in hand. Another cascade of police gunfire killed him instantly.

Distracted, Zlatko was focusing on the action surrounding Limon's final moments when Lopez slapped him on the shoulder. *"Carajo*, that's him," Lopez blurted. "Bastard's on the roof! *The roof!*"

A bearded, portly figure had emerged out of the bedroom window and hopped to the tile roof of the adjoining building, as had Limon. The bushy-haired man was bare-footed, wearing faded blue jeans and a dark blue T-shirt. And he was armed.

Zlatko quickly adjusted his sight picture back to the new figure that was moving across the slate tiles.

Peering through the Zrak scope, Zlatko saw gunfire from the street sparking off of the rooftop walls. The figure was physically reacting to the shots. Although clearly wounded, he was shouting defiantly and returning fire with a handgun.

The Bosnian quickly placed the scope's reticle on the moving target of the figure's head and floated it to the external canal of the left ear. Trusting to both luck and skill, he gently pressured the trigger, rushing the shot.

The rifle bucked slightly as the 198-grain bullet left the muzzle traveling at more than 2,700 feet per second. Almost instantaneously, the projectile struck the target's left ear. Coursing through the man's head, it exited out of his right ear. The slug then pranged off of the red brick wall and ricocheted out into oblivion.

Pablo Escobar dropped to his knees, a dazed look of surprise in his eyes. After a momentary pause, he sagged to his right and sprawled out onto the roof. His pistol clattered harmlessly away from his hands.

"*Dobro*," Zlatko whispered.

A throaty roar of appreciation rang up from the Search Bloc cops in the street – followed immediately by chants of "*Viva Colombia!*"

Lopez slapped Zlatko on the shoulder once again. "Good shot!"

"That's what I said," Zlatko mumbled, pulling the Zastava back and tucking it into its case.

"You got the bastard! Son of a bitch, you *are* El Sicario today," Lopez exalted, watching the Search Bloc cops begin to scale the wall to the roof where the body lie. "Nevertheless, let's haul ass. Like now."

As Zlatko recovered his weapon, Lopez keyed the radio. "*Puro*," he told Aachen. "*Puro*. Clear the area."

"Roger and out," Aachen responded tersely.

At once the Org radios acknowledged the transmission and went silent as the teams began the exfiltration scenario.

Lopez and Zlatko took one final glance at the scene before them and then followed suit.

= TWENTY-SEVEN – RUEGA =

Cemetario Jadines Monte Sacro
Itagui, Colombia
December 4, 1993

It had been raining steadily earlier in the day. By mid-afternoon however the rain had slowed to an intermittent drizzle. The air was still damp and redolent of freshly turned earth.

The inclement weather had not dampened the ardor of the thousands of locals who had shown up for the burial service. A heavy contingent of Colombian military police, replete with helmets and rifles at the ready, were also present. They were a show of force, the government's attempt to maintain order in what was fully expected to be a madly chaotic scene.

They were not to be disappointed.

At long last, a hearse appeared on the Autosur 25 to the musical accompaniment of a mariachi band. The vehicle slowly turned into the grounds of the *Cemetario Jadines Monte Sacro*. As it did so the assembled crowd exploded into choruses of screams and plaintive wailing. The remainder of the lengthy procession did its best to wedge into the grounds of the cemetery behind the lead vehicles.

Lopez and Zlatko were seated in a blacked out Chevy Suburban on the opposite end of the graveyard, parked amidst a bevy of police trucks. From there they viewed the noisy developments with fascination. As they looked on bemused, attendants opened the rear doors of the hearse and extracted a shiny silver coffin.

The rainfall started anew. Heavy droplets began to splatter off the top of the coffin as it was exposed to the sky.

"*Viva Pablo!*" a group of men shouted enthusiastically. "*Viva Escobar!*"

"*Ay, pobrecito!*" an old woman cried. "*Mi querido!*"

"*Mi angel!*" another elderly woman keened sorrowfully. "*Le han matado!*"

A frenzied looking man whipped a Colombian flag back and forth in the wet air, chanting above the noise of the mariachis, "*Don Pablo, Don Pablo. Ruega por nosostros!*"

Zlatko, who had been laboring to learn some Spanish while in country, glanced at a well-thumbed phrase book in his lap. "This word: *ruega*," he said. "It means what?"

"Pray," Lopez answered, his eyes fixated on the scene before them. "*Ruega por nosostros...* Don Pablo, pray for us."

Zlatko snorted sardonically.

"Hey, don't sell their emotions short Zee," Lopez cautioned, watching the undulation of the assembled masses. "You need to walk soft my friend. These people – these *Paisas* – if they knew, they would eat you up and shit you out... And those would be the nicer ones."

The coffin, then free of the hearse, was jostled by the crowds as they forcibly pushed themselves in. The press of their numbers knocked aside the officiating priest and members of the Escobar family alike. A number of people, caught in the scrum, struggled and failed to maintain their footing on the increasingly slippery ground.

The burial was the culmination of an all night wake that had recently been concluded in Itagui, a small city just southwest of Medellin. The wake itself had been heavily thronged, to the extent that the press of mourners had broken out several windows of the funeral home in the course of their ardor.

It had been almost exactly forty-eight hours since Pablo's death.

Zlatko had seen more than his share of death in Bosnia, but nothing to compare to the scene unfolding in front of him. "Why such love for this piece of shit?" he wondered aloud.

Lopez shrugged. "The Robin Hood effect," he said. "He was a murdering, drug smuggling bastard, but he spread a lot of cash around in the slums. A lot of people benefitted."

Seeing that the situation was rapidly getting out of control, the military closed in to protect the burial party from the grasping hands and arms of the crowd. The Escobar family was now effectively separated from the coffin. To avoid being trampled, they retreated back to the relative safety of their vehicles.

The military provided a cordon of bodies around the burial party, as the coffin was carried up to the top of a muddy hill. Once there, it was hurriedly placed atop of its final resting place.

"I'm serious Zee," Lopez continued. "Escobar's gone but the Cartels will live on… You can never mention your role in this to anyone. Not even to other people in the Org."

Zlatko maintained his gaze on the frantic spectacle at the top of the hillock. "Yeah," he replied flatly. "*No problemo.*"

Finally the assembled Escobar supporters lowered the coffin into the moist grave. That completed, they were forced back by the military police as workmen began to shovel dirt on top of the vault covering.

At long last the remains of Don Pablo were left in the family plot, now in the company of his ancestors. The grave would remain as an attraction to tourists, the faithful and the merely curious.

Pablo Escobar-Gaviria, a one time petty thief, had been a millionaire by the age of twenty-two, a member of the national congress, and the most feared drug lord of his age. The organization that he developed grew to control eighty percent of the global cocaine trade.

At the time of his death *El Padron* – who had once declared his preference for a grave in Colombia over a cell in America - was forty-four years old.

-END-

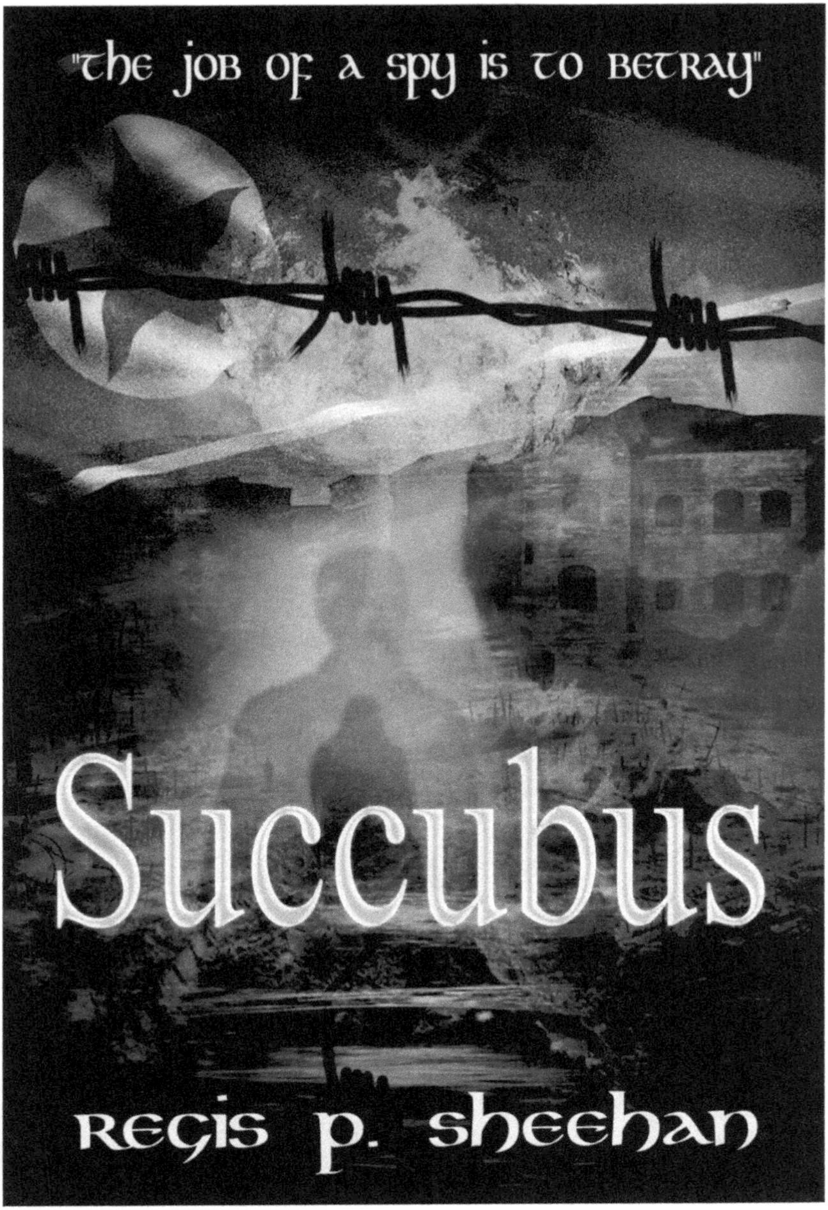
"THE JOB OF A SPY IS TO BETRAY"
Succubus
REGIS P. SHEEHAN

SUCCUBUS

A novel by
REGIS P. SHEEHAN

DEDICATION

To the People of North Korea
The True Victims of the Kim Family Regime

Acknowledgments

With special appreciation to

Mitch Price
Special Agent (Retired), United States Secret Service

For his consultation on the issue of North Korean counterfeit
Supernotes
-&-
Jessica Rohr, RDH
Registered Dental Hygienist
For her consultation on dental procedural matters
-Also-
For background information on the North Korean prison
camps:

Human Rights.gov - Web site

Kang, Chol-Hwan – "The Aquariums of Pyongyang: Ten Years
in the North Korean Gulag", Basic Books, 2005

US Congress - Hearing Before the Congressional Executive
Commission on China – 112th Congress – Second Session – March
5, 2002

For glimpses of life in North Korea:

Demick, Barbara – "Nothing to Envy", Spiegel and Grau, 2010

French, Paul – North Korea: State of Paranoia", Zed Books,
2014

Kirkpatrick, Melanie - "Escape from North Korea – The Untold
Story of Asia's Underground Railroad", Encounter Books, 2016

Lankov, Andre – "The Real North Korea", Oxford University
Press, 2014

Lee, Jin Seo - "North Korean Political Prison Camps", Radio
Free Asia Korean Service, 2016

NK News – "Life on the North Korean Borderlands: A Collection of Essays and Articles by NK News Contributors", 2015

Sweeney, John – "North Korea Undercover: Inside the World's Most Secret State", Pegasus, 2015

Tudor, Daniel, and Pearson, James – "North Korea Confidential", Tuttle Publishing, 2015
-And-
Hood, William - "Mole", Ballantine Books, 1983

"Like war, spying is a dirty business. Shed of its alleged glory, a soldier's job is to kill. Peel away the claptrap of espionage and the spy's job is to betray trust. The only justification a soldier or spy can have is the moral worth of the cause he represents."

William Hood, "Mole", 1983

ONE: JILIN

Along the China/North Korean Border
October 16, 2003

October in China could be cold. October in far northeastern China, astride the border of North Korea, could be damned cold. And so it was.

Night had just fallen, bringing with it the sharp winds that were just now beginning to whip across the flats. They sailed effortlessly up the slope and into the Westerner's face. It didn't help that he had just wedged himself into a break in the lightly snow-encrusted trees. The position, wet and frigid, was an uncomfortable but rather well chosen vantage point for the job at hand.

Reaching back to his daypack, the Westerner withdrew a small, encrypted mil-spec radio. He ensured it was turned on and was properly tuned. That done, he rested it against the dampened base of a tree. Next xxx out of the daypack came a pair of binoculars, which he gently perched atop a dry patch of ground. Finally came an Infrared penlight which found its place next to the binoculars.

Preparations done, he paused briefly to listen for movement – human or animal – in the environment. Agreeably, all was quiet.

The man was commonly known to his colleagues and friends, the latter now ever fewer in number, as "Bear". His Christian name was Michael Paul Medved. He had been in this line of work, in one form or another, for a very long time.

Bear slipped off his gloves and placed them carefully on the ground at eye level where he could quickly find them again. After rubbing his hands together to generate a bit of heat, he grasped the rubberized binoculars and trained the lenses on the near distance below.

A dark strip of frozen terrain extended away just below his lair. Patiently, he twisted the focus rings as he adapted his night vision to the view.

And there it was.

Before him was a very narrow strip of water called the Tumen. Largely unheard of in the West, it served as the border area of the region encompassing North Korea, China and Russia.

To the south of his position in Jilin Province, China, was the better known, though now largely forgotten, stretch of the Yalu River.

The Yalu, or Amnok, was the waterway that was more familiar to Americans – or at least to those of certain age – thanks to its 1950's Korean War fame. The Yalu was the geographic boundary most often cited as the demarcation line between a police action and a serious land war engagement.

On June 25, 1950, the forces of North Korea crossed the 38th Parallel that divided their country from South Korea, thereby initiating the Korean War. Seoul, the South Korean capital, collapsed a few days later. The United Nations quickly dispatched forces, primarily in the form of American troops, to combat the Communist incursion.

By the autumn of 1950 the war was not going well for the North Koreans. General Douglas MacArthur had landed at Inchon, recaptured Seoul and chased the North Koreans back to the Yalu.

In response, 300,000 Chinese alleged volunteers swarmed across the Yalu in mass formations. By November of 1950 American and Chinese troops were in direct combat with each other.

More than one US military leader wanted to strike the enemy north of the Yalu, that is to say, in China. They were deterred from this action by their political leadership. The latter feared such action would cause the Chinese – and maybe the Soviets as well – to drop the pretense of volunteer action and result in a full-scale war. Maybe even World War III.

American fighter pilots in particular were often warned not to go "north of the Yalu". But go they frequently did, and in so doing won air superiority for the UN troops fighting below.

Now Bear was north of the Yalu. This was not his first time in Asia. His initial visit to the region was in the mid-1960's as a US Army Special Forces soldier and a member of the MACV-SOG recon teams. Although the authorities would never admit to it, he had never stepped foot into China way back then. At the time, the clandestine mission had been to assist in the insertion of a road watch team into the People's Republic who doubled as telephone tappers.

Bear was a good bit heftier now than he had been in his MACV-SOG days. He was pushing sixty in not so many more years. His longish blond hair was thinning and streaming to gray.

Nevertheless, the former commando turned undercover narc knew he could more than hold his own when the situation required him to do so. He just hoped that the need would not arise that night.

Lowering the binoculars, he peeled back the Velcro cover of his tactical watch and briefly studied the luminous dial. He had been in position now for close to an hour. They were running late. Verging on being uncomfortably late.

Being off schedule did not necessarily mean disaster. As he knew, there were a number of reasons that...

The noise of a thickly muffled explosion caught his attention. Off to his right, far to the south along the river, a yellowish-red fireball flamed briefly above the trees.

Bear keyed the mic on the radio, sending a pre-programmed burst transmission out into the atmosphere. Seconds later he was rewarded with an acknowledging response from his teammates.

Nodding to himself, he lifted the binocs back to eye level. "Okay," he breathed to himself. "And here we go."

TWO: R/35/L

A three story, whitewashed brick building sat in the pleasant, far outskirts of Leesburg, Virginia. It shamelessly proclaimed itself to be the offices of the Kovach Group Insurance Brokerage. It was a title that was sufficiently dull so as to deter the idly curious. For those who persevered, however, Kovach offered enough legitimate business activity to accommodate them.

The true nature of the Kovach Group's activities had less to do with reinsurance business coverage and more to do with the coverage of developments in the foreign news media.

The Kovach Group was what the CIA called an "off-site location". It housed a dozen or so employees who worked in their comfortable quarters under conditions of a fairly loose cover arrangement. They were part of the CIA's Directorate of Intelligence, or the DI.

Erik was one of the analysts who worked on the second floor of the building. A relative newbie to the Agency, he was a member of the branch that covered the Western and Central European open media sources.

It was a Friday and he was looking forward to maybe hooking up with the new girl he met downtown last week. Dinner. She was a paralegal with one of the many DC law firms. At the very least, they would have dinner. Maybe dinner in Georgetown – as expensive as that would be.

In any event, he thought, hope springs eternal. Even in the CIA. *Especially* in the CIA.

The more significant news circulating in the ether that day was the capture of the so-called DC Sniper – the individual who had literally terrorized the Northern Virginia area since the beginning of the month. In the end, the feared sniper had actually been a pair of amateur killers.

The local and national news feeds were abuzz with the capture of two men named John Allen Muhammad and John Lee Malvo.

4

Both were arrested without incident at a rest area on I-270 in Maryland. To date they had scored a total of ten victims, all innocents who were shot from ambush.

The realty, as exposed by the facts of the capture, ran contrary to several weeks of alleged sightings and law enforcement press releases. The shooters now in custody were two people, not one. They were black, not white. And they were using a dark blue Chevy Caprice sedan, not a white panel van. Other than that...

One could take it as a cautionary tale for all intelligence staffers.

Erik turned his attention back to his classified system, satisfied that he was now less likely to be shot through the head while fueling his car later in the day. Within minutes of scrawling through the database however, even dinner in Georgetown was fading into the background.

"Wow," he mumbled quietly as he squinted at the display glowing on his computer screen.

Erik tapped his fingers on the keyboard to double check what he was seeing. Then he did it again. Same result.

"This one has whiskers on it Patty," he said to his silver haired partner who occupied the adjoining cubicle. "An oldie but a goodie... Unbelievable really."

Patty, verging on retirement, was frankly more interested in her annuity planning than in the European media developments at this point in life. "You sure?" she asked absently.

"Yeah... Looks like."

"Then take it upstairs and show it to him."

"Hmmm," Erik mumbled. He hit the print button and pushed his chair back to fetch the hard copy article.

* * *

"You sure?" the supervisor asked. He swiveled about in his chair to take in the view of the fall foliage beyond his top floor window as he regarded the scrap of paper in his hand.

"Sure am," Erik replied. He remained standing in front of his boss' desk. "This is a verified true hit on Romeo/Thirty-Five/Lima," he said. "For real."

The supervisor replaced his glasses on the bridge of his nose, the better to focus on the printout. "This Romeo series hasn't been used since ah...?"

Erik glanced at the 3x5 index card in his hand. "Not in the past four years," he said. He looked at the card again. "Four and a half years to be exact."

"Your exactitude is noted and appreciated," the supervisor commented flatly. He turned his attention back to the brief note on the paper.

"This is in response to the honored Fellows of the Search Committee," it read. "I am intrigued by the Research Proposal that you have outlined with regard to the Agena Project. I would be honored to participate. My professional CV will be supplied under separate cover... Respectfully, Dr. A. L. Peron."

"And that is the correct verbiage for this entry?" the supervisor asked.

"It is," Erik confirmed. "Word for word. Exactly."

As they both well knew, R/35/L was a largely forgotten method of contact from what the Agency thought of as a "Media Walk-In." The goal was to attract people who would be of interest. People who wished to voluntarily make contact with the CIA.

By design, the uninitiated would have no access to this channel. Those who responded would have had, by definition, some degree of inside knowledge to be aware of the annunciator ad procedure in the first place.

In addition to being knowledgeable of this protocol, one would also need to know that an ad must be placed in a Friday edition of the International Herald Tribune in hopes that the US Government would take note of it.

In this case, it did.

When the CIA initiated the Media Walk-In program a decade or so earlier, it did so with the realization that it was a risk. It could be susceptible to clever fraudsters, paper mills and – even worse – provocations by hostile intelligence services. On the up side, it would also provide an avenue for true sources of intel who could safely reach out and make contact in no other way.

"Refresh my memory," the supervisor said. "What is the response procedure for Romeo/Thirty-Five/Lima?"

6

Erik didn't need to refer to his 3x5 card. "Reply next Friday via an ad in the international edition of Le Figaro," he said. "Using the pre-established language format."

"Okay. Do it."

THREE: THE AGREED FRAMEWORK

National Security Council Staff
Washington, District of Columbia
November 21, 2002

Jerry Saltzman was a thirtyish NSC staffer. A bachelor and a political junkie with a Master's in international relations, he now happily found himself occupying a small office in the ornate Old Executive Office Building, or OEB.

The OEB, which in a simpler time housed the former Departments of War, Navy and State together, was now an extension of the Presidential support staff. It shared the compound grounds with the White House. The latter was just across the narrow driveway that separated them.

Ever since the Bush II inauguration, Saltzman had been assigned to work on the NSC's Asia portfolio. And November had been a pretty busy month.

The year, as was the case with all years, began with the President's State of the Union Address. At that time, POTUS named North Korea, along with Iraq and Iran, as part of an Axis of Evil, which together posed a grave threat to the peace of the world.

As if obliged to play their role in the unfolding drama, North Korea under Kim Jong Il – the Dear Leader – dutifully continued to fulfill the evil genius persona that so many feared.

The year 1994 had been considerably more upbeat, Saltzman knew. He reached for a familiar briefing book relating to that period and flipped it open. On the first page was the optimistic October 21, 1994 quote. Some eight years earlier, it had been uttered by then-President William Jefferson Clinton. "I'd like to say just a word about the framework with North Korea that Ambassador Gallucci signed this morning," Clinton began with just a bit of the characteristic head swagger.

"This is a good deal for the United States," he continued. "North Korea will freeze and then dismantle its nuclear program. South Korea and our other allies will be better protected. The entire world will be safer as we slow the spread of nuclear weapons."

On that date, the United States and the Democratic Republic of North Korea (DPRK) signed what was diplomatically called The Agreed Framework.

Under the agreement, the DPRK stipulated it would dismantle its graphite reactors. They would also halt activity at their uranium enrichment reprocessing facilities and move to seal them and eventually dismantle them altogether.

Likewise, they agreed to allow the return of the United Nations nuclear inspectors – the International Atomic Energy Agency (IAEA)- to resume their routine and unannounced inspections of their facilities.

In return, the DPRK would enjoy some global largesse. For starters, they would be provided with two light water reactors (LWR), similar to those used in the United States. Both projects would be a gift - paid for by an international consortium.

By the end of the following year the DPRK would also receive some 150,000 tons of heavy fuel oil. The oil was to be used for domestic heating and the generation of electricity. They would also receive 500,000 tons of fuel oil annually until the first LWR successfully went on line.

And, not inconsequentially, the US promised neither to threaten nor to use nuclear weapons against their Pyongyang bargaining partners.

But that was then.

This was now.

Within the past week, the North Koreans had openly admitted to having restarted their nuclear facilities. The United States Government, in turn, declared its termination of the fuel oil shipments to the DPRK.

And just yesterday, the North Korean Government avowed its right to implement a nuclear weapons program.

To Saltzman, it looked as though the Nuclear Club was getting ready to expand. The vibes were not good.

FOUR: DUE DILIGENCE

**Leesburg
Loudoun County, Virginia
November 26, 2002**

Erik reluctantly trudged back up the worn wooden steps to his supervisor's third floor office. It was a chilly Tuesday morning and he had no good news to offer. From his point of view, at least.

He knew it was no knock on him or his job performance, but still he would have preferred to have had the opportunity to hit this one out of the park. At the very least, it would have been a good war story for future recounting. That didn't happen, though.

Nonetheless, Thursday was Thanksgiving. There was that.

He peremptorily tapped on the doorjamb of his supervisor's office, then entered and dropped into a chair opposite the other's desk.

"Let me guess," the supervisor offered absently. "This is about, uh, Romero Something Or Other?"

"Romeo/Thirty-Five/Lima," Erik supplied. "The Herald Tribune."

"Yeah. That's the one... So, what happened?"

"Not much," Erik admitted.

"Let's have it then."

"Uhm. As you know, the IHT ad went active on Friday, October 25th. Following the procedure, I put a response in the Friday November 1st international edition of *Le Figaro*."

"Good man," the supervisor said. "And then?"

Erik frowned. "Well, uh, nothing."

"Nothing," the supervisor replied. "That's not much else. And so?"

Erik crossed his booted feet nervously. "Well, our guy should have replied to our message a week later – November 8th - in the Jerusalem Post. But it was a no go... Nothing on the 8th, where it should have been. Nothing on the 15th or the 22d either... All quiet."

The supervisor tilted his head back and forth understandingly. "Okay. Good enough. We made our due diligence effort. Put this

Romeo contact out to the Community to see if anyone wants to chase this... But it's not for us."

"Okay Chief," Erik relented. "Will do."

FIVE: ACCOUNTABILITY REVIEW

Washington, District of Columbia
December 10, 2002

The US Commerce Department is a sprawling edifice occupying the corner of Constitution Avenue NW and 15th Street NW in downtown Washington DC. Just a shade to the south of the building is the towering Washington Monument.

A glance across the street and to the north finds the heavily secured grounds of the White House. The area is naturally a major focal point of tourist activity.

The man who was biding his time in the bowels of Commerce was not there for tourism. Indeed, he'd much rather have been somewhere else. Anywhere else.

The lone individual occupied an uncomfortable chair in the exterior of the Secure Compartmented Information Facility, or SCIF. Chalice, as he was known, was a compact figure with a closely cropped head of graying hair and a weathered, olive complexion.

Chalice was not unfamiliar with operational performance reviews, though none in his experience had been conducted at this high a level of interest. A former Army Special Forces Warrant Officer, and later a Military Intelligence HUMINT agent handler, he was now a case officer for a civilian covert federal agency.

The agency with which he was affiliated was officially labeled the Joint Interdepartmental Committee on Special Activities, or JICSA. Among those members of the Government who were read in to the program, relatively few in number, it was more colloquially referred to as the Org.

Headquartered in the McLean suburbs, JICSA easily blended into the milieu of the other so-called Beltway Bandits under the cover name of Global Threat Analysis, Inc. While it presented itself as a corporate risk assessment and advisory firm, in reality it was a clandestine entity that answered to the Executive Branch via the National Security Council.

From a purely bureaucratic perspective, the major strength of JICSA was its ability to morph its structure in response to the missions at hand. This it accomplished with a small core staff of professionals who were reliant upon a constantly fluctuating collection of contractors with highly diverse skill sets.

From a purely political perspective, operating quietly under the auspices of the NSC, JICSA offered a degree of legitimate deniability to the larger, well-known intelligence agencies.

JICSA's modest size and flexibility routinely earned favor from the budget people who predictably from time to time were looking for financial targets.

Chalice was presently less interested in existential threats to his agency than he was regarding to his own future. He had been the case officer for a previous Org operation code named SOLO APEX. As was all too tragically clear, the project did not end well.

In a sense, the tasking of JICSA in the case of SOLO APEX was a bit of an anomaly. More frequently, the Org neither collected nor developed intelligence; rather, it acted upon developed intelligence – and aggressively so.

The purpose of SOLO APEX had been to insinuate a trusted American agent into the ranks of a burgeoning Jihadist group. This Chalice did with great success. The agent, a South African national by birth, penetrated the target group and made his way as far as a leadership compound in Algeria by April of 1999.

Prior to that time, fittingly enough at a 1998 Halloween meeting in a safe house in Prague, the agent had advised Chalice of a vague Jihadist plan to attack Western targets in some sort of aviation context. The specifics of the plan were unknown. And, at the time, they were unknowable.

Although unmasked at the Algerian compound and subjected to a brutal interrogation, the agent was nonetheless able to signal his distress, calling for an emergency extraction. In response, Chalice dispatched a rescue force to pull the agent out of the compound.

The resulting attempt failed. It culminated with the loss not only of the agent but of the entire rescue team and their aircrew as well.

The only positive aspect of the tragedy was the successful application of the cover story to conceal the operation. The terrorists themselves were not seeking to publicize their vulnerability. And, aside from several Allied intelligence organizations, most especially the French who had an agent on the ground, the world moved on unaware of the episode.

The Org did likewise.

* * *

Like all Americans, Chalice vividly recalled the morning of Tuesday, September 11th, 2001. In his case, he had been working out in a suburban Northern Virginia gym when the television announced that an aircraft had struck the north tower of the World Trade Center in New York City.

Chalice had resumed his workout, assuming it was a freak aviation accident involving an inexperienced private pilot and his single engine plane.

Eighteen minutes later what was clearly a commercial airliner hit the second tower, eventually destroying it. At once there was no doubt; this was clearly a terrorist attack upon the United States.

It took no great leap of imagination for Chalice to draw the connection between what he was seeing on TV with his ingrained memories of the SOLO APEX operation. It was beyond obvious that this was exactly what his agent was trying to communicate to him nearly three years before the fact.

This unprecedented assault is what Chalice could have theoretically prevented. But he did not.

Shocked and numbed, Chalice stumbled back into the gym's dressing room. He made it as far as the showers where, still fully clothed, he began retching violently into the stall for what felt like an eternity.

* * *

As was the case with several other members of the Org, Chalice had been called to testify in front of the Review Committee. For an expanse of eighteen hours over a three-day period he had been relentlessly grilled on all facets of the operation. It seemed that every conceivable issue had been covered, from the selection and deployment of the agents to the project's eventual disastrous demise. The questioning had been pointed and distinctly unsympathetic. It had been an exhausting and troubling process.

And supposedly, they had reached the day when the Committee would announce their conclusions.

The catastrophic result necessarily triggered a procedural review process. In the State Department, such a procedure was called an Accountability Review Board, or ARB. Needless to say, a State ARB drew widespread publicity as to its membership and results. Such was not the case with secretive JICSA procedures.

The covert agency had its own covert review process. Nevertheless, it was a process that delved carefully into the facts of the case. Its findings were passed along to the NSC for administrative action.

* * *

The door to the SCIF creaked open, allowing JD Tucker to emerge from its stuffy confines. Chalice, the former Warrant Officer, respectfully climbed to his feet in the presence of the former Army General Officer.

Tucker had retired years earlier from the Army as a brigadier general; a one-star officer. In his time, he had also successfully commanded the legendary Delta Force, or SFOD/Delta. He still looked every bit the part. He was also the no-nonsense director of JICSA.

The two Army veterans made eye contact for a few silent moments before Tucker allowed his face to crack in the briefest of smiles.

"Relax," Tucker said, clapping Chalice on the shoulder. "The Review Committee gave us a pass on SOLO APEX. They ruled that all foreseeable precautions to safeguard personnel had been taken. They just ended in mission failure. And death. Fortunes of war."

Chalice exhaled in an involuntary gasp of relief. "Thank God," he muttered quietly. He immediately felt a recurrence of the familiar sense of guilt over the deaths of so many people.

"Yeah," Tucker agreed. "Him too."

Wordlessly, the members of the Review Committee began to file out of the SCIF. One or two gave Chalice and Tucker a fleeting, appreciative smile. The majority ignored them in their hurry to exit the building and be done with the process.

Tucker waited until they were again alone in the anterior room. He fixed his redeemed case officer with an unemotional stare. "You've had your wings clipped for a good long while now, Chalice," he said. "You about ready to go back on the board?"

"Yes sir, I am."

Tucker smiled openly. "Okay. We may have something for you then."

SIX: THE FM

Georgetown
Washington, District of Columbia
December 23, 2002

A Diplomatic Security Service motorcade was staged in front of the Four Seasons Hotel. They were in the pricey Georgetown area of Washington. The motorcade consisted of four vehicles - a Metro DC Police car, the DS lead car, the Cadillac armored limo, and the Chevy Suburban follow.

Nick Oliveri, a Special Agent of the Diplomatic Security Service, was the Shift Leader on this particular detail. He had posted himself at the right rear passenger door of the limo as soon as he heard the Agent in Charge (AIC) warning of an imminent departure over his earpiece. He had already cracked the heavy door open a few inches in preparation for the protectee's appearance.

The protectee, the FM (or Foreign Minister) of a critical Mid-Eastern nation, was an important partner of the United States. While an exemplarily devout Muslim when back home, he was a bit of a playboy when out and about in the West.

"In the box," crackled the earpiece. The AIC and the FM were now in the elevator and coming down to the lobby.

"Copy," Oliveri replied into his mike. "Limo ready."

Two days in New York at the UN with this guy and one day in Washington and he was routinely late for every appointment. Now, with the Secretary of State on the agenda, he's running early. Figures, Oliveri thought.

"And coming out."

Almost immediately, the doors of the Four Seasons popped open and the advance agent came out onto the sidewalk. Right behind him was the Foreign Minister with a trusted staff assistant at his side. Two more DS agents flanked the FM on his left and right. The AIC was closely bringing up the rear within an arm's length of the Minister.

Within moments the FM was safely buttoned up in the back of the limo and they were rolling off toward Main State.

* * *

Twenty minutes after departing the Four Seasons, the FM was on the seventh floor of the State Department, and seated in the well-appointed office of the Secretary. Needless to say, the primary topic was Saddam Hussein and his regime in Iraq.

The Secretary, as befitting his military background, conducted his meeting with the Foreign Minister at a correct but fairly brisk pace. As was usual, the agenda was dominated with a discussion of Iraq and the possible options to deal with issue of Saddam Hussein.

Of particular interest was the recent response from Saddam Hussein's government in Baghdad to the United Nations. The UN had asked for an accounting of the Iraqi weapons program.

Citing what the Secretary termed as a total failure, he recounted the Iraqi omissions with reference to anthrax and other biological weapons, the nuclear issue and the alleged mobile chemical weapons production units.

What the Secretary did not share with the Foreign Minister was the fact that the American suspicions of Saddam and his weapons of mass destruction program were buttressed by reports from a German intelligence source code-named Curve Ball.

All told, given the intelligence coming in from American, German and British intelligence sources, it appeared the Iraqi leader was on the path to a serious weapons program. Saddam's proclivity to utilize such weaponry was not in doubt.

As the Foreign Minister well knew, on that very same day UN inspectors were due to begin interviews with Iraqi nuclear scientists in Iraq itself. How successful they might be was a matter of pure speculation.

Satisfied with the productive meeting, the FM shook hands with the Secretary and assured him of the best wishes from his king. His most important meeting of the trip now concluded, the FM was whisked back down to the lobby where Oliveri and the rest of the DS detail awaited him. His next stop was Dulles International and then onto his personal jet for the long ride home.

After the Secretary bid farewell to the FM, he summoned one of his senior policy advisors for a post-meeting conference.

"And?" the advisor asked.

"They're on board with Iraq," the Secretary said. "They'll support us in New York and Geneva. No doubt of that."

The advisor nodded. "Okay. Good news then."

"Not all good news though," the Secretary said, furrowing his eyebrows.

"No?"

"His service has somehow picked up snippets about the North Koreans," the Secretary said. "Sounds like they are accelerating their nuclear program... He expressed his concern. He thinks we're losing focus there."

The senior advisor brushed an imaginary piece of lint off of his blue serge pants leg. "I imagine that they're just getting Pyongyang's latest batch of propaganda. Probably nothing to worry about."

"I hope so," the Secretary of State offered. "Iraq is more than a full plate all by itself... We don't need any extra bullshit from the North Koreans just now."

"Agreed."

"Have someone look into it though."

"Will do."

SEVEN: JICSA

McLean, Virginia
December 27, 2002

It was late in the morning. JD Tucker had just returned from the gym, his hair still damp from the shower. Despite his justifiable claim on senior citizen status, the former Delta Force commander still prided himself on a degree of physical fitness that many of his juniors would envy.

As he slipped into Conference A, which is how the JICSA people referred to their one and only SCIF, he caught sight of his two primary advisors. Both were already seated at the conference table.

Kurt Meyerhof, his deputy and a man with a near genius level IQ – at least according to him - a retired member of the Office of Naval Intelligence. During his career, he had specialized in foreign naval leadership personalities and doctrinal issues.

The woman, still a shapely and alluring redhead in her early forties, was Angela – or Angela the Analyst, as she was known. She was the chief of the small but critically important JICSA analytic element.

Prior to coming aboard with JICSA, the Georgetown graduate had been a hard targets analyst with the Defense Intelligence Agency. Her time with DIA included a stint with their HUMINT handlers in the Clarendon office tower in Arlington.

As Tucker settled into his beige colored executive chair he took appreciative note of the silvery coffee pot atop the table.

"Cold out there?" Meyerhof asked the boss.

Tucker nodded, filling a mug with black coffee. "Cold enough to freeze a ..." he glanced at Angela. "Yeah, it's cold out."

Actually, the need for delicacy between Tucker and his Chief of Analysis was for show only. They had a history.

A few years back, during the SOLO APEX timeframe and earlier, they had been involved in a heated romantic affair. Although their couplings were usually conducted out of town and out of sight, it was not the sort of thing that could be condoned.

19

Meyerhof knew of the affair. Although he never mentioned it to either party, Tucker knew that he knew. As always, he appreciated the discretion of his deputy.

Although they remained professional colleagues, each party had since gone their own ways. Tucker remained the divorced man about town while rumor had it Angela was now seeing a well-positioned real estate developer.

But the passage of time did not erase memories.

Tucker took a sip of the still steaming coffee and cupped the mug in both hands. "So," he began. "What have we got?"

"We have a read out on the Romeo/Thirty-Five/Lima issue," Angela said.

"And that is?"

"The bit of stale crumb the Agency recently threw our way," Meyerhof replied.

"Correct," said Angela. Her face was glowing in the way that it did when she was onto a promising new project. Or when cuddling after an exuberant sexual encounter, Tucker recalled. "But this discarded crumb may turn out to be better than the entire cake."

"Okay. Enlighten me," Tucker prompted.

Angela adjusted herself in her seat. "What they are calling Romeo/Thirty-Five/Lima is a media walk-in," she explained. "In fact, the individual was attempting to reach them in what is a fairly outdated mode of contact. The Agency duly sent the prescribed response but the reply never came. So, they lost interest."

"We went to our friends at The Fort," Meyerhof continued. "The NSA was able to run down the ID of the possible contact fairly quickly."

"So, who is it?" Tucker asked.

Wordlessly, Angela slipped the text of the NSA TOP SECRET/COMSEC report in front of him.

"Hmmmm," Tucker mused as he scanned the single sheet of paper. "Is the Agency aware of this development?"

"No," Meyerhof retorted. "Certainly not."

"Let's keep it that way."

Tucker read through the message more closely a second time. "This could be politically sensitive," he said. "We'll need to go and see the Wizards."

"I'll set it up," Meyerhof answered. Rising from his chair he added, "As to the case officer, Kirby is back and ready for assignment. Go with him?"

"No, I think not," Tucker countered. "Chalice has just been cleared by the Review Board... He needs to get his head back into the game. Give this one to him."

"You got it."

EIGHT: ARGENT SUCCUBUS

Off-Site Location
Shepherdstown, West Virginia
January 6, 2003

Shepherdstown is located at the northern end of the Shenandoah Valley, along the Potomac River. The oldest town in West Virginia, it traces its founding back to 1762. In those days, long past the city was known as Mecklenburg.

In keeping with their standard practice, the Wizards were meeting in yet another off-site locale. In this instance, it was in a storied wood frame house that sat discreetly two blocks off West German Street, not far from Shepherd University. The Org located this venue when it was seeking remote locations for their executive sessions in the general DC area. They determined they could do little better than this frequently overlooked rural niche.

In a somewhat unusual turn of events, JD Tucker asked Meyerhof to attend this session of the Wizards with him. Most often, the Org director jealously safeguarded his singular relationship with what amounted to the JICSA governing board of directors.

Tucker and Meyerhof were waiting inside the house when the Wizards arrived in a nondescript Ford van. All four men were former senior members of various elements of the national security establishment.

As was the norm, a pair of the Org's technicians had surveyed the property earlier in the day and swept the facility for electronic eavesdropping devices. A team of casually attired security officers thereafter discretely posted the site. They were there to ensure that it continued to remain free of hostile surveillance gear throughout the course of the meeting.

"Thank you for coming out here today," Tucker said as the four managers settled into their chairs. "I hope the trip was uneventful."

"My wife and I have been to Shepherdstown a few times," Barry Duguid replied with a wave of a hand. "Beautiful area. Always happy to be here."

Duguid, the newly appointed chairman of the Wizards, was a retired career CIA officer. He was a gaunt figure with the lanky physique of a long-distance runner. Duguid had assumed the chairmanship when the former chair, a veteran Air Force general, died as the result of a stroke.

"To business then," Tucker intoned.

"Go ahead," Duguid replied.

For the better part of the next two hours Tucker and Meyerhof took them through the latest developments in current Org plans and operations. The Wizards were understandably keen on Tucker's appreciation of the recent SOLO APEX Review Board conclusions.

After a short break, Meyerhof briefed the oversight board on the Org budget and fielded their questions, which were few.

"What is the new issue today?" Duguid asked at last, changing topics.

Meyerhof passed four classified folders to the Wizards as Tucker prepared to speak.

"ARGENT SUCCUBUS is the assigned case name," Tucker said. "To be honest, we aren't quite sure how deep this one will go. But if it has legs, it will also have political ramifications. State would certainly be concerned."

"Background?" Adolfo Torres asked. The newest member of the Wizards, Torres was a Cuban immigrant who rose to the rank of brigadier general in the Army's Military Intelligence branch.

Tucker explained the CIA media walk-in procedure – with which Duguid was familiar – as well as the results of the NSA identity linking research. The operation, he explained, would begin with an initial approach to the targeted individual to ascertain his intentions.

"Who did NSA identify as the target?" Richard Kaufman asked. The ruddy-faced attorney had formerly held a senior position in the Office of the General Counsel at the National Security Agency. He retained a lively interest in the activities of his old employer.

"To the best of our estimation," said Tucker, "it is a North Korean named Ro Jae-Ki."

"The name means nothing at all to me," Kaufman sniffed, displaying a bit of impatience at the director's perceived showmanship. "Who is he?"

"Mr. Ro appears to be the Deputy Chief of Mission of the DPRK embassy in Rome," Tucker revealed. "Their DCM."

There was a moment of reflective silence among the four Wizards.

"The number two North Korean diplomat in Italy wants to defect?" Ambassador Wardlaw, the fourth member of the Wizards, said at last, breaking the silence. "I would think that to be unlikely. Highly unlikely. But if true, then the State Department would most definitely be concerned with this approach."

"Respectfully," Meyerhof began, "just this past October a top North Korean nuclear scientist actually did defect in London. Six years ago, in 1997, the North Korean ambassador to Egypt also defected. He and his wife both sought asylum at the Embassy in Cairo."

"That same year," said Tucker, taking up the theme of the story, "the elderly head of the ruling Korean Workers Party sought asylum in Beijing, of all places. Three years before that, an army colonel who was responsible for procuring personal luxuries for Kim Il Sung throughout Europe defected in Vienna."

"So there certainly is historical precedent for this one," Meyerhof concluded.

Wardlaw shrugged noncommittally.

"I would have thought this was related to the on-going developments in Iraq," Kaufman observed. "The Administration seems to have a certain objective in mind there."

Duguid nodded to his colleague. "I agree, but if so let's not join them in target fixation, if that's what they have," he said. "The world continues to turn, Iraq or no Iraq."

"Yes."

"I don't see any harm in making contact with this Ro fellow to sound him out. Find out what's on his mind," Torres said. "If he's the one who actually placed the original ad, that is."

Duguid glanced about at the other two men, who silently assented.

"Okay then," he said. "Let's reach out and touch Ro Jae-Ki in Rome. See what develops and let's take it from there."

"We can do that," Tucker agreed. "And we will."

NINE: SOTU

The Capitol
Washington, District of Columbia
January 28, 2003

Preparations for the annual State of the Union address were, as always, extensive. Security matters were paramount, as the totality of the national leadership would be gathered together into one room for a short period of time.

The frigid January night saw numerous street closures in the District. This was especially the case in the area blocked by Independence and Constitution Avenues and Southeast 2d and Northeast 3rd Streets. The closures were accompanied by generous overtime authorizations for officers of the DC Metropolitan Police Department and members of the US Capitol Police.

Not to be outdone, the US Secret Service and the State Department's Diplomatic Security Service both sought their own privileges. Each was intent on safely transporting high level officials and senior members of the foreign diplomatic community into the Capitol to witness the President's third State of the Union address.

The result was a flood of black motorcades continually streaming through the District up and onto Capitol Hill. Upon arrival, they disgorged their protectees and security agents under the portico. The retinue were then duly whisked into the building by their advance people.

While they would not openly admit it, the fictional scenario of a nine-year-old novel hovered in many of their minds. It was certainly known to the management of all of the relevant federal agencies.

In 1994, a popular Tom Clancy release described a suicidal attack of a hijacked airliner into the US Capitol. The imagined result killed the President, most of the Congress, the members of the Supreme Court and scores of others. It was nothing more than an entertaining fictional prospect in 1994. By 2003 however, a mere two years after the 9/11 attacks in New York and Washington, it described a possibility that was more than simply concerning.

The President kicked off his speech covering the usual topics: education, tax relief, heath care reform, drug addiction and the war against terror. He also cited the formation of his new Department of Homeland Security.

Turning attention abroad, he spoke of Iran and Iraq. And in between those topics, he brought up the subject of North Korea.

"On the Korean Peninsula, an oppressive regime rules a people living in fear and starvation," he said. "Throughout the 1990s, the United States relied on a negotiated framework to keep North Korea from gaining nuclear weapons. We now know that that regime was deceiving the world and developing those weapons all along.

"And today the North Korean regime is using its nuclear program to incite fear and seek concessions... America and the world will not be blackmailed."

The President paused for the applause.

"America is working with the countries of the region - South Korea, Japan, China and Russia - to find a peaceful solution and to show the North Korean government that nuclear weapons will bring only isolation, economic stagnation and continued hardship.

"The North Korean regime will find respect in the world and revival for its people only when it turns away from its nuclear ambitions.

"Our nation and the world must learn the lessons of the Korean Peninsula and not allow an even greater threat to rise up in Iraq. A brutal dictator, with a history of reckless aggression, with ties to terrorism, with great potential wealth will not be permitted to dominate a vital region and threaten the United States."

The assembled politicians and appointees cheered him. Baghdad took notice.

As did Pyongyang.

TEN: VIALE DELL'ESPERANTO

Rome, Italy
January 29, 2003

A blue Fiat was parked in a shaded sideway in central Rome. The two men in the car were Bosnian Muslims. Both were veterans of the BiH Army's defense of Sarajevo. And beyond. Although ethnically Muslims, both were decidedly secular in terms of their religion. And both were long-term Org assets.

They were intently watching the gated entryway of the compound at Viale dell'Esperanto, number 26. It was the address of the embassy of North Korea - also known as the Democratic Peoples' Republic of Korea, or the DPRK.

The Italian government was proud of the fact that they were enjoying diplomatic relations that had been established with North Korea only three years earlier. In so doing, they had followed the examples of Sweden, Denmark, Finland, Austria and Portugal.

The man in the driver's seat of the Fiat was a bony figure with an angular face, a prominent nose, and a balding head. Zlatko Piric by name, he was a former sniper in the Bosniak military, the *Armija*, and a hardened veteran of the internecine Yugoslav wars.

Zlatko aimed the lens of his camera at the compound and snapped off several quick frames.

"Three establishing shots," he said. "Left front wall of compound. Main gate. Right front wall," he said.

"*Da*. Got it," replied his partner, jotting in his notebook. His fellow Armija veteran was known to his comrades by his wartime nickname of Escobar.

Escobar was ironically unaware of the relationship between his war name and the past Org activities of his work associate - Zlatko. His partner was eager to keep it that way.

The metal gate slowly ratcheted open forty long minutes later. After a brief pause, a black Audi sedan eased out and began a left turn as Zlatko repeatedly triggered the camera. "Looks like him," he commented.

Escobar picked up his radio to call Chalice, who was parked a block or so away. "Moving now," he said. "Black Audi. Dip plates. Three Asian males. Two up front. One in back."

"Got it, thanks," Chalice responded.

Knowing it was a cardinal sin to correlate his movements with that of the target, Zlatko did not move the Fiat at once in an attempt to follow the Audi. Chalice and the others would take care of that.

"I confirm that we have Yankee visual," came Chalice's voice over the radio. "Pooch, go on and get up ahead of him."

"*Va bene*," a third voice replied. "Rolling."

The muted chatter of the distant voices began to fade as the covering vehicles maneuvered out of range, juggling their positions to keep pace with the Audi.

This was their second week of surveillance covering the DCM of the North Korean embassy. As was often the case with surveillance activities, it meant the use of multiple vehicles and stationary positions. Further, it entailed a lot of static watching and limited activity. This was even more so the case with the reclusive North Koreans, who showed scant interest in life beyond their compound.

Once the Org received authorization to go active on Ro Jae-Ki, the limited electronic monitoring assets that were normally focused on the North Korean Ambassador were repurposed onto him. In so doing, they learned quite a bit about the diminutive DCM.

From past research, the Org already knew Ro was a member in good standing of the North Korean nomenklatura. A distant cousin of Kim Jong-Il, the Dear Leader himself, he enjoyed privileges that far exceeded those of the normal citizen of the DPRK.

In fact, the DCM's familial connections awarded him a greater degree of unquestioned freedom than was available to the ambassador himself.

The Org learned that Ro enjoyed the good life and did not miss home at all. His wife and children had remained comfortably behind in Pyongyang while he comfortably made do abroad.

Research had also indicated Ro had maneuvered to decline an ambassadorship of his own somewhere in Africa in order to spend a few more years in the more opulent Roman surroundings.

The man in the front passenger's seat of the black Audi was called Tae. He was the DCM's personal security officer. More than that, he was Ro's confidant.

Tae had spent twelve years of relentless commando training in North Korea's Reconnaissance Brigade. The training had been in preparation for the long anticipated, but as yet unrealized, final assault on the South Korean puppet regime. The experience left him hard-edged and humorless, yet open to opportunities.

Embassy service with the wily Ro Jae-Ki imprinted many new lessons on Tae. Under the former's example, Tae came to appreciate that there were many opportunities to be had, unseen corners to be cut, and new relationships to be exploited.

He also learned there was money available to be made. Real money. Hard foreign currency. Money far in excess of anything a former commando captain could have begun to imagine.

DCM Ro Jae-Ki enjoyed everything about Rome, especially the available women. A man of eclectic tastes, he frequented Asian, Africans and Europeans alike. But the best of all, in his estimation, were the Italians.

To Tae – and to Tae only – Ro referred to these outings as his cultural events. The security officer held the opinion that his superior was somewhat reckless in this aspect. But he wisely kept that judgment to himself.

As the DCM often paraphrased a past Roman pope - "The Lord has given us the papacy. Let us enjoy it." And so it was with his diplomatic mission.

Tae nodded and continued to do his duty.

ELEVEN: CAFFE BAR

Rome, Italy
January 30, 2003

Among the pleasantries of Italian daily life that so appealed to Ro Jae-Ki were the so-called caffe bars. They were everywhere, most often appearing as small niche establishments that served both the small, pungent cups of espresso-like coffee, as well as sandwiches and snacks. Needless to say, this was not a perk that was available back home in Pyongyang.

As in so many things, the adaptable Ro did as the Romans did. He chose to stand at the bar while he savored his drink, rather that seating himself at one of the few scattered tables. And the cost of the coffee at the bar was about a third of the price that was charged for taking a seat. It was a bit odd. But it was *Italia*.

Cosi che va, he mused silently. So it goes.

The DCM had stopped at his favorite caffe bar while en route back to the embassy. He had just come from a brief visit with his counterpart at the Farnesina Palazzo, the home of the Italian Ministry of Foreign Affairs, or MFA.

He had been to the Farnesina to deliver a demarche, or diplomatic note, to the MFA. The note was a response to the Italian government's criticism of Pyongyang's actions of the past month. The criticism specifically referred to North Korea's initiative in breaking the seals of the International Atomic Energy Agency's inspectors and restarting one of their nuclear reactors. The North Korean argument, that it was essentially an internal political matter and certainly not any business of the Italians, was short and sharp.

Ro's MFA counterpart was not surprised by the reaction. It was expected.

Ro glanced at his watch. His driver was parked around the block – the closest parking spot that he could find. The faithful Tae awaited him patiently on the sidewalk. There was still time for a second cup.

As he signaled his intention to the barman, he became aware of middle-aged Italian male who saddled up to the bar alongside of him. While smiling politely, the new arrival maintained a respectful distance from the DCM. The Italian was casually dressed and sported a short salt and pepper beard. A woolen scarf was fashionably draped about his neck.

The man nodded to the barman's unspoken question. "Si," he said. "Cappuccino. Per favore."

Ro suppressed a smirk. He had been in Italy long enough to know that no respectable patron, other than a tourist, would order a cappuccino after the noon hour.

The barman shot the newcomer a sidelong glance but wordlessly complied with the request.

As the coffee machine began to hiss and sputter, the newcomer turned his attention to Ro. "*Ciao*," he said agreeably. "*Come stai?*"

"*Bene*," Ro said tightly.

"*Bene*... Good," the Italian newcomer smiled. "You speak eh, English?"

Ro accepted his second cup and stirred a bit of sweetener into it. "Yes," he said without enthusiasm. "I speak English."

"And very good you do too," the man observed. "Maybe better than mine. I think this."

Ro did not reply.

"And our city, this *Roma*," the man continued, gesturing happily. "You are enjoying it?"

"I am," Ro said looking at his watch again. Perhaps it was time to get back to the embassy.

"This would maybe help you to enjoy," the man said as he slid something along the counter toward Ro's saucer.

It was an embossed business card, light gray in color with rose gold edging. The simple message read:

NOTTI ROMANE MEMORABILI
~La Bella~

A cellphone number was inscribed on the third line.

Although usually a master of his emotions, Ro was momentarily stunned. And it showed.

Memorable Roman Nights.

He did a mental translation a second time to ensure he was not misreading the message. It was the very phrase that the Americans had alerted him to watch for.

The responding message had finally appeared several long months after he had placed his ad in the International Herald Tribune. In truth, he had all but given up on the venture.

"Look on the back," the man murmured, accepting his cappuccino from the barman in return for a few copper coins.

Ro Jae-Ki did so. The reverse side of the card displayed a hand-written note. It listed what was apparently a room number in the Albergo Cesari, one of the more elegant downtown hotels.

Ro slipped the card into his pocket without meeting the other's eye.

"Call *La Bella* when you are ready to see her," the man said, his English suddenly improving. "But not too long please."

The Italian finished his cappuccino with a single gulp and clattered the cup back onto its saucer. "*Scusi,*" he said, and left.

In tradecraft parlance, Ro had just been *bumped* by the Org. The next move was his.

TWELVE: TURTLE BAY

The United Nations
New York City, New York
February 5, 2003

Momentous events were stirring in Turtle Bay, the moniker given to the Midtown Manhattan neighborhood that was the home of the United Nations headquarters. After months of painful diplomatic maneuvering, the Secretary of State was about to address the UN Security Council. He would be presenting the case for confronting the regime of Saddam Hussein once and for all.

Just the previous day, the British Prime Minister and the French President met in Le Touquet, a small commune near Boulogne-Sur-Mer on the French coast. The meeting was an effort to devise a unified response to the Saddam problem.

In Le Touquet the two leaders easily agreed that the Iraqis must be required to eliminate their weapons of mass destruction. What they disagreed upon, however, was the need for allied military action to bring about this result.

Outside of the headquarters building, the frenetic action duplicated the level of activity normally seen in the annual UN General Assembly (UNGA) meetings in the Fall of the year. The resulting imposed traffic restrictions did nothing to enhance the patience of the native New Yorkers.

One after another, a series of motorcades came down the so-called chute, an artificial traffic pattern that was constructed on First Avenue leading to the UN. Approaching the entrance at East 43rd Street, their NYPD marked lead and tail cars broke off, allowing the limo and follow car combinations to turn off First Avenue and into the UN grounds.

Killing the sirens and overhead light bars, the vehicle pairs traversed the grounds and eased to a stop at the entrance of the General Assembly building. There, under temporarily draped blue canvas tentage, an awaiting advance agent met each motorcade.

Exiting their vehicles, the dignitaries, their senior staffers and protective agents were escorted past the scrum of press photographers. They quickly moved through the doors, up the central escalator and into the Security Council chambers.

The assemblage settled into their seats around the circular table with a taut sense of expectancy. The United States delegation today was headed not by the Ambassador to the United Nations, but by the Secretary of State himself. Seated directly behind the SecState, to publicly display his support for the material that was about to be presented, was the Director of the Central Intelligence Agency.

Following the usual diplomatic niceties, the SecState launched into his well-prepared presentation.

"The material I will present to you comes from a variety of sources," he began. "Some are US sources. And some are those of other countries. Some of the sources are technical, such as intercepted telephone conversations and photos taken by satellites. Other sources are people who have risked their lives to let the world know what Saddam Hussein is really up to."

His international colleagues waited quietly for what was to come.

"I cannot tell you everything that we know," he continued. "But what I can share with you, when combined with what all of us have learned over the years, is deeply troubling.

"What you will see is an accumulation of facts and disturbing patterns of behavior. The facts on Iraq's behavior demonstrate that Saddam Hussein and his regime have made no effort - no effort - to disarm as required by the international community."

More than an hour later, the SecState concluded his remarks saying, "Saddam must be left in no doubt as to the serious situation he now faces ... time is now very short."

Citing the failures of the League of Nations, he warned that it "... had failed because it could not create actions from its words. We owe it to our history, as well as to our future, not to make the same mistake again."

After a number of responses, the Iraqi Foreign Minister countered by saying that the American presentation contained "...incorrect allegations, unnamed and unknown sources, as well as assumptions in line with the American policy towards one known objective."

Only the most self-deluded international diplomats failed to see what was coming.

THIRTEEN: LA BELLA

Rome, Italy
February 8, 2003

The radio abruptly came to life with the sounds of Zlatko's reedy voice. "Confirmed that Yankee is now coming to you," he said. "Maybe fifteen minutes now. Or maybe less."

"Copy. Understood," Chalice replied. "Thanks." He replaced the radio on the coffee table and looked over to his bearded Italian partner. "She's ready?"

Nardo Puccio, also known as Pooch, was the beefy Org asset who had initially bumped Ro in the caffe bar. An experienced operative, when not on contract with JICSA he worked as a private investigator in his Tuscan hometown of Florence. Puccio claimed, without a shred of verifiable evidence, to be a descendent of the famed Medici banking family, the rulers of Florence during the Renaissance era.

"Savina?" he answered. "Yes, she is ready."

They were patiently wiling away the hours of a fine Saturday afternoon in room 515 of the Albergo Cesari. The Cesari was an historic hotel in central Rome, not far from the famed Trevi Fountain.

Ensconced in the adjoining room was the woman named Savina.

Savina was yet another Italian Org agent. Now easing gracefully into middle age, she nevertheless retained her stunning beauty. Her dark, almond shaped eyes and raven hair never failed to turn heads on the street.

A former journalist, Savina had worked with Chalice eight years earlier during an operation in Bosnia. At that time, she played a dangerous role, essentially posing as bait in the behind-the-lines rendition of a Bosnian Serb war criminal. Today she would be the initial witting contact between the North Korean DCM and JICSA.

Chalice sat silently in his armchair. All of the arrangements that could have been made were made. He was focusing on nothing, or no mind, as his martial arts instructors phrased the concept.

Like the surface of the theoretical Zen pond, he was not anticipating the ripple that would be formed when the theoretical pebble splashed through its surface. He would only react.

The room next door was thoroughly wired for recording. Still, his agent Savina would be alone with the DCM. As a contingency, nevertheless, he and Puccio would be able to respond quickly in the case of emergency. Unlikely as that was.

Whatever the case, there would be no police involvement. The Italian authorities were unaware of the little drama enfolding on their soil. In the judgment of the Org, it was a need-to-know situation and they didn't have the need.

Idly, Puccio turned his attention to the sports pages of the latest edition of the *Corriere Della Sera*. Like most Europeans, he was an avid soccer fan. At the moment, he was he was searching for an update on the Italian national team, the *Azzurri* or the Blues, as they were locally known.

He was about to draw Chalice's attention to the photo of a local TV starlet who was sporting a remarkably snug Azzurri jersey when the radio crackled again.

"He's at the lobby elevators now," Zlatko reported. "His friend is settling into a chair down here. All normal looking."

"Okay. Got it," Chalice replied.

He picked up the phone and dialed the extension to room 513.

"*Pronto*," a female voice answered after two rings.

"It's time," Chalice told her.

"Yes," she said, hanging up the receiver.

Puccio tossed his newspaper aside and fitted a pair of headphones over his head. Smiling, he gave Chalice a thumbs-up. "It's okay. We are recording," he confirmed.

"Alright. Good."

* * *

As was typical with his so-called cultural event outings, Ro Jae-Ki did not employ an embassy driver that day. This was one of his standing practices. He designed it as such to limit the number of people who were privy to the more private aspects of his life.

Instead, the faithful Captain Tae fulfilled the driver's function as well as that of bodyguard/watcher. Needless to say, this personal degree of flexibility would have been impossible for other DPRK embassy officers. Given Ro's impeccable familial connections however, the ambassador wisely refrained from probing too deeply into the non-official activities of his boss.

Leaving Tae to his own resources in the lobby, Ro took the elevator alone to the fifth floor. Pausing to ensure the corridor was empty, he approached the door of room 513 and tapped on it lightly.

This was, he knew, the true edge of his betrayal. In the back of his mind was a nugget of fear that the entire Notti Romane Memorabili encounter was a pretext to entrap him - despite his lofty familial connections – and haul him back to the DPRK in disgrace. Relatives of the Dear Leader had been executed for less than this. Far less.

After a delay of several tense moments, the door swung open.

Ro smiled in relief. There were no North Korean agents immediately apparent. At least, none as far as he could see. Moreover, the woman behind the door was far more attractive than he had previously imagined.

"You are *La Bella*?" he asked.

"*Si, grazie*," she answered. Switching to English, she added, "Welcome. And please, do come in."

Ro stepped into the room, glancing about warily. What he immediately noticed, aside from the fact that they were ostensibly alone, was the bottle of eighteen-year-old Macallan scotch sitting on a fashionable end table. Next to the whisky was a pair of hefty crystal glasses and a bowl of freshly cracked ice.

Tea be damned. The single malt scotch was by far his favorite drink. However, knowing the Americans and their ways, Ro was not at all that surprised to see it.

As he made his way to the proffered chair, Savina broke the seal on the bottle. The perfect hostess, she filled his glass with a generous dollop of the Macallan over ice. For herself, she poured quite a bit less.

"*Salute*," she said at last, clinking the edge of her glass thickly against his.

"*Salute*," Ro responded. Cautiously, he took the first satisfying taste of the whisky. So far so good, as the Americans say, he thought.

Savina settled herself across from him and crossed her legs. She was, as always, well aware of the effect she had on men.

"And so," she began. "Why are we here together this afternoon?"

"Ah, *Bella*," Ro said with a hint of coyness. "We are here because you invited me to this suite."

Savina smiled graciously. "With respect, *Professore*. You invited yourself to this meeting. You initiated the contact over four months ago in fact. We are merely giving you an audience to be heard... That is so. Yes?"

He nodded affirmatively.

"So now, what is it that you want?"

"You say 'we'.... And we are...?"

"You know very well whom I represent," she countered. "And we know that the amount of time that you can be away from the embassy is somewhat restricted. Even for you. So, let's not waste your limited availability on pointless banter."

Ro took another sip of his scotch. "Well... so it is," he said. "*Cosi che va.*"

He sat his glass down with exaggerated care and took a moment to preen his lapels and tie with both hands. "We will talk primarily about me then," he said. "I represent an important faction of the Democratic Peoples' Republic of Korea... A faction that is, I think, not easily accessible to American intelligence."

"Yes?"

"And in these days, I believe I am of much value to you and to those you represent. Of very much high value."

"Go on," she said, raising her glass. "I am listening."

As the tapes rolled, Ro spoke and answered questions, to the degree that he was willing to do so. This went on for the better part of an hour. The majority of his answers dealt with his personal history. He was clearly reluctant to provide much in the form of sensitive intelligence.

When he was finished with what he was prepared to deliver, he noticed the Macallan bottle was more than half empty. "And that is all?" Savina asked.

"For today," Ro answered. He looked pointedly at his wristwatch. "It is still early though," he observed.

"Early?"

"Time enough maybe for a, uh, memorable Roman afternoon?"

Savina smiled. "That, *Professore*, is not on offer... At least, not for now," she said, knowing the implication would never be fulfilled.

"Oh," he said with a mock grimace. "That is so sad."

Savina reached into her purse and handed him a folded index card. "This is how we will contact you," she said. "And we will be contacting you. Soon."

"I look forward," Ro replied.

* * *

Chalice and Puccio made their way to room 513 following Zlatko's advisory that Ro and Tae had safely cleared the area.

Chalice dropped onto the sofa and glanced out of the window at the Via di Pietra down below. "Well, that was an interesting encounter," he said at last.

"I would agree," Puccio said.

Savina finished what was left of the whisky in her glass. "Interesting for an initial meeting," she observed flatly. "But there is certainly more there to exploit."

"Regardless," Chalice said, "he is ours now."

"Yes?" Puccio prodded.

"No matter what else happened, I doubt that the Dear Leader would react well to hearing a tape of today's meeting."

Nardo Puccio, the alleged Medici, grinned in agreement and helped himself to the Macallan bottle.

FOURTEEN: OFFICE 39

McLean, Virginia
February 11, 2003

JD Tucker and his senior operational staff members were gathered in the SCIF of the JICSA headquarters. Satisfied that everyone was finally settled around the ovoid conference table, he nodded to his Analytical Chief. "Go ahead," he said.

As the lights dimmed on cue, a colorful PowerPoint presentation flashed onto the screen. It was labeled as TS/HCS - or Top Secret/HUMINT Control System. The caption indicated the information had been derived from sensitive human agents, as opposed to technical resources.

The briefing wordlessly began with a series of surveillance photographs of Ro Jae-Ki. Several of the shots featured his security officer, Tae, in the background. The majority of the photos however, were tightly focused on the features of the DCM.

"So, this is the ARGENT SUCCUBUS case," Angela - the chief of JICSA analysis - said as she began her narration. "As we all now know, Chalice and his team successfully made contact with the target a couple of days ago in Rome."

Angela advanced the frame. Zlatko's surveillance shot of the DPRK embassy's main gate filled the screen.

"We have confirmed our target is one Ro Jae-Ki. He is the DCM, or deputy chief of mission, of the North Korean embassy in Rome," she said. "We are also confident he is the same individual who made the Romeo/Thirty-Five/Lima contact with the Agency back in October... He is definitely our guy. We are now focused on him and operationally locked on."

Another photo of the DCM flashed onto the screen. "What we have confirmed," Angela continued, "is that, aside from being a career diplomat, he also has his fingers in a raft of illegal practices. A trait not entirely unknown to North Korean diplomats."

Tucker caught sight of a sizable ring on Angela's finger in the soft gleam of the SCIF lighting. He pushed aside a twinge of repressed jealousy and focused on the content of her brief.

"Ro affirmed that he wants to defect and is seeking our assistance," Angela said. "While he is theoretically able to walk away from his people in Rome at any time, he knows he would be doing so at some significant personal risk. He is clearly willing to submit to a series of debriefings but he also wants long term protection in the United States as part of the deal."

"He's in Italy!" one of the staffers at the table exclaimed with a touch of exasperation. "Why doesn't he just get on a plane tomorrow and leave, for Christ's sake?"

Angela was unable to suppress a brief glare in the staffer's direction. "I can think of two reasons for starters," she cracked. "One. Someone else, somewhere else, could eventually get on another plane some day and proceed to hunt him down. And kill him.

"Two. He has an assigned personal security officer at the embassy named Tae Soon. Tae's a former captain in the North Korean Army's Reconnaissance Brigade. A trained commando in other words.

"While we know that Tae Soon is complicit in Ro's corrupt practices, he is also there to keep an eye on him. Essentially, he's playing both sides of the fence."

"Then this Tae character is a problem for us?" someone asked.

"He's an obstacle," Angela replied equivocally.

"We can deal with obstacles," Tucker said flatly, jotting a note down on his pad.

"What about the risk to his family members if he succeeds in bailing out?" a voice asked.

"Our guy has a bit of a sociopathic personality," Tucker observed, looking up from his notes. "He doesn't give a flying shit about them. To put it mildly."

A map of central Pyongyang appeared on the screen.

"Not surprisingly, Ro is very well connected back home in Pyongyang," Angela continued. "His family is directly related to the Dear Leader himself, Kim Jong-Il. Thanks to those connections, they all have favored government positions and the social privileges that go with them. As an example, Ro's immediate family members all have residences along or adjacent to the highly favored Mansudae Street in the capital," she said.

"How is that significant?" another staffer asked.

"Only the regime elites live in that neighborhood," she clarified. "It's a very high rent neighborhood... If they were to pay any rent at all. Which they don't."

"Fringe benefits," someone observed. "They're an odd bunch over there."

"So odd in fact, that they have their own system of numbering the years," Angela said as an aside. "They are called *Juche* years, with Year One being 1912, the year of Kim Il Sung's birth."

"So that would make this..." someone began to speculate.

"Juche year 92," she supplied.

"Like I said," the other added. "Odd bunch."

Hearing no more questions, Angela pushed ahead with the presentation. "Of significant interest, Ro reported he is not only the deputy chief of mission in Rome – he is also a senior operative of a North Korean bureau known as Office 39."

One or two of the faces at the table remained vacant.

"A little elaboration on this Office 39, please," Tucker interrupted. "For the sake of our colleagues who are not so familiar with North Korean trivia... Juche years and all that."

"Right," Angela said. "Officially they are known as Office 39 of the Korean Workers Party... The North Korean Communist Party. In actuality, however, the Party has nothing to do with it. They report directly to the Dear Leader. Their primary objective appears to be the aggressive gathering of hard currency reserves for the ruling family. The funds raised are both for the family's personal use, such as Kim's estimated expense of $800,000 per year for Hennessy Paradis cognac, as well as for their foreign policy objectives."

"How so?" a voice at the far end of the conference table asked.

"Office 39 had its origins in the late 1970's," Angela replied. "At that time, their embassies abroad were directed to find means of self-financing their operations. That effort soon evolved into a complex web of front companies, including straight out criminal activities such as money laundering, counterfeiting and drug smuggling."

"I'm familiar with the counterfeiting issue," Meyerhof interjected. "According to the Secret Service, the North Koreans are cranking out nearly perfect copies of our hundred dollar bills. My contact says the counterfeits are so well done that they are all but impossible to detect. The Service calls these bills Supernotes. It's a nightmare for them. Absolute nightmare."

A map of the provinces of North Korea flashed onto the next screen. "Uh, that far northeastern province next to the Chinese border is called North Hamgyong," she said. "It is their main poppy growing area. It's also a prime smuggling area for all kinds of goods moving to and from China.

"The opium produced in North Hamgyong is shipped over to the provincial capital in Chongjin City. Once in Chongjin, under the tutelage of Thai specialists, they turn out significant quantities of a fairly low-grade heroin... Methamphetamine as well."

"Opium in North Korea?" a staffer asked incredulously.

"Yes. In fact, they produce about one percent of the world's total opium supply," Angela replied. "They're pikers though, when compared to their competition. About seventy-six percent of the world's opium comes from Afghanistan and another eighteen percent from Burma, as an example."

"Yeah, but still..."

"They take advantage of their connections with Chinese Triads, the Japanese Yakuza and Russian Mafia members to move the product across borders," she continued. "Between the front companies and foreign banks in places like Macau, Switzerland and Austria, they bring in a fortune in hard currency."

"Like how much?"

"We're talking in the billions of dollars," she said. "Billions."

The assembled staff silently reflected on that factoid for a moment.

"But would they involve one of their more senior diplomats – like our guy Ro here – in actual drug trafficking?" Tucker asked.

"Without a doubt," Angela said. "Dozens of other North Korean dips have done it in multiple countries... Several have been arrested in possession of both heroin and meth."

"This crowd sounds like a group of Bond villains," one of the staffers cracked.

"Except this crowd is all too real," Meyerhof growled.

The next slide displayed an enhanced satellite photograph of a highly secure North Korean government facility.

The site was situated some sixty miles north of Pyongyang. A well-developed, fenced-in compound, it was surrounded by a bleak, nearly moon-like landscape. The green Kuryong River looped south of the buildings, partially encircling the facility and essentially creating an inland peninsula. A modest town sat to the northeast of its perimeter.

"This is the Yongbyon Nuclear Scientific Research Center," Angela said. "It's the home of their first nuclear reactor. It, and their nuclear weapons program in general, is one of the primary beneficiaries of Office 39's fund raising efforts."

Angela zeroed in on the main building with a red laser pointer. "And this is the grand prize," she said. "Ground zero. This is the structure housing their five-megawatt reactor. In other words, their plutonium production reactor."

"Meaning?"

"It is the site that produces weapons grade plutonium. Quite useful for making nuclear explosives."

"Thank you, Angela," Tucker said, assuming control of the briefing.

He stood up and moved over to the screen.

"The North Koreans began construction of this reactor around 1980," he said. "Technically, they achieved critical mass in 1986. That's a key step on the road to weaponization... However, in 1994 the reactor was shut down as part of the diplomatic process called the Agreed Framework.

"So far, so good, right? And so it was until this past October. That's when the DPRK announced they were restarting the reactor and withdrawing from the Non-Proliferation Treaty."

The JICSA director tapped at the screen with his knuckles. "We are essentially blind here folks," he admitted. "Yes, we have overhead photography and technical monitors. But the truth is, the Intelligence Community has no direct knowledge of what's going on *inside* that site."

Even in the darkened room, the senior staffers could detect a feral smile on Tucker's face. "According to Chalice, however, Ro Jae-Ki added a sweetener to the deal."

Pausing for dramatic effect, he added, "The DCM has a niece who is a research scientist at the Yongbyon weapons lab... And she wants out too."

FIFTEEN: NOMENKLATURA

Rome, Italy
March 8, 2003

Ro Jae-Ki was playing the role of the sophisticated gentleman diplomat, free of any stereotypical notions associated with North Korean hermits. This time he did the honors, cracking the seal on the Macallan. Twisting the capped cork out of the bottle's neck, he made an elegant display of charging Savina's glass before attending to his own.

Handing her the glass, Ro caught the scent of an expensive French perfume. It was one he had always favored on his Western women.

"*Grazie*," she said as he took his seat across from her. She was purposely dressed in a tight black skirt and a red silk blouse. While buttoned to the neck, the blouse nevertheless served to accentuate her curvature, as was the intent.

They were conducting their second meeting under the same cultural event pretext as before, largely for the benefit of Tae. This time however they were located in a luxury hotel room on the southern side of the city, not far from the ancient Roman Colosseum.

Ro hoisted his glass politely in her direction. "La Bella," he said.

"Professore," she replied in kind.

"I see that congratulations are in order for your people," he offered obliquely, pausing to take a drink.

"Congratulations?"

"For the capture of Khalid Sheikh Mohammad, or KSM as the Americans call him... The Al-Qaeda man. Connected to the attack in New York, the plot to blow up airliners in flight and so forth. Your people took him in Rawalpindi, Pakistan just a few days ago. A wonderful catch."

"I did not know that," Savina said honestly.

"Yes," Ro smiled. "I am sure of it. He is somewhere in American custody this very day." He sat his glass down on the side table. "In any event, we share the same view of the Islamist threat, your side and mine. They are a sickness – a danger to be exterminated."

"I thought we were on the same side now," Savina offered.

Ro nodded affably. "Let us say that we are still negotiating."

He raised his glass slightly once again. "In any event, let us drink to the capture."

"*Alla cattura*," she responded.

Setting her own drink aside, Savina continued with her structured interview. "Tell me a bit more about the situation in North Korea. Surely it's a good life that you are thinking of abandoning."

"Of course, it is," he admitted. "For us. My family is part of what the Russians call the *nomenklatura*."

"The establishment elite," Savina added.

"Yes," he said. "In the North, they – we – have a system called *songbun*."

"Songbun?" she repeated. "I've never heard of it."

"Yes. Songbun was formulated by the first Kim, Kim Il Sung, back in the 1950's. It generally divides all people into three classes," he explained. "At the top of the system you have the core or loyal class. They enjoy the highest living and educational standards."

"Yes?" Savina prompted.

"Below that is what is called the wavering class. This is the largest group. Peasants, workers and so forth... People whose loyalties to the regime can be reasonably questioned."

"And?"

"At the bottom is the hostile class," he said. "These are the anti-revolutionary people, the former landowners, the former pro-Japanese families, various criminals. It also includes the families of defectors."

"But your family is, of course, among the core group," Savina said. "The loyal class."

"Yes. We are well connected. And being well connected, we are also well informed."

And, Savina silently reflected with a degree of unstated irony, *thanks to your actions here today your entire family is about to cascade from the heights of the core class down to the living hell of the hostile class. At best.*

She left this observation unvoiced, for obvious reasons.

Ro took another sip of his scotch. "You must understand however, any analysis I may have regarding the ruling family and

46

their policies and ambitions will await my safe arrival in America... And for, uh, sufficient compensation for my consultancy."

"I understand," she agreed. "We would not expect anything else... But we would like to know just a bit more about your relatives in the North. You are directly related to the ruling Kim family, you said?"

"I am a first cousin of what we call the Dear Leader. Our families are very close."

"And therefore, very privileged?"

"Of course," he said. "Nomenklatura."

"Examples?"

"My family is very well situated with our cousins, the Kims," Ro said. "For example, my younger brother is a mid-level official with *Jojik-Jidobu*, or the Organization and Guidance Department."

"What is that?"

Ro crossed his legs into a more comfortable position. "It is the body that controls everything in the country," he said. "Very influential. The OGD has existed since the end of the war against Japan but our Kim re-empowered it in 1973. It is everything. It oversees political and military appointments and keeps watch on the activities of anyone of interest to the Kims. Most importantly, it manages the personal security of the Kim family."

"Is your brother aware of your contacts with us?" Savina asked.

"Obviously not," Ro answered.

"Are you certain of that?"

"I am alive."

Point taken. Savina wondered if the DCM's level sophistication included insight into how patient a skilled securi service could be as they played cat and mouse with one of th suspects.

"And your niece?"

"Miss Hwa," he said. "You more familiar Westerners would her Nari."

"Nari," Savina agreed. "Let's call her that. Tell me about he

"As I told you at our last meeting, Miss, uh, Nari is a res scientist at our Yongbyon nuclear facility. Her specialty is we design."

Exactly, Savina reflected, happy to hear the DCM con earlier claim. Chalice had previously advised her that while a good catch for political intelligence, the niece could be the gold standard, insofar as life and death issues were concerned.

"Age?" she asked, making notes for his benefit. She knew the background tapes would be the primary record.

"Twenty-eight, thirty maybe," he said.

"Married?"

"No."

"Children?"

"Of course not."

"Any current romantic involvements?"

"No. Not that I am aware of."

"What foreign languages does she speak?"

Ro paused for a moment. "She is a highly-educated woman," he said. "She speaks Chinese. Enough English. Maybe a little French or German."

"And her reason for wanting out of the DPRK?" Savina pursued.

"To have a life equal to those in the South. And to survive."

"To survive you say... Literally?"

'She noted that several of her colleagues who expressed socially al ideas have disappeared from sight. She does not want to · their examples."

na rose to add a bit more of the scotch to Ro's glass. Taking ⸍ once more she pressed on, conscious that she was the limits of what Ro might be willing to freely provide.

 st time we met, you said you and Tae were involved in ʔyongyang might not approve of..."

⸍f lered his response for several long moments. "I am

ty . yes?"

eir ⸍

I have access to the covert financial operations of

call ⸍." Savina said, risking a more blatant approach.

rnote program."

r." sing his legs and easing back in his chair. "You

earch with Deng Xiaoping's description of Beijing's

apons ly defined it as socialism with Chinese

irm his s call it authoritarian capitalism."

Ro was

48

"In any case," Ro countered, "one might say that Tae and I have been pursuing, uh, socialism with entrepreneurial characteristics..."

Or embezzlement, Savina thought.

"And one other thing of possible interest to you," Ro added.

"Yes?"

"Last week we re-started our nuclear reactor in Yongbyon."

SIXTEEN: SHOCK AND AWE

Persian Gulf
March 20, 2003

Lieutenant Commander Ed Nowak, call sign Switchback, was now flying abeam the carrier and heading due south. It was the middle of the night, and he was high over the waters of the Persian Gulf. From his visual perspective, both the sky and sea merged to form an undifferentiated expanse of blackness.

From the view of Nowak's cockpit, the huge warship was but a small blur of red superstructure lighting. The illumination glimmered in the darkness on his port side as a welcomed visual point of reference. Despite his many years in naval aviation, Nowak always found it difficult to conceive that such a mammoth ship, so full of life, activity and machinery, could ever appear to be so insignificant.

Nowak tugged on his shoulder harness to tighten it up in preparation for landing. It was a needless, yet comforting exercise. The harness, locking him into the ejection seat, was as tight as it was ever going to be.

His destination was the deck of the USS Kitty Hawk.

Commissioned in 1961, the Hawk was the oldest American warship still in active service. It had been on a routine deployment elsewhere in the region when its commander was ordered to divert to the Gulf to deal with the situation that was emerging ashore. The carrier duly arrived on station a month earlier, in February, prepared to deal with this very moment.

As scheduled, Nowak checked in with the onboard flight controllers to confirm his position in the recovery pattern. They replied in reassuringly professional, clipped tones of voice.

In the early days of his naval flying career, night carrier landings had terrified Nowak. Of course, he never for a single moment let his fellow jet jocks know he came close to losing it the first time he tried the procedure.

Some of the guys at least claimed to be very comfortable with the night procedure, given that all visual distractions were removed in the darkness. That had never been the case for him.

Much earlier, Nowak had been catapulted off the end of the carrier deck and shot up into the evening sky. Following a pre-planned aerial refueling, he and the other members of his flight then made their way to their designated position over the southern Iraqi city of Basra.

Upon arrival, it had been time to execute the mission. On cue, Nowak dropped his ordnance on a telecommunication site in the center of the urban area. That done, he wheeled about in a tight left turn away from the target. The members of his flight did likewise. A multiple string of explosions blossomed up colorfully in his wake.

While he had left a lot of noise and devastation in his wake, he never knew if he had actually killed anyone. And he didn't want to know.

Nowak preferred to think of his actions as *servicing the target*. Nothing more than that.

Listening to the soothingly emotionless radio chatter in his ears, Nowak turned his F/A-18 Hornet left once more and onto his base leg. He paused momentarily and then turned a final left, lining the plane up for its final approach to the carrier deck.

He was now some three miles astern of the Kitty Hawk and closing fast. Regardless of its size, from where Nowak sat the 86,000-ton carrier was nothing more than a dot of white light in the middle of the distant nothingness.

As always, Nowak knew another qualified Navy pilot was stationed at the aft end of the carrier to help guide the returning flyers safely back onto the deck. While officially termed the Landing Signal Officer, or LSO, the officer holding that slot was more routinely known as *Paddles*.

"Switchback," came the steady voice of Paddles. "Call the ball."

"Roger ball," Nowak replied flatly after a brief pause. In so doing, he confirmed he was centered up on the ship and coursing down along the controlled glideslope.

Simultaneously, he double checked to ensure the plane was in what was generally termed a dirty configuration, which was to say that his gear and tail hook were down, with full flaps extended.

Irritably, Nowak realized that his scalp was now getting itchy under his helmet. And his butt was getting tired of being clamped into the ejection seat. It was not an ideal time for such distractions.

Not with the landing lights of the deck looming up brightly ahead of him.

Per the usual protocol, Nowak was aiming to latch the tail hook of his Hornet onto the third of four arresting cables at the approach end of the deck. Successfully doing so would bring his Hornet to a sudden, jarring and immediate halt.

Coming in slightly too high however would result in his missing the cables entirely. This would result in him becoming a bolter. That would cause him to flash down the deck and immediately soar back into the air under full power for a go-around and yet another try.

Coming in a bit too low, a far worse fate, would result in his slamming into the back of the carrier with dramatically fatal consequences. It was a terminal error, clearly to be avoided at all costs.

"A little low, Switch," Paddles observed calmly. "Add power."

Eyes fixated on the sequential line of white dots ahead of him, Nowak edged the throttles forward a few millimeters.

"Power," Paddles repeated.

Nowak reluctantly gave it a wee bit more juice.

"Power."

Nowak nudged it yet a bit more forward.

"Okay, Switch. You're in the groove," the LSO commented approvingly. "Hold it right there... Rock steady."

Nowak held the landing configuration a few tense seconds longer until the wheels of Hornet slammed onto the deck. He pushed the throttles all the way forward in preparation for a bolt as the tail hook bit into the desired cable and jerked the Hornet to a shockingly abrupt stop.

Breathing heavily with relief, Nowak relaxed his shoulder muscles and awaited the directions of the deckhands to taxi off the centerline.

It was an historic night. The Liberation of Iraq had begun.

SEVENTEEN: RYONGSONG

Pyongyang, North Korea
March 20, 2003

It was late morning. A routine Thursday. The Dear Leader, Kim Jong Il, was at his desk in the Ryongsong official residence just outside of Pyongyang. He was fixated on a pad of paper and a smaller collection of hand scrawled notes while awaiting his lunch.

Located some seven miles north of the city center, Ryongsong was but one of Kim's several lavish residential compounds. Perhaps more befitting a royal personage than a socialist chieftain, it encompassed several square kilometers. Protected by electrified fencing, special army units and – some said – minefields, it contained a variety of office buildings, houses and gardens as well as an underground tunnel complex linking it with neighboring government fortresses.

Kim was diligently laboring over the text of a speech he was to deliver to the Supreme People's Assembly in the coming week. Although a pro forma delivery, he was intent upon making it a quality presentation.

Kim Jong Il had a varied collection of titles. Aside from the *Dear Leader* appellation for instance, he was also officially acclaimed as the *Superior Person*, the *Shining Star of Paektu*, as well as the *Guiding Sun Ray* and far more. The titles were by no means uttered in jest.

According to the official mythology, Kim had been born in 1941 atop the highest peak on the peninsula, a semi-mystical mountain called Mount Paektu. It was a geographic feature that had been venerated throughout Korean history. The birth event, allegedly, was heralded by the appearance of a double rainbow and by a new star in the sky.

The truth of his birth was more pedestrian. It occurred in a far corner of the Soviet Union along the Amur River where his father, the now deceased and grandly deified Kim Il Sung, was waiting out World War II in a Red Army brigade with other Korean exiles. There had been no recorded astronomical wonders to accompany his son's birth.

More to the point, however, Kim Jong Il was also termed as the *Bright Sun of Juche*, for Juche was to be the topic of his speech.

Juche, or self-reliance, was the all-pervasive national ideology of the DPRK. Although his father originated the concept in the 1930's, it only gained serious traction in the 1950's when the elder Kim aspired to carve out a niche for his country between the Communist giants of China and the USSR.

Perhaps as much a secular state religion as a political philosophy, Juche touted the importance of national sovereignty and the supposed pre-eminence of the working classes under the guidance of a ruling father figure. What the supposed self-reliant ideology ignored was the vast amount of financial aid the country annually received from the neighboring Soviet Union. That aid suddenly ended when the USSR collapsed in 1991, taking the North Korean economy down with it.

Kim knew there was little he could say about Juche that the members of the Supreme People's Assembly had not heard before. That did not matter. Though nominally the highest governmental body in the DPRK, the Assembly was little more than a rubber-stamping talk shop that never disputed or contrarily debated any issue placed before them by either of the Kims.

Beyond any doubt, the Assembly members would obediently listen to his speech with rapt attention. At its conclusion, they would predictably rise to their feet attempting to outdo each other with loud and enthusiastic applause. That was all that was required of them. Nothing more.

The door of his private office banged open unexpectedly, signaling the flushed arrival of Myo, his most trusted senior advisor. Kim looked up in surprise. This type of behavior was very far from the norm in his presence.

"Forgive me," Myo sputtered anxiously, "but please... The television!"

Kim Jong Il continued to gape in confusion as his senior advisor powered up the large screen office television set.

"It's the Americans," Myo explained as the set came to life. "They have gone insane!"

Kim watched owlishly as the wide screen TV revealed ghostly scenes of filmy, green tinted footage. Mushrooms of white light bloomed in the background, temporarily bleaching out the screen. The South Korean TV commentator droned on with the assumption that the viewer was already aware of the theme of his coverage.

Kim turned again to Myo with a questioning look on his face. "Where is this?" he asked.

"Baghdad," Myo said. "The Americans are attacking Baghdad! ... Right now!"

"They are bombing Iraq?"

"Yes," the advisor answered. "The bombing was preceded by missile strikes from their naval ships." He hesitated. "Worse, it appears the initial American attacks were an attempt at national decapitation."

"At decapitation?" Kim repeated, still trying to grasp the events unfolding before him.

"To begin the war by killing Saddam Hussein."

Kim turned his attention back to the television, now watching with a growing sense of horror.

The allusion was immediately clear. Only a few months earlier, in reference to possible military operations in both Iraq and North Korea, the American warmonger Rumsfeld himself had said, "We are capable of fighting two major regional conflicts. We're capable of winning decisively in one and swiftly defeating in the case of the other. And let there be no doubt about it."

If the Americans planned to begin their Iraqi war by killing Saddam, Kim reasoned, could they not immediately start a new Korean war by suddenly killing him as well?

Reading his eyes, the senior advisor prompted, "We cannot wait. You must be evacuated. Now!"

Kim nodded at once. "Give the word."

Myo made a quick call in response to the order. Within moments a security team of the Supreme Guard Command swarmed into the office. They quickly surrounded Kim. Two of them apologetically hoisted him from his chair while another one draped a ballistic vest about his bulky frame.

That done, the security team hastily led him out of his office and down into the tunnels to the below ground railway. From that point, they transported Kim another several miles north to the Cheol Bong Li command and control site. The latter location was buried deep beneath the Guk Sa Bong mountain.

There, securely wrapped under the protective layers of rock and dirt, Kim was forced to wait out the American decapitation strike against the DPRK.

It never came.

EIGHTEEN: OVERLOOK

**Mount Washington
Pittsburgh, Pennsylvania
March 25, 2003**

Pittsburgh is rarely thought of as a tourist haven. For those who do seek it out, however, the heights of Mount Washington offer the most well-known views of the city. The natives agree.

The more knowledgeable photographers, both professional and amateur, eventually find themselves astride the circular overlook platform that extends precariously into space along the edge of Grandview Avenue.

Previously known as Coal Hill, the crest of Mount Washington affords the famed postcard views of The Golden Triangle. It is the seminal shot of the downtown area where the Allegheny and Monongahela Rivers converge to form the westward flowing Ohio. It had been known as the Gateway to the West since colonial times.

A thickly built man with flowing locks of graying hair and a beard to match was perched alone against the railing. Although now in his mid-fifties, he was still an imposing physical presence. The chill wind ruffled his hair as he squinted his ice blue eyes at the familiar view. He appeared to be studying the scene below. In reality, his mind was focused elsewhere.

Paul Michael Medved, better known to friends and adversaries alike simply as Bear, knew the city all too well. A native of the area, he was a former member of the Allegheny County Police. In that capacity, all those many years ago, he had served as one of the ACP's most successful and longest lasting undercover narcotics investigators.

Although widely admired for his ability to blend with his street targets and penetrate their networks, his superiors and peers alike came to suspect he had been irrevocably sliding over to the dark side. Undeniably, even to himself, the aspects of his undercover persona were overtaking what remained of his real life. As a result, there were few in the department who thought he would ever be able to forsake his undercover identity and rejoin the force in any conventional capacity.

Bear watched as the boxy red and gold carriage of the Duquesne Incline pulled into its upper station along the ridgeline off to his right. The Incline was a piece of history, having begun operations in 1877. It ran from the lower station on West Carson Street below to Grandview Avenue up here.

Bear well remembered the Incline as the location of one of his many cocaine deals back in the day. Back then, he and a doper suspect from the Garfield area had ridden it up and down several times in the same afternoon while negotiating a six-ounce buy. The discussions were conducted in hushed, abstract terms.

During the extended conversation, the nervous doper had twice nervously uttered the phrase, "You ain't a cop are ya?"

Each time, Bear assured him that he was not. Then as now, total honesty was not a prerequisite of making drug cases. Both sides played the game effectively.

Although Bear could summon up the smell and the grizzled features of the doper, he could not remember his name. He did recall, however, the gentleman's colleagues had brutally murdered him before his arrest warrant had been finalized by the DA's office. Fittingly enough, the doper's body had been found out by the Pittsburgh Zoo.

Prior to his time in the County Police, Bear had been a Green Beret - a Vietnam era Special Forces soldier. More to the point, he had been a member of the shadowy Military Assistance Command, Vietnam - Studies and Observation Group. As such, he was one of those men who had repeatedly participated in the near suicidal reconnaissance missions with MACV-SOG beyond the fence into Laos, Cambodia and North Vietnam. Unlike a significant number of his SOG teammates, Bear had survived the war intact.

Physically.

Never much of a socializer to begin with, Bear was well suited to the often-solitary life of the undercover narc. He became even more reclusive and task-focused after the sudden deaths of his wife and son in a rain slick traffic accident.

And then The Org had presented itself.

Bear's initial contact with JICSA came while he was detailed to the Drug Enforcement Administration for an undercover venture into the narco sanctuaries of Haiti. In the course of that investigation, Bear was approached by the Org and recruited as an asset.

The conclusion of the Haiti operation also marked the inevitable end of his career with the County Police. Bear had been in Florida at the time of his decision. He phoned in his resignation, which was accepted with nothing more than pro forma objections.

Since then, he had performed a variety of lucrative contract assignments with the Org. Most notably, he was part of the hunt for the Medellin Cartel chief Pablo Escobar in Colombia. As he had been repeatedly cautioned however, the less that was said about that particular endeavor, the better.

These days Bear supplemented his income both by running a small private security firm and by serving as an adjunct instructor with a number of regional police training academies in Pennsylvania. He was doing okay, he thought. Probably better than he deserved.

Glancing to his left, he caught sight of a familiar figure ambling down the Grandview sidewalk in his direction. Casually, he turned his attention to a pair of river barges down below as they churned their way through the waters of the Ohio ahead of a tug.

At last the olive-skinned man came up alongside of him on the railing.

"Right on time," Bear commented to the man who was his usual Org case officer. He looked at his watch. "*Mas o menos* anyhow."

The two men had first met operationally at a bordello in Bogotá in 1993. That had been at the start of the hunt for Escobar. The conclusion of their efforts in that case had been favorable.

"Good to see you too," Chalice replied, taking in the expansive scenery. "How've you been?"

"Okay," Bear said. "Busy enough. You?"

"Yeah. Same." Chalice pulled out a Sony Cybershot camera to take a couple of obligatory photographs of the city below. "That's the historical location of Fort Pitt down there at The Point?" the former Army warrant officer asked.

"What's left of it," Bear said. "Just the last of the fort's original blockhouses. You should go see it."

"Maybe next trip," Chalice said. "I'm flying out this afternoon. How's your fiancée by the way?"

"Kelly?" Bear said. "Yeah, not a fiancée though." He shifted the zipper of his windbreaker up closer to his throat. "We're living in sin, that's about all... She's doing good though."

"Right." Chalice snapped another shot or two and dropped the camera back into his jacket pocket. "As long as you're happy, I'm happy."

Bear nodded agreeably. He peered about to ensure they were still alone on the wind-swept platform. "But enough about me. Obviously, I got your message... Something about an upcoming gig over in Asia?"

"Yeah," Chalice replied. "That area in general."

"Great. I love a mystery, but just between us can you tell me any more about it?" Bear asked, watching a police helicopter buzzing around the far shore of the North Side. "Like, uh, details?"

"Not a lot at this point," Chalice admitted. "But it'll include riding herd on a possible body snatch. The good news though is that this body wants to be snatched."

Bear nodded. "Permissive environment?"

Chalice shrugged, making a frown. "Ah, on your end, not so much."

"Yeah. Well, what fun would it be otherwise?" Bear observed bleakly. "When does it kick off?"

"Date uncertain," Chalice said. "Not for a few months at least... But we'll probably need you on board for some training and mission prep time for a couple of weeks before then with the others. Can do?"

"Can do easy," Bear said. "I'm flexible... The usual fee for services?"

"Plus twenty percent this time around."

"Sweet," Bear said, giving Chalice a half grin.

"That's danger pay, Big Guy."

Chalice slapped Bear on the shoulder and turned to leave. "Give my love to Kelly. We'll be in touch. Real soon."

"Yeah," Bear said. "Real soon."

NINETEEN: KILO SITE

Denver International Airport
Denver, Colorado
April 6, 2003

Chalice stared at the Arrivals board in the main hall of the Jeppesen Terminal. Unfortunately, the delays were starting to pile up. Thanks to a combination of thunderstorms and high winds, the United Airlines flight from San Francisco was now expected to arrive an hour and forty minutes late.

He shrugged. Not completely unexpected, it being the Mile-High City and all that. At least the flight was still coming his way.

Producing a cell phone from his corduroy jeans, he hit one of the speed dial numbers.

"Yeah?" the other answered immediately. It was Bear's voice.

"They're making good time," he said. "Should be here in the next half hour."

"Got it," the other said, disconnecting the call abruptly.

"Yeah, bye," Chalice said into the dead phone. As he well knew, social graces were not high among Bear's skill sets.

Chalice killed the intervening time by nursing a cup of cappuccino and perusing a copy of the morning's Denver Post in a local shop. When he could stall no longer, he positioned himself at the top of the escalator that fed incoming passengers up from the below ground automated railway and into the main terminal.

He waited for another fifteen minutes until he caught sight of them. They were three youngish Asians traveling together as a group. He readily recognized them from their file photos, as they did him.

Chalice greeted them as they cleared the top of the escalator. "I'm Cody," he said, giving them the cover name they were told to expect. He pulled them aside and shook hands with the senior member of the group. "Welcome to Colorado."

"Chol," the slender, intense looking man said. "Thank you for meeting us."

"My pleasure."

Chalice knew the thirty-two-year-old Chol had been trained as a mechanical engineer in Daejeon. As a young child however, he had been an escapee from North Korea with his parents. Unfortunately, neither of them had survived the border crossing effort. Now he was with the Org.

"I am Jina," said the only female member of the trio. An attractive, diminutive woman in her mid-twenties, she was a former grad student in Seoul. Although she had never been to the North, her parents were also refugees from the Hermit Kingdom who successfully made their way south two years before her birth.

As Chalice shook her hand politely, she guided his attention to the blocky, hard-faced man who waited patiently next to her. "And this," she said, "is Seok."

"Seok," Chalice said, shaking the man's flat, unyielding hand. "Good to see you."

"Sir," the latter replied without expression.

Seok, Chalice knew, was a twelve-year veteran of the Republic of Korea, or ROK, Marine Corps. Unlike Jina, he had actually visited the North a number of times in past years, albeit illegally and by way of small coastal raiding craft.

"Let's find your luggage and get moving," Chalice said. Wordlessly, they filed in behind him.

A half hour later, all baggage collected, Chalice led them outside of the terminal building, where they found Bear awaiting them.

Garbed in a light fleece jacket and a blue woolen watch cap, the former MACV-SOG soldier peered at his new charges studiously. He was patiently standing next to a Ford van with mirrored windows in the rear passenger compartment.

"This is Tim," Chalice told them, relaying Bear's cover identity.

Wasting no time on pleasantries, Bear loaded the three Koreans into the van along with their luggage. He then unceremoniously slammed the door shut behind them and locked it.

As the three Korean agents settled into the rear seats they were immediately aware of the fact that the windows were blacked out. As such, their view of the outside world was completely obstructed.

Settling in, they decided to take advantage of their enforced solitude to catch up on their sleep. It had been a long day of travel thus far.

Satisfied with the arrangements, Chalice clambered into the van's passenger seat and fastened his seatbelt. He gave Bear a thumbs-up and they pulled out of the DIA grounds and headed toward the high country.

* * *

Bear traveled north past the confines of Denver. Turning onto Route 72 they began the northwesterly climbing trek in the direction of the Continental Divide. After an hour of driving they were well within the folds of the Rocky Mountains and climbing.

Their destination was a point at 9,000 feet of elevation in Boulder County. It was located between the town of Nederland and the tiny commune of Ward. The surrounding area was that of woodlands and bright, snowcapped mountainous peaks.

Kilo Site, as it was called, was one of the only two permanent Org locations – the other being the headquarters in McLean. Part of the Congressional Black Budget, it was also partially funded by other members of the Intelligence Community who made use of its facilities on an as-needed basis.

As they neared the area, Chalice reflected on an interaction he had with one of the locals at a bar a few years ago. "Boulder," the man recounted, "is for the people who can't handle the pace of life in Denver. Nederland, on the other hand, is for those who are too stressed out by the liberals living in Boulder. And Ward is finally for those who are too stressed out by Nederland."

Perceptive analysis, he thought.

Finally, Bear steered the van off 72 and onto an unmarked, hard-packed dirt road that appeared to lead nowhere. For those travelers who persevered however, they soon came to a fenced site with a rusting sign that read: "United States Government Property - Environmental Research Site – No Admittance Without Prior Authorization".

Dismounting, Chalice approached the padlocked gate and unlocked it. Although the gate appeared to be deserted, it was in fact being monitored both by surveillance cameras and hidden ground sensors. Chalice allowed Bear to pull the van through before closing and re-locking the gate.

A further two hundred yards later, after rounding a bend, they reached another line of fencing, the latter clearly of more recent and sturdy design. Above the second gate, this one manned by an armed sentry, was the sign "United States Government Property - No Entry – Hazardous Materials Testing."

After the sentry verified Chalice's credentials, he waived them through the barrier, sealing it once again behind them. They were now entering Kilo Site. Although it was April, patches of dirty snow dotted the sides of the roadway.

Residents in the surrounding county were vaguely aware of the Site. Many thought it to be a research facility, as advertised. Others referred to it loosely as the Spook Place. A handful believed it to be the final resting place of the aliens from the Roswell UFO crash site. The majority however, following the mountain lifestyle of live and let live, simply didn't care.

A handful of buildings formed the core of Kilo. Upon entering the secure area, Bear pulled up to Building One, which was the administration and headquarters facility. Across the circular loop was the largest structure in the Site, Building Two, which was the conference facility, housing classrooms and meeting rooms.

Bear dropped Chalice off at One and proceeded down the paved road to Building Three, which was the dormitory. There the Koreans were checked into their individual military style rooms. They would find the cement block lodgings to be clean and modern, but basic in the extreme. A small gym was located on the first level for those who felt the need for additional exercise.

Not far from the dorm was Building Four, which was the dining facility. This included a self-service bar and lounge, replete with television, pool tables and Internet computers.

Further recessed into the dark woods was Building Five. This was primarily an indoor shooting range. Five also included an armory, a weapons vault and an adjoining electronics shop. Its neighbor, Building Six, was the central logistics office.

Even deeper into the woods, secluded within its own internal set of fencings, was Building Seven. Nobody talked about Seven.

A bearded figure with a multi-colored knit watch cap on his head exited the admin building to greet the new arrivals.

"Chalice," he said, extending his hand in greeting.

Chalice took the hand of his old acquaintance and shook it warmly. "How are 'ya, Wahhabi?"

TWENTY: WAHHABI

Kilo Site
Boulder County, Colorado
April 7, 2003

Following breakfast the next morning all three of the Korean agents were individually fluttered, or polygraphed, by an examiner from Headquarters. The purpose of the exercise was to do a final check on their reliability prior to initiating them with the details of the ARGENT SUCCUBUS operation. Each of them passed the ordeal.

There had been some prior discussion as to the value of including an interpreter with the polygraph examiner. In the event, it was deemed to be unnecessary, as all three were sufficiently conversant in the English language. Jina was significantly more so, while Seok was somewhat less.

There were many in the Government who regarded the polygraph with a devotion that bordered upon the religious. Others, more skeptical and somewhat less committed to the process, spoke of the polygraph only as a useful investigative tool.

Chalice was on the fringes of the latter group. He had no real confidence in the machine itself. He rather saw its primary value as a psychological intimidation device capable of extorting honesty from its test subjects. But, in the trite phraseology of the day, the poly exam was what it was.

* * *

That afternoon, the reliability question being settled, the team was now officially considered to be in seclusion. They would not be released until the end of the operation.

Seven people were gathered in one of the classrooms in the conference center. Along with Chalice, Bear, and the three Koreans, was the man who was nicknamed Wahhabi. Also, recently arrived from McLean, was Kurt Meyerhof.

Wahhabi was the administrator of Kilo Site. A forty-something man with permanently reddened cheeks and a full reddish colored beard, he was a veteran of the Org's covert operations. Born of Mormon parents in Utah, it was while serving years earlier in Tajikistan that a colleague dubbed him with the odd moniker. The tag was prompted by what his partner judged to be his somewhat Jihadist appearance.

The current generation of Org people knew him by no other.

Having been sidelined with an injury while abroad, Wahhabi now lived with his wife, kid, and three dogs in a comfortable home in the heights overlooking Nederland. It was not what he signed up for, but he was still in the game. It was enough.

As chief of Kilo, Wahhabi was deemed to be in the need-to-know category with regard to the Succubus case. He was therefore invited to join in on the initial team brief. Nevertheless, he was highly impressed that the deputy director of JICSA would come out to personally brief the agent team. He had not seen the like of it before.

After a series of somewhat awkward greetings and hand shaking, everyone seated themselves around a rustic wooden table. A set of folders awaited them, each packed with photos, map sheets and other study materials.

Meyerhof went straight into the subject matter, without bothering to introduce himself in any detail to the Korean agents.

"First of all," he said, "I want to express my appreciation to each of you for your willingness to participate in this operation. Needless to say, it is not without risk... Not at all." He paused to look at each of the Koreans in the eye. "But we would not put any of you in danger if it were not worth the effort."

"We understand the risk," Chol said, filling the silence. "We are here."

Jina nodded silently in agreement.

"Good," Meyerhof said. "Okay then. Let's start."

He opened the folder before him. The others did likewise.

"This is an operation that has several aspects. But from your perspective, it is basically this: we have reliable source reporting that a research scientist at the Yongbyon nuclear facility in the DPRK wants to defect. We need you to make contact with her and bring her out safely."

"Her?" Jina repeated.

"A young woman," Chalice interjected. "Just about your age in fact."

"How are we to do this?" Chol asked, seemingly unbothered by the daunting project ahead of them.

"For your team," Meyerhof continued, "there are four parts - insertion, contact, target recovery and exfiltration."

Meyerhof directed their attention to the first map sheet in their folder. "As of now, you will go in by land across the border from China. The entry point will be in the far northeast of the DPRK. In North Hamgyong Province. A trusted Chinese smuggler will get you across and handle the initial logistics."

Seok digested that last factoid uncomfortably. He did not like the Chinese. And he did not trust them at all. But he was not the commander of this mission and so he held his tongue.

"For obvious reasons, neither Cody nor Tim will be crossing into the DPRK with you," the deputy director added, using the names by which the Koreans knew Chalice and Bear.

"We just don't think a pair of white boys like us would fit in there real well," Bear supplied with a small grin.

Devoid of the intended humor, the Koreans nodded, blankly signaling their understanding.

"Speaking of fitting in," Wahhabi interposed, "there's more than just the ethnic issue here. Admittedly, I don't know a hell of a lot about conditions in North Korea these days, but isn't our guy Seok here a little, uhm, large for a North Korean male?"

Chalice cracked a smile. "Yes. Indeed, he is that. And that's why Seok will be carrying credentials identifying him to be a well-cared for officer of the SSD, or the State Security Department... With those creds, and the supplied covered vehicle, he shouldn't be questioned by anyone on the street."

Seok frowned momentarily as he struggled for the words. "SSD?" he repeated.

"*Bowibu*," Jina translated for him.

"Ah," Seok nodded, understanding.

"That explains getting in," Chol said politely. "How do we hit the target and come back out?"

"The precise details will be provided later," Meyerhof replied. "But in general terms, the plan is for your team to travel down to the Yongbyon area and there you will contact and recover the target.

"Before you arrive in Yongbyon, the target will have been advised to expect you and cooperate with you. The initial contact will be made by Jina, who we assume will be able to present a less threatening image to her."

Jina nodded agreeably.

"Coming back out," Meyerhof continued, "we have three primary options. Plan A, which is preferred, is to take her to a designated point on the western coast. Korea Bay, just north of the Yellow Sea. A boat will be meeting you there to pull you out."

"Okay," Chol said.

"Plan B is to travel south to a designated point along the Demilitarized Zone and cross into the Republic of Korea on foot. An Org team would be waiting on the DMZ to cover and receive you."

Meyerhof still had their undivided attention. This was not a surprise, as the topic was a literal life or death matter to the three of them.

"Plan C," he continued. "Move over land to the north. After reaching a designated point, cross back into China on foot. You would then be met and taken out of China.

"Finally, and least preferred, is what we call the go to hell plan," Meyerhof said. "If all else fails, you walk cross-country to a specified geographical location on the eastern coast, along the Sea of Japan. If it comes to this, you would then conceal yourselves in the coastal area as best as you can while we arrange to make a pick-up."

There was momentary silence.

"But you would still come for us?" Chol prompted.

"You would not be abandoned," Meyerhof assured him. "We have never abandoned an agent team in a denied area. And we certainly won't start now."

"We will have means of communications?" Jina asked.

"Of course. And it will be continuously monitored."

Seok cleared his throat at last. "Sir," he began. "What if our target, the lady, changes her mind?"

"Changes her mind?"

"If she says she will not come with us... We do what then?"

Meyerhof turned his attention to the team leader. "That will be your decision, Chol. You will be the man on the spot. Not me. Not Cody and not Tim. You must do whatever is needed for the safety of the team. If that includes aborting the mission, no-one back here will ever question your decision."

Chalice remained expressionless. But he had his doubts about that last bit.

TWENTY-ONE: FROZEN DEAD GUY

Nederland, Colorado
May 23, 2003

It was late afternoon on a Friday. The cold weather was breaking, slowly evolving into the promise of Spring.

Chalice and Wahhabi were sharing a corner booth in a tavern on the south end of Nederland. Based on Wahhabi's recommendation, each had a bottle of Fat Tire, a local Colorado brew, on the table in front of them.

"*Prosit*," Wahhabi offered as a toast, clanking his bottle against Chalice's.

"*Slainte*," Chalice responded. He took a grateful swig of the cold beer. "You have my thanks for the work of all of your guys... All's well that ends well."

"Ended well on my side anyhow," Wahhabi said. "Now they are free spirits. Loose out in the big, wide world... With you and yours."

The training regimen of the three South Korean agents, under the auspices the Kilo staff, had just come to an end. Trainers and trainees alike were worn out by the highly-condensed experiences of the past month.

Earlier that day Bear, the agents' constant companion at Kilo, had departed Colorado on a flight back to Pittsburgh. He was going to catch up on some down time with Kelly before starting the next phase of the operation.

Although all were already experienced field agents, Chol, Jina and Seok had been put through their paces and then some in preparation for the ARGENT SUCCUBUS deployment.

Each day at Kilo began with a bout of physical training and conditioning runs in the high-altitude environment. As was expected, Seok - the ex-ROK Marine - excelled in this and other hands-on phases of the training. In that respect, the other two continuously struggled to keep up with him.

Their skills-based regimen included classified map and satellite photo studies of the DPRK. The focus of the study was on the Yongbyon area and potential exfiltration routes. The latter subject extended to various border crossing scenarios, such as conducting several frosty nighttime swims in a river north of Fort Collins. This they did while hauling the inert form of Bear, role-playing a hapless defector, in tow.

Next came several days of escape and evasion/field survival skills exercises in the neighboring Arapaho National Forest. At the end of the wilderness phase, the trainees, all of whom were inevitably captured, were put through an uncomfortably realistic and often painful forty-hour session in methods of resisting hostile interrogation techniques.

Regardless of the skills taught, the implicit training point was quite clear. Do not get caught by the Opposition, whoever they were. Ever.

An intensified weapons course back at the Kilo Site followed. The goal was to familiarize them with the handling of likely North Korean firearms they might come across during the course of the mission.

The weapons exposure included use of the Type 68 7.62mm semi-auto pistol, the Type 88 assault rifle (a variant of the ubiquitous AK-47), a shorty, pistol grip Russian shotgun, and the Type 73 light machinegun. As was frequently emphasized by the instructors, the weapons training segment was for contingency use only. If the shooting ever started, they and their mission were likely finished.

Emergency medical treatment, basic vehicle commandeering methods, use of their issued communications gear and essential unarmed combat tactics were next on the crowded agenda.

Although each had native fluency with the Korean language, throughout the course they were constantly coached and drilled on current North Korean idioms and accents. The instructor, an austere North Korean defector who was herself on loan from the CIA, was a demanding mentor. She was eventually satisfied they could pass casual inspection inside the DPRK.

Training ended with a multi-day surveillance detection and avoidance exercise ranging from Denver to Colorado Springs. The team was matched with Org role players and set against experienced Air Force OSI special agents who avidly portrayed their counterintelligence pursuers.

At long last the team was judged to be ready to go. Or at least as ready as they could be, given the constraints of time. Results of the training were submitted to Headquarters. JD Tucker signed off on them at once.

An old Bob Marley song suddenly blared out from the tavern's jukebox, bringing the two men back to reality. "You kind'a get to like that shit," Wahhabi commented apologetically. "Almost."

Chalice pointedly eyeballed the tattered white baseball cap on Wahhabi's head. "And Frozen Dead Guy?" he asked. "What's up with that?"

Wahhabi pulled the cap off to glance at the familiar logo. "Yeah, man. The Frozen Dead Guy," he said, replacing it. "Where the hell you been?"

"Not around here long enough. Obviously."

"He's Grandpa Bredo," Wahhabi said. "A local cult figure. He died in Norway in the late 90's. His body was frozen and eventually sent here for storage up in the hills."

"Storage?"

"Till a cure for what ailed him can be found and he can be reanimated."

"Okay," Chalice offered tentatively.

Wahhabi smirked. "Just between us, word is that Grandpa has already thawed out a couple of times. So, ah, I'm not completely optimistic as to his chances of coming back."

"Yeah," Chalice agreed. "What's the message then?"

Wahhabi finished his beer in a single long pull. His left leg was hurting again. Reaching into his jeans pocket, he pulled out a twenty and threw it onto the table. "Don't let your people thaw out too early my friend... Not where they're going."

TWENTY-TWO: LUPANARE

Pompeii, Italy
June 10, 2003

Chalice carefully negotiated the irregularly cut, chunky gray cobblestones under his feet. He had difficulty absorbing the reality that they had actually been emplaced more than two thousand years earlier. But so they had, by the hands of the original Pompeiians ages past.

An avid history buff, Chalice had dreamt of visiting the ancient Roman settlement of Pompeii since first reading about it in his childhood, many years ago.

And now here he was. At long last.

Aside from satisfying his historical yearnings, Chalice was there to get a first-hand debrief on Savina's latest meeting with Ro. Neither he nor Puccio had been available to cover the unexpected session in Rome that had taken place two days' earlier. Circumstances had thus provided the opportunity to accomplish two objectives at once.

In the case of Savina, the area was not in the least bit foreign. The former journalist was a native of Maiori, a small town on the Amalfi coast. She had grown up not that far from the ruins of Pompeii.

While the surrounding Campania region had been populated since the Bronze Age, Pompeii's true historical claim to fame was traced to its massive destruction on August 24th, 79 AD. That was when the volcano to its northwest, a monster called Vesuvio (or Vesuvius), disastrously erupted.

To the initial amazement and growing terror of the locals, the volcano continued to violently flare for another two days. It horrifically dominated the landscape to a degree that can only be imagined today.

The expanding plume blackened the sky for miles around and inundated the area with rocks, cinders and other boiling hot lethal debris. When it was finally exhausted, the blast had covered the town under a deep layer of smothering volcanic ash.

Archeologists now estimate roughly 2,000 people were killed in the town. Some of those, the more fortunate ones, were slain outright. Others, the far less fortunate, died more slowly as the result of being trapped and suffocated under the collapsed structures.

In general, the dead were comprised of two groups: those who were unable to escape the horror, and those who chose to ride out the crisis in hopes of protecting of their wealth and properties.

Those souls in the latter group were probably not that much unlike the victims of modern-day hurricane parties in Florida who opted to ride out the storm while hoping for the best, Chalice reflected.

Pompeii silently maintained its secrets for nearly two millennia until modern excavations began in 1748.

Upon entering the gates of the protected area, Chalice overheard an elderly guide addressing an awaiting tour group. He told them that a significant percentage of the area purposely remained untouched. That was to be left to succeeding generations, the guide said, and their presumably superior methods of archeological research.

Savina was waiting for him by the modern water fountains.

"Welcome to the past," she said, taking his hand with both of hers. "I will be your guide today."

"*Grazie mille*," he said in reply. "I've been wanting to see this place forever."

"You cannot be blamed for that," she said. "Come along."

Chalice had flown into Naples the past evening upon hearing that Ro Jae-Ki unexpectedly announced his need to again meet with Savina. While Chalice had planned on coming into Italy within the week in any event, the new development advanced the schedule by several days.

As she walked him over to the site of the Quadriportico dei Teatri, she began to report on Ro's current state of mind in a hushed tone of voice.

"Sorry, but there are no tapes this time," she said. "Our friend asked for an unplanned meeting. And he selected his own hotel... I was hesitant, but I thought it best to comply."

"It's okay," Chalice replied. While he would have preferred otherwise, by this point in the operation he was fairly confident Ro did not present a physical threat to Savina.

"So, what are his issues?" he asked.

"He has several," she answered in a muted tone of voice. "He seems to be getting – uhm, what is the English expression – anty?"

"Antsy?" Chalice supplied.

"Yes," she confirmed. "Antsy, I would say. He is worried about the length of time this is all taking... He said that he thought that it would be faster. He assumed – he hoped – that by now he would be in America. Safe."

"But he understood from the beginning that this process would take time," Chalice interjected. "Especially considering the matter of his... relative."

Savina made a face. "Okay. Maybe he knows this intellectually. But emotionally, no.... I think he feels he is juggling his chances of a future between becoming an American millionaire over there and losing his head back home... Or losing it here."

Chalice paused to let a knot of his fellow sight-seers move slowly past them. "Highly doubtful that the resettlement program will make him a millionaire," he observed at last. "But I know what you mean."

The Quadriportico, as the name implied, was an open grassy field bordered by a square of one-story buildings on all sides. A semi-circular theater adjoined the area to the northwest.

"This, as you see," Savina said, reverting back to her role of guide, "is quite representative of its time."

"How so?"

"It was basically the training school for the gladiators of Pompeii." She motioned toward the unadorned surrounding rustic enclosures. "They, the fighters I mean, lived imprisoned in these cells. They trained on this field. And they fought in the nearby larger amphitheater to the east of us."

"And died there," Chalice speculated.

"Some," Savina countered. "But not all... In the end, they were costly business investments for their owners. Expensive properties, not simple slaves to be wasted in every encounter."

Following the example of a handful of nearby tourists, Chalice produced a camera from a fanny-pack on his waist. Like them, he captured a collection of views, one after the other. At last, the immediate group finished their own photos and began to move further on.

"And then there is the matter of our friend's assistant," Savina continued discretely as they moved along as well.

Chalice knew she was referring to Ro's security officer, Tae. "Aren't they partners in crime?" he asked. "And I mean that literally."

Savina suppressed a laugh. "They are," she agreed. "But he seems to fear his assistant is coming too close to our, uh, special project."

"As in too close, how?"

"He knows the assistant is happy to share in whatever private proceeds they may develop on their own. Aside from the knowledge of their employer, that is. But maybe our friend thinks that the ultimate objective will be more than the assistant can abide."

Chalice shrugged. "Okay. Then maybe we need to find a way to manage the assistant."

"It would seem so. Yes."

Walking side by side, they stepped out onto the ancient Roman street. The sense of history was overwhelming as they made their way over the irregular, time-worn stones of the roadway, taking care to avoid a twisted ankle – or worse – in the smooth-edged gaps between the stones.

After trudging along for another few blocks along the narrow surface of the Vicolo del Lupanare, Chalice and Savina found themselves standing before a very well-preserved, ancient two-story structure that was perched on the corner of three intersecting streets.

This was the famous Lupanare. It was the best surviving example of the many public brothels that had once enjoyed a thriving existence in Pompeii.

Despite its notoriety, the Lupanare was a rather small building. Stepping inside, Chalice found the series of individual rooms in the interior of the ground floor to be verging on the claustrophobic. They offered little more than a stone bed and pillow combination that must have once been covered with some sort of matting.

Faded paintings over the entryways displayed the various specialties that had been offered to the long-lost customers. The upper level was structurally off limits to visitors.

"Just amazing," Chalice said, absorbing the view.

"And given my cover, not out of place," Savina said with a hint of a smile. "Wouldn't you agree?"

Chalice grimaced but did not reply.

Exiting the Lupanare, he stepped back out onto the uneven Roman street following his Italian agent. The intersection was swarming with tourists, their chatter effectively masking any conversation between the two.

In so doing, Chalice didn't bother to observe for hostile coverage. He knew both Zlatko Piric and Nardo Puccio were trailing them on foot not far behind, providing security and keeping watch for surveillance. Likewise, Escobar was loitering on the street a block ahead of them performing the same function.

Savina continued in her role of agent/guide. "So, in this direction is the old forum of Pompeii," she said.

"Please. Continue."

"Our friend offered a bit more insight into his connections with the various programs of his organization," Savina said, continuing with her tale as she weaved through a gaggle of elderly Spanish touristas.

"Like?"

"Macau," she said, after gaining breathing space from the others. "He was there five years ago as part of something called the Zokwang Trading Company... Does it mean anything to you?"

"Nothing."

"Our friend said Zokwang answers to his Office 39."

"Which is the group he actually reports to," Chalice added.

"Yes. He said this, uh, Zokwang was founded in 1974 in Macau. While it provided a sort of consular function for the home country, it was also involved in arms sales and illegal technology transfers. He mentioned two other companies doing similar things."

Like trading in missile technology, Chalice reflected. "And all this went unnoticed by the Chinese?"

"No," she said. "Not according to him... He said in the mid-90's, prior to his arrival, staff members from Zokwang were actually arrested by the Macau police."

"For what reason?"

"Trading counterfeit American currency," she said. "They were using a local Macau bank called the Banco Delta Asia."

Supernotes, Chalice surmised. He had previously learned these bogus $100 bills had also started appearing in Bangkok, Thailand, circa 2001. The latter was apparently a new focal point of North Korean activity by that time.

The constricted roadway finally emptied out into the open expanse of the Pompeiian forum. As Chalice peered about, the standing columns of the old temples appeared to be fragile in the extreme. That they remained standing for so long was a wonder.

And over them all, clearly dominating the distant landscape, was the brooding colossus of Vesuvius.

The volcano was quiet now, but still alive. Still a threat.

Which brought Chalice back to the more immediate matter of Tae.

"It seems to me that the main problem right now is the issue of our friend's assistant," he said.

"I would agree."

Chalice took several more shots before tucking his camera away. "Then let's start dealing with him directly. Soon."

TWENTY-THREE: ETRURIA

Orvieto, Italy
June 28, 2003

It was a fine, warm Saturday afternoon in Umbria. While the sun showered the countryside, the air was mercifully lacking in humidity.

Tae, formerly a captain of the Korean People's Army Reconnaissance Brigades and currently a special security officer assigned to the DPRK Mission to the Italian Republic, now found himself strolling along the unfamiliar heights of the Orvieto plateau.

On this date, had he been back home in North Korea, he would doubtlessly be taking part in the annual *Struggle Against US Imperialism* month-long celebrations. Instead, here he was, soaking in the heritage of an ancient pre-Latin civilization in a foreign land.

Having feigned illness and the need for a restful weekend, Ro Jae-Ki covertly instructed his trusted associate to undertake the ninety-minute drive northward from Rome and into the Umbria region. Tae's assigned goal was to attend a clandestine meeting with an ostensible pair of East European criminals on behalf of the DCM. And on behalf of his own financial interests as well.

Despite the limitations of his North Korean upbringing, Tae was fascinated by historical matters. His foreign protective assignments with Ro facilitated his unofficial studies. As such, he had taken the time to research the background of his Umbrian meeting place.

Between two to three thousand years earlier, as he had learned, Orvieto had then been known as Velzna. In those distant days of the misty past, Velzna was a significant part of the empire of Etruria.

Etruria was a land held by the ancient Etruscan people. It was a civilization that preceded the Romans by half a millennium or more. Etruria included the modern Italian cities of Volterra, Perugia, Arezzo and several others.

But it was in modern Orvieto that a branch of the Etruscans had constructed a secure home for themselves high atop the flat volcanic plateau. Beneath the streets of Velzna, wedged into the soft tufa rock, the ancients dug a series of protective tunnels and storage areas that still exist today.

There they withstood all threats, until the Romans defeated them, some two hundred years before the birth of Christ. The city was later to become a fiefdom of the medieval Papal States and a refuge of the Roman Popes themselves.

The history was undeniably overwhelming. As fascinating as he found it to be, Tae was earnestly focused on the here and now.

Bringing himself back to the present, he understood the men he would be meeting with today were interested in diverting a significant quantity of the North Korean counterfeit $100 Supernote bills for their own – criminal - purposes.

Tae had no idea, nor any concern for that matter, as to the ultimate destination of the channeled funds. He only knew that he, as well as Ro, would be a financial beneficiary of the deal. He was no stranger to such negotiations, as his hidden bank account in Geneva could well testify.

Tae had no way of knowing this meeting was a drama that had been constructed solely for his own benefit. Chalice, via the Savina channel to Ro, had developed the scenario for the purpose of diverting any suspicions Tae might have had regarding the DCM's encounters with the Westerners.

At high noon, as appointed, Tae was standing on the flagstones in Orvieto's Piazza del Duomo. Before him was the duomo, the 14th century cathedral that had taken some three hundred years for the faithful to build.

A golden frontage above the main doors of the cathedral gleamed in the bright sunlight. Behind him was a modest museum containing several floors of Etruscan artifacts. Despite their provenance, they were of no interest to him at the moment.

Warily stepping into the cathedral, Tae was again amazed that such a large and ornate structure could have been assembled by hand so many centuries ago. Adhering to its medieval design, the wide nave of the interior was devoid of pews and other such modern additions. The faithful would worship on the cold stone. A number of chapels, containing valued frescoes, adorned either side.

Most strikingly in his view, the walls and pillars were formed of alternating layers of black and white stone. The pattern reflected a Muslim artistic influence, he recalled. It was for reasons that were more than he could conceive.

After casually wandering about the interior for several minutes, Tae caught sight of a lanky young Asian man lingering near the main altar.

Tae paused, ostensibly admiring the carving of a pieta near the front of the cathedral. The pieta was a depiction of the mourning mother of the slain Christ. Amazingly in his eyes, it had been carved from a single block of marble.

While doing so he observed that, other than a handful of other Asians in the cathedral, the young man at the altar was alone.

Tae casually moved forward until he came alongside the younger man. He followed the other's gaze at the bright frescoes covering the walls. "This cathedral is magnificent," he said in Korean.

The younger man nodded in agreement. "But the one in Siena is far superior," he added.

Satisfied with the prearranged verbal exchange, Tae continued, "And you are with the gentlemen from the East?"

"Yes," Chol said. "And you are with the gentleman from Rome?"

"I am."

"And so here we are."

"That is good," Tae said, satisfied with the contact.

"Come and walk with me then," Chol said. "It's just a short distance from here... And that view is also magnificent."

* * *

Wordlessly, Tae trudged along with Chol for several blocks until they reached the stark eastern limit of the tufa plateau. There, overlooking the flatlands below was the Pozzo di San Patricio, or Saint Patrick's Well.

Contrary to legend, the feature had nothing to do with the patron saint of Ireland who had never set foot in Italy. Rather, it had been dug by order of a Pope in the 16th century as part of a planned strategic refuge. The well was some two hundred feet deep.

Replete with a cylindrical path for mule-drawn carts, it was designed to support the town with a vital water supply in the event of a long siege – not an unlikely event at the time.

A tree-lined walkway led to the circular top of Saint Patrick's Well. Inset into the green hedges along the way were several flat benches.

Two middle-aged European men were lounging on one of the benches. They were patiently awaiting their Korean contacts. While doing so, they were eyeballing the more attractive female tourists visiting the attraction.

Unbeknownst to Tae, the two men were both Org assets, Zlatko and Escobar.

"Up there. Those two are your contacts," Chol quietly advised Tae as they approached. "They speak some poor English, but no Korean of course. I'll be translating for you."

Tae grunted his agreement emotionlessly.

Both men rose slowly to their feet as they caught sight of Tae and Chol. Neither appeared overly eager to meet the newcomer.

"These are the people from the East," Chol offered by way of introduction.

Tae nodded curtly and reached out to shake their hands.

"I am Fedor," Zlatko said. He motioned off-handedly in Escobar's direction. "And this is my associate."

Tae, standing mute, did not return the favor.

After exchanging coldly appraising stares, Zlatko gestured at the passing tourists. "Too many eyes and ears here," he said. "Let's step over there and talk business."

Tae and Chol accompanied Zlatko to the far wall of the precipice. Escobar lagged several feet behind, ever playing the role of the taciturn bodyguard.

Upon reaching the chest high rock wall at the edge of the sheer drop-off, Zlatko rested his elbows and peered out at the expansive distant scenery. "This view," he observed, shaking his head appreciatively. "It's very striking. You agree?"

Chol translated.

"Yes," Tae agreed. "So it is. But I have not come here for the view."

"Still," Zlatko observed, "such beauty does not appear by itself. It requires money to produce and maintain. Much money."

Tae shrugged wordlessly.

"So, as a Communist, I'm guessing you do not like money?" Zlatko prodded.

"I like money," Tae admitted, ignoring the jibe. "Well enough."

"As do I, as a member of a former Communist family... From what I know, I think that maybe you are becoming an independent Capitalist these days."

Tae did not reply.

"And that is what brings us together today," Zlatko continued. "Your boss in Rome has sent word to my boss in Belgrade... He says he can supply us with what they call the Supernotes. Those high-quality, counterfeit American hundred dollar bills your country produces."

Tae nodded. "That is true."

"And you have done this before?"

"Many times."

"And can do so again?" Zlatko prodded.

"Of course."

"Good. That is what we hoped and expected," Zlatko said. "What is your price?"

Tae did not hesitate. "Our price for you? Seventy-five percentage points on the dollar. As the Capitalists would say."

Zlatko already knew that the Supernotes, due to their unusually high quality, and therefore popular demand, often commanded between sixty to eighty points on the dollar. That is to say, as much as eighty genuine dollars for a counterfeit one-hundred-dollar bill. Nevertheless...

"That is a crazy figure," Zlatko protested. "My boss would go no higher than fifty points... And that would be extortion in any case."

Tae peered into the distance for what he assumed to be an appropriate amount of time. He then conferred briefly with Chol for a better definition of the word extortion.

"Maybe, he offered finally, "if your boss were to see the quality of our product, he would think differently. Your profit, I think, would be quite great."

"Exactly," Zlatko said. "But let us take it one step at a time."

"How so?" Tae responded.

Zlatko frowned theatrically. "Okay. I propose that you deliver a small amount of your Supernotes for us to analyze back home. If all is well, then we will proceed to purchase a good quantity of your bills. Many such notes."

"Yes?"

"And so, if we can successfully move those bills through the marketplace, we will come back to you for a very substantial buy."

Now Tae took his time to appreciate the proposal. "How much is this supposedly substantial purchase of which you speak?"

Zlatko affected a pose of deep study. "Maybe, let us say, one million dollars. American?"

"Yes?"

"Of course," he said. "Maybe more later. Of course."

As he watched Tae mentally calculating his share of the take, Zlatko knew the fish was hooked.

"So, get back to me," Zlatko said, gesturing toward Chol. "This man will tell you how to contact us."

A glean of genuine interest finally appeared in Tae's eyes. "I will," he said. "Very soon."

"Good. Then do so," Zlatko replied. With a preemptory handshake, he turned and marched off with Escobar and Chol trailing along behind him.

Tae absently watched the departure of the East European criminals, but his mind was on his potential Swiss bank deposits.

TWENTY-FOUR: YODOK

McLean, Virginia
July 3, 2003

JD Tucker was at his desk just after sun up. Arrayed in front of him, alongside his work files, were a pot of coffee, a sesame bagel and an unopened container of blueberry yogurt.

It would be a short workday for him as he expected to be leaving for North Carolina later in the morning. Tucker planned to spend the Fourth of July weekend in the Fayetteville area with some old Army buddies from his Delta days. The get-together had been arranged for months and he was looking forward to the diversion.

Swiveling in his chair, he powered up his high side, or secure, computer. After the usual delay as the ethers exchanged data, he logged into the CIA daily interagency feed. That done, he began to scan the current topics of interest. Not surprisingly, Iraqi-related developments topped the list of concerns on CIA's corporate mind.

Tucker began with a piece referring to the recent insurgent attack on the Baghdad power grid. He was a bit surprised to see the Administrator of the Coalition Provisional Authority (CPA) had reversed himself in reaction to the attack.

The CPA now decreed that a new security force would be established to provide security to utilities and other powers facilities. Contrary to his earlier decisions, the Administrator determined that former members of the Iraqi Army would staff this new force.

In another entry, he noted that the French were still voicing complaints both publicly and through confidential diplomatic channels with regard to the US and UK military actions in country. The open media had already reported the irritation of Congress, highlighting the replacement of the French Fries in their cafeteria with so-called Freedom Fries.

Further down the feed, Tucker saw that Operation Sidewinder, launched several days ago, was continuing apace. The goal of Sidewinder, led by the Army's 4th Infantry Division, was to dislodge the Saddam loyalists and paramilitary fighters who were clearly behind the deadly attacks on Coalition forces.

On the upside, CIA reported the Polish Defense Minister's announcement that his country would be sending several thousand troops into Iraq. Tucker was already familiar with the capabilities of their well-trained Special Forces personnel. The GROM, as they were called, would be a welcomed asset to the theater commander.

Skipping past several items, he finally saw that INR, the Intelligence Community component of the State Department, had weighed in once again on the WMD issue. They released a report expressing their doubts as to the accuracy of the earlier intelligence pertaining to the mobile biological weapons lab in pre-invasion Iraq.

Tucker assumed this had to be a fairly troubling development down at Foggy Bottom, as the lab had been a crucial point of the Secretary's testimony to the United Nations General Assembly back in March.

For that matter, the possible WMD ties between Iraq and his North Korean ARGENT SUCCUBUS case was an open question. Tucker jotted down a note adding that to Chalice's priorities list.

Tucker next clicked on the Asia tab of the CIA news feed. He searched the page until he found the report that one of his staff had mentioned the previous afternoon. And there it was – the CIA debrief of a former prisoner who somehow survived the hellish life of the North Korean prison camp called Yodok.

The man, simply referred to by the Agency as "PJL", was described as a former schoolteacher who was now in his late 'thirties. PJL had reportedly been dissatisfied with life in the DPRK and was unhappy over a failed romantic relationship. In response to both, he opted for the commission of one of the more serious crimes in the eyes of the state. He illegally fled the country by crossing the northern border and entering into the People's Republic of China (PRC).

What PJL could not have then known was that China and North Korea shared a secret mutual agreement dating back to 1986 – if not earlier. That agreement called for Chinese assistance in the return of North Korean escapees to their home country. It also established a series of procedures for enhanced security in the border region.

More than that, it specified the Chinese would turn a blind eye to some of Pyongyang's own cross-border activities. The secret agreement essentially gave the North Korean Bowibu – the State Security Department - a relatively free hand to monitor North Koreans in the PRC. The SSD could hunt them down and even abduct them for forced repatriation.

The Chinese, for their part, routinely advised their counterparts in the Western embassies in Beijing that the return of DPRK escapees was a routine law enforcement matter. No harm ever came to them, they said with assurance.

To the case in point, PJL had successfully led a low-key existence in the city of Shenyang, just north of the border. There he mixed easily with the so-called *Chosonjok*, or ethnic Koreans of China. For nearly three years PJL eked out a living among the Korean minority population with his hands, most often working as a common laborer on various construction projects.

His life in China had been hardscrabble and lonely but not all that bad, relatively speaking.

Then one afternoon at his worksite he was unexpectedly accosted by uniformed officers of the Shenyang Public Security Bureau – the police – and unceremoniously taken off to jail. There he spent a fearful night, unable to sleep or eat. The next morning, he found himself in the presence of a grim-faced agent of the Bowibu.

Within days of his arrest PJL was transported to a Bowibu interrogation center back in the DPRK. At that point, his life changed forever. PJL was placed into isolation. He was shackled, humiliated, and repeatedly struck with wooden batons. This was all done to correct his demonstrated anti-social behaviors.

Accused of being no better than a stray dog, PJL was told he was a disrespectful thief and traitor. The DPRK officials claimed astonishment that he could commit such crimes despite all of the bounties the Dear Leader had generously bestowed not only upon him but upon his family as well. Fearing the worst, he wisely held his silence.

The pressure was intensified during his third night of incarceration. PJL was man-handled into a cramped and painful sitting position. A short length of raw board was forced behind his knees. His hands and feet were then secured behind his back with a pair of steel cuffs.

JPL was left in that agonizing position in a darkened enclosure for an expanse of two days without food or water. When they finally pulled him out of his hole, he readily agreed to sign a paper confessing to whatever crimes they alleged.

Despite his pain, he was gratified to see his prescribed confession did not include any admission of espionage or terrorism against the state. The results of such charges, he well knew, would be terminal.

Following an eight-minute trial the next day, JPL was summarily found guilty of his crimes. He was then immediately dispatched into the *kwanliso* system of political prison camps. In his case, JPL was shuttled off to the Yodok camp.

Also known as Camp 15, Yodok was situated in the Ipsok River valley in South Hamgyong province. The camp was scenic in its mountainous setting, for those who had the luxury of enjoying the view, but it was unceasingly brutal and degrading in its daily practices for the majority of its inhabitants.

As PJL soon learned, the camp was divided into two zones: the total control zone and the revolutionary zone. Fortunately for him, PJL was sentenced to the latter, which was marginally less severe and at least held the possibility of a future release. Such was not the case for the unfortunates who were delivered into the total control area for what remained of their lives. Indeed, it was said, many feared a life sentence in the camps even more than they feared an outright order of execution.

Nevertheless, even in the lesser regime side of the camp, beatings, privations, and near starvation were the accepted order of the day. The guards were free to exercise discipline over the inmates with such severity as they saw fit. And as they saw fit.

Subsistence in Yodok – there was no *life* as such – consisted of heavy labor from dawn to dusk, routinely enforced with physical punishment. In return, the prisoners were provided with one set of shoes and ragged clothing, a crude hut for sleeping, and a meager diet of corn and rice.

Layered onto the harsh conditions of the camp was the ever-present element of uncertainty. Rare was the prisoner who actually knew what the extent of his or her sentence was. Beyond that, additional years could be added for trivial offenses.

PJL was assigned to a mining crew that worked in the gypsum quarry within the spacious confines of the camp. As with all prisoners, his team was assigned a daily work quota. Failure to meet the quota was met with physical punishment and a reduced food ration. For many, the self-perpetuating cycle of insufficient work production, resulting in less food to eat, leading in turn to still lower work production, was a de facto death sentence.

Starvation was hardly the only cause of death at Yodok. Other inmates became the subjects of public executions. The death penalty could be and was handed out for a variety of reasons. All prisoners were forced to witness the event, after which a handful of them carried the bodies to the mass gravesite – which, with black humor, they called the *flower garden*.

By default, all of the Yodok victims in the flower garden unceremoniously passed into eternity naked, having been stripped of their rags and footwear by their fellow prisoners for their own use. PJL admitted to doing this himself more than once.

Always in the back of his mind, PJL had reported, was the fate of his family members on the outside. Assuming they were still on the outside. It was common practice for the authorities to hold family members guiltily responsible for the actions of their criminal relatives. They often ended up in the camps themselves.

And then, after twelve years of suffering, PJL was released from confinement. His release, though welcomed, was almost as abrupt as his arrest.

With Yodok behind him, PJL went into the larger prison that was North Korean society itself. And he did so with his name indelibly stained as a former camp inmate.

As Tucker noted, the news item ended at that point. The CIA did not deign to comment upon PJL's life after Yodok. Nor did it mention, even in this classified format, how he was able to finally exit the DPRK. Assuming he did in fact leave the country.

Tucker signed out of the CIA feed and sequenced into the program holding the JICSA current operational case files. Within moments he opened the ARGENT SUCCUBUS folder and called up the photos of his three Korean agents. Under each photo were their true names, work histories, familial connections and detailed biographies.

The Org Director reflected on what would befall them, were they to be captured while inside North Korea. Certainly, it would surpass anything experienced by PJL, whoever he was. And JD Tucker was the man who was sending them in there.

Tucker had been putting off this moment for several days, as it grinded up against both his personal ethics and soldierly instincts. But, finally, he knew it was unavoidable.

The single page classified memo lay prominently on the corner of his desktop. Sighing, he hurriedly scrawled his name above the signature block and dated it.

It was done.

The body of the memorandum was brief in the extreme. It simply read: "ARGENT SUCCUBUS – Prometheus Deployment authorized."

Accordingly, just prior to their entry into the DPRK Chol, Jina and Seok would each be outfitted with a small glass vial. The vial itself was shielded within a thin but sturdy latex membrane. The greenish fluid contained within the vial was a rapid effect suicide potion.

The lethality of the fluid far exceeded that of the old L-Pill of the OSS era or even the later day shellfish toxins of the CIA. Its actual use would be an individual decision on each of their parts.

Tucker silently prayed that Logistics would be able to reclaim all three vials for destruction at the end of the case.

TWENTY-FIVE: SURVEY GROUP

Tikrit Area, Iraq
July 28, 2003

The US Army Blackhawk helicopter churned steadily northward through the humid morning air. They had lifted off from Baghdad Airport less than an hour ago and were nearing their destination – a hastily secured compound just south of Saddam's hometown of Tikrit. Thus far the flight had been fairly nominal.

Aside from the aircrew, the helo carried only two passengers on this hop. Both were garbed in the civilian clothing, cargo pants and dark shirts, that was increasingly common to the community of contractor personnel. Although seemingly fit men, the pair were nevertheless older than the usual grunts the crew normally ferried around the Iraqi countryside.

On this particular trip both passengers - Chalice and Bear - were Army combat veterans now under National Security Council (NSC) cover. Strapped tightly into their webbed and aluminum framed seats, they were monitoring the ongoing radio chatter in the earpieces of their flight helmets.

The Blackhawk pilot, an Army Chief Warrant Officer, keyed his mike, calling ahead to the reception committee at the compound. "Charlie Rico Three, this is Harper One-Five inbound to your poz," he transmitted. "Estimate arrival in five mikes. How copy? Over."

There was a momentary delay. "Good copy Harper. We're standing by here."

"Sitrep?"

"All quiet. You're clear in."

Chalice peered out of the open right-side door of the craft to take in the view. Or at least as much of the view as he could see over the broad shoulder of the door gunner.

They were tracking along as planned, basically following Route One. The mustard yellow expanse of the ground below was relieved by the narrow Tigris River, which paralleled the road immediately to the east. Although Chalice couldn't see it, the landing zone was rapidly coming up just ahead of them.

The LZ was within a walled compound that encompassed a number of warehouses as well as a few smaller detached buildings. From the perspective of the two Blackhawk pilots, there was nothing special to recommend the desolate looking place.

"Like old times, huh?" Chalice called to Bear over the noise of the wind whipping past the door.

"Kind'a sort'a," Bear replied, propping a booted foot up on a metal ammunition box. "My old times were a lot greener than this place, though."

"Yeah," Chalice agreed, turning his attention back outside. "I hear you."

"Harper," the LZ team called with a sudden bit of excitement. "Wave off! Hold your position!"

"Talk to me, Charlie Rico," the pilot replied tightly, gripping the cyclic stick a bit more intently. His co-pilot was also scanning the ground more carefully for signs of trouble.

"Stand by, Harper... We're now taking sporadic small arms fire coming in from the northwest... Need you to orbit a bit to the south and hold there."

Obediently, the pilot pulled the Blackhawk to the left and assumed a tight racetrack pattern south of the compound. There he waited for the ground pounders to resolve the problem.

Even from his constricted seat, as the helo tilted over Chalice could see the repeated flash of tracers jetting out from the compound toward a row of shrubbery a few football fields distant. As he did so, he heard the pilot's dispassionate voice again in his earphones.

"Charlie Rico, we see your shooter's general area in that line of vegetation," the pilot said. "We're gunned up right now. You want some assist on that target? Over."

"That's a rog, Harper," the ground team responded. "An assist would be much appreciated."

"'Kay... You seeing that Teddy?" the pilot called to the door gunner.

"I see 'em," the gunner replied emotionlessly.

"Put some in then," the pilot ordered.

"You got it, Chief."

As they came back around, the gunner charged his machine gun and opened fire on the presumed hostile target.

The pilot held the ship steady for a moment and then pirouetted to the north, turning right to give his gunner a continued view of the target. Teddy took advantage of the angle, pounding the scrub of greenery with a belt-load of 7.62mm armor piercing rounds. The noise within the passenger compartment of the Blackhawk was deafening, dampened only by the internal fibers of their helmets.

"Check fire, Harper. Check fire," came the voice from the ground moments later. "I think we're good here... Wait one."

"Holding," the pilot replied.

The gunner fell silent as the pilot resumed flying the racetrack.

After a few minutes the ground team came back up on the air. "Okay, Harper. Target's down... We're good. Bring it on in."

"Roger."

The pilot circled back to the north again and brought the helicopter into the LZ on a southerly heading, allowing the gunner yet another chance for suppressive fire if need be. It was not needed.

As the wheels of the Blackhawk touched down, Chalice and Bear freed themselves from their safety restraints and hopped out of the aircraft. They crouched forward, shielding their faces from the swirling dirt storm as the Blackhawk lifted back up again and loudly soared away from the compound.

A helmeted Army Sergeant First Class, eyes obscured by dark sunglasses and skin darkened by the sun, out of the dust appeared to greet them. "Welcome to ISG-North, gents," he said cheerily, reaching out to shake their hands. "How's your day going so far?"

"This kind of reception normal?" Bear asked, gesturing back toward the site of the sniping event.

"Aw that," the SFC said dismissively. "That's just Haji saying hello... If he was seriously pissed we'd be seeing RPG fire or mortars... So, come on. Let's go see Mr. Jonas."

The two Org personnel followed him.

* * *

Without further discussion, the SFC escorted them through the doors of the warehouse and back into the secure area.

ISG-North, they knew, stood for the Northern Sector of the Iraq Survey Group. The Survey Group was the immediate successor to the now-defunct UN weapons inspection team. Composed primarily of Americans, Brits and Aussies, they were the post-invasion WMD hunters. A lot of political juice was riding on their efforts.

After a few minutes, they were shown into a small office area. At least, and appreciatively, the enclosure boasted a window air conditioning system that struggled mightily against the environment.

The man behind the desk rose to greet them. He was a thickly built, light complexioned Black man. He had a compact head of silvery hair and a matching beard.

"I'm Jonas," he said. "And I guess you are the two NSC staff investigators that I was told to expect?"

"We are that, sir," Chalice said, as he and Bear presented a pair of NSC credentials bearing their cover names.

They knew that Hector Jonas, a GS-15 Civil Service type, was a senior Defense Intelligence Agency analyst on loan from DIA to the Iraq Survey Group. While conducting liaison meetings in the Baghdad Green Zone in search of Pyongyang's ties with Saddam's weapons of mass destruction program, they were directed to Jonas. He, they were told, was the authoritative figure on North Korean–Iraqi relations currently in country. Hence the flight to Tikrit to find him.

"Have a seat then," Jonas offered. "How can I help you?"

The wooden chair legs screeched against the concrete floor as the visitors settled themselves in.

"How's the hunt going?" Bear asked.

"Nothing solid yet, but we're hopeful," Jonas answered guardedly. "There's a lot of nooks and crannies in this country. Plenty of places to hide things."

"I bet."

"The call from Baghdad on you two was a little sketchy on the details. Since you're up here now, I presume you're interested in the Iraqi WMD issue?" Jonas began.

"Only insofar as their connection with the North Koreans is concerned," Chalice said. "We've just been put on the NK account."

"We're told you are the guy," Bear added.

Jonas reached into a mini fridge next to his desk and pulled out three cans of Diet Coke. "Best I can do is give you a history lesson," he said passing two of the chilled drinks to his guests. "Nothing current that I'm aware of. Of course, there's no Iraqi government at the moment for the Koreans to deal with either."

"Whatever you have is more than we do," Bear offered, pulling a small Moleskin notebook and a pen from a cargo pants pocket. "Fire away."

"Okay then," Jonas said, popping the top of his Coke can and taking a swallow. "So, yes, it's true enough. Saddam has been in bed with the North Koreans to kick-start his weapons programs. No question there."

"So, Saddam and the North Koreans go way back?"

Jonas shook his head. "No, not really. Ironically enough, the North Koreans had relations with the Iranians going back to the '80's... They even sided with Tehran during the Iran-Iraq War."

"And that war went from...?" Chalice probed.

"Around 1980 to '88."

"There were a lot of Iraqis killed during that time, as I recall," Bear said. "Any estimate of the casualty rate?"

"Somewhere up around half a million - over the course of the full eight years," Jonas estimated.

"You're saying the North Koreans were on the side of the people who killed a half million of his troops and then Saddam later decides to buddy up with them," Bear observed skeptically. "So then, I guess that Saddam must have been the forgiving type."

Jonas smirked at the sarcasm. "Yeah, well... not so much – as the many dead souls here could attest. In any event, there is no doubt Saddam was seeking a weapons program for a good long time. Even back then. Maybe *especially* back then."

"Nukes or chemical?" Bear prompted. "Or both?"

"We already know he had chemical weapons," Jonas said, "He used them on Iranian troops during the war and later he used them again on his own people, the Kurds..."

"Thanks to Chemical Ali," Chalice observed.

"Right. Better known as Ali Hassan al-Majid. Saddam's cousin and holder of various top-level jobs in the regime. Iraq was a family-run business."

"Where's he at now?" Bear asked.

"We're still looking," Jonas said. "In any event," he continued, "there is a lot of evidence Iraq was dedicated toward rebuilding its banned missile program. He was always after nukes and the rockets to deliver them."

"When did the UN sanctions actually begin?" Chalice asked.

"August 1991," Jonas said. "Starting with their invasion of Kuwait. Specifically, I believe it was Security Council Resolution 707 that called for the Iraqis to stop all nuclear activities until the UN could confirm that they were in full compliance."

"Okay."

"But even earlier than that, in February, the United Nations specified via Resolution 687 that the Iraqis could not have any missiles with a range exceeding about 90 miles."

"What good is a short range ballistic missile like that?" Bear mused.

"Well, that's what Saddam thought," Jonas agreed. "So, he turned to our old friends, the Russians, for help in development of something better. And help they did – or at least tried to. Even to the extent of throwing their weight around in the Security Council in '97 and '98, unsuccessfully, to get the sanctions lifted."

"And that's where we see the SCUDs coming from," Bear guessed.

"Not directly... The international community, and especially the US, put so much pressure on the Russians that they backed off the program. And that is when Saddam found his way to the North Koreans. His people held several meetings with them between 2001 and earlier this year."

"I'm assuming Kim Jong-Il was happy to help," Chalice said.

"For a price," Jonas answered. "Like ten million dollars up front."

"Nice price," Bear observed.

Jonas nodded. "I'm guessing that KOMID was involved in this venture. Its right up their alley."

Chalice shook his head. "Sorry. Name means nothing to me."

"KOMID," Jonas repeated, "is a North Korean government entity. Stands for the Korea Mining and Development Trading Corporation."

"Okay."

"Of course, it has nothing at all to do with mining but a lot to do with trade. It's Pyongyang's main arms dealer and exporter. Especially with regard to ballistic missiles and weapons technology. They've been active in the Mid-East, Africa, Latin America. All over really."

"Right. So just what did Saddam get for his ten million?" Bear asked, persisting on the money issue.

"It was a two-phase project. Firstly, he wanted a missile that could push a warhead out far enough to do some real damage. Kim offered what the Koreans called the Nodong rocket. It's based on the Russian SCUD-D concept. Has a range of around 600 miles and a payload of about 2,000 pounds of explosives."

"That beats the 90-mile limit nicely," Bear said.

Jonas nodded. "We know the Iraqis built a dozen or so clandestine sites to work the problem. With North Korean assistance, Saddam even invested $400 million in a SCUD plant in Sudan. He also tried to convert a couple hundred Chinese Silkworm ship-to-ship missiles to a land attack configuration."

Chalice broke eye contact to scrawl more notes into his book.

"Phase two was to get their hands on a nuclear weapon to put on the top of those rockets," Jonas went on. "Big question is whether they ever succeeded."

"But?" said Bear.

"But, as was the case with Russia, there was a lot of international pressure. Kim decided he couldn't take the heat and deserted the project. But he kept Saddam's $10 million just the same."

"Sweet," Bear said admiringly.

"That's about all I can give you off the top of my head," Jonas concluded. "For more granular detail, we would have to get together back home in DC. That's where my files are."

"Let's plan on doing that," Chalice said, closing his notebook. "We appreciate your time."

Jonas peered at his wristwatch. "I don't believe your ride is coming back for you for a few more hours. In the meantime, let's have lunch here – such as it is – and I can bring you up to date on the WMD search."

"Sounds good to us," Chalice said. "Lead on."

TWENTY-SIX: YONGBYON

Yongbyon, North Korea
August 23, 2003

Ro Jae-Ki was in Yongbyon to spend a bit of quality time with his favorite niece, Hwa Nari.

Ostensibly, this was a side visit for which he was eligible as a member of the privileged elite. In truth, it was the primary reason for his return visit home.

Covering the meeting with his niece was his earlier appearance in Pyongyang to participate in the annual August 15th celebrations. The day was important to Koreans both North and South as it commemorated the emancipation of the peninsula from the Japanese in 1945. In the North, it was known as Liberation of the Fatherland Day. To their cousins in the South, it was more simply called Liberation Day.

Ro spent several days in Pyongyang, conducting official consultations with the Europe desk officers in the Ministry of Foreign Affairs. Of their advice, he could have frankly cared less. The objective of the exercise was to see and be seen among other members of the Nomenklatura.

Thoughtful presentations of Italian wines, chocolates and silks ensured he was well-remembered by his peers and professional competitors alike.

While in the capital, Ro also contacted one of his counterparts in a subdivision of Office 39. Following an acceptable bribe, nothing too generous, his colleague provided him with a small quantity of unaccounted for – and diverted - Supernotes. These were to be used by Tae for the initial test exchange with the supposed East European criminal he knew as Fedor.

Both tasks accomplished, Ro was comfortable in announcing to the MFA that he longed to see family members before returning to his duties in Rome. This, of course, would include his sister's daughter at her prestigious location in Yongbyon.

To eyes that have grown accustomed to the style and grace of classical Italian architecture, Yongbyon presented an austere tableau. Situated in a mountainous area, purposely remote, it was

97

clearly not designed to attract foreign tourists and their euros. Travelers to the closed Russian cities of an earlier day would have recognized it's features at once.

The Nuclear Scientific Research Center was a large, sprawling emplacement. Despite its importance to the regime, the Center was rather common and tawdry in appearance. Originally built with Soviet assistance in the early 1960's, it was a conglomeration of blocky concrete structures and rows of intimidating fencing.

As was the case with the majority of the Center employees, Nari lived on the compound itself. In her case, she was granted the privilege of a separate, private apartment.

Given Ro's position in the government, he could have easily gained access to the facility, but he preferred not to elevate his visibility to that degree. Instead, they agreed to meet in a small park in the adjoining town.

It being a Saturday, the Research Center was not working at full capacity. She was free to pursue her own interests.

Ro was waiting in the small park when he caught sight of his niece's approach. He smiled, appreciating the fact that the years had been good to her. Nari was fairly tall for a Korean woman, with thin and attractive angular features. Despite her penchant for science, in other circumstances, in other countries, she might have had a shot at fashion modeling.

Her face broke into a wide smile when she saw him. "Uncle!" she said, hurrying to embrace him.

Ro returned the embrace with genuine affection. "Nari," he said as he pulled away to study her face. "It's been many years. You are a beautiful woman now. Your mother must be very proud."

Nari blushed demurely. "Not beautiful. I am merely average."

Ro handed her a canvas tote bag filled with cosmetics and perfumes from Italy and France, shaking his head. "For you. Now you will be even more beautiful."

"You are too generous, Uncle," she said, accepting the gifts with an appreciative slight bow.

"Let's walk," Ro said, touching her gently on the shoulder. "We have something to discuss. And then we should eat."

"Yes, Uncle."

Ro surreptitiously surveyed the surroundings of the park as they slowly strolled down the broken walkway. This was, after all, one of the most secure tracts of land in the country. Nevertheless, he saw nothing of concern. But then again, he wondered, would he?

"I've come about the special matter. The one we have communicated about," he said softly as they continued moving. "You recall it, I'm sure."

"Yes, Uncle," she answered after a pause. She could feel the flow of adrenalin began to release in her system.

"I have news," Ro said. "About that same matter."

"And?"

"It can be done... No. It will be done. And soon."

Nari caught her breath, not fully knowing how to respond. It was what she wanted. It was what she had asked for. But now... it was close to becoming reality. Almost. And it was suddenly terrifying.

"How are we to do this?" she asked, trying to tamp down her fears and maintain an even appearance.

"The details will come when they are due. But you should begin to ready yourself now," he told her. "When it is closer to the time, I will contact you, as I have done before."

"You will be here?"

"No," Ro said quickly. "Not me. But someone will come. She will come here and meet you in this very park. She will be a Korean woman. Someone close to your own age."

Nari could not restrain herself from glancing about for hidden Bowibu agents. "How will I know her?"

"When you meet her, she will greet you and say these words: 'Your Uncle Sung sends you his best and fondest regards...' Repeat that back to me."

Nari's throat was dry. Swallowing nervously, she echoed, "She will say to me 'Your Uncle Sung sends you his best and fondest regards'. And then I will know it is them who have come for me."

"Exactly."

"And then?"

"And then you must do whatever she and her brothers instruct you to do. Absolutely without question. Do you understand me on this, Nari?"

Nari lowered her eyes. "I am afraid, Uncle," she whispered. "This is very dangerous."

"Look at me, Nari," Ro commanded. When he had her full attention, he continued. "You must do whatever they say.

Immediately. It is the only way for this matter to succeed. For both of us."

"Yes."

"You understand me?"

"Yes," she answered. "But these people... You trust them? Have they done this before?"

In truth, Ro had no idea who the Americans would send or what they had ever done in the past. Nevertheless, to calm his niece, he gave her his most confident and engaging diplomatic smile. "Of course," he said with profound assurance. "These same people have done this twice before.... With great success."

"Then, Uncle," Nari said, "I put my life in your hands."

Ro bobbed his head in satisfaction. The negotiation was settled.

"Come," he said, motioning to the far end of the park. "Let me escort you to dinner in what I am told is the finest restaurant in Yongbyon. On behalf of the Ministry of Foreign Affairs."

She agreed.

TWENTY-SEVEN: CLOSE TARGET RECON

Camp Hialeah
Busan, South Korea
August 30, 2003

Like Ro, Chalice had also chosen a Saturday afternoon for his meeting with one of the key players of his evolving drama. This individual was a man who had truly been there and done that. In other words, the man had performed the Org's proof of concept mission in the North.

Camp Hialeah was a US Army logistics base at the southern end of the Korean peninsula. It had been established in 1945, in the days when Busan was still called Pusan. As such, it served as the point of supply flow for material equipping both the Korean War of the 50's and the later continuing Cold War with the DPRK.

Chalice made his way through the largely deserted facility until he found Building 111, a transportation admin office. Stepping inside, he saw the American officer that he was there to meet.

"I'm McGurk," the man said, rising to grip Chalice's hand in a large, beefy paw.

"Simmons. NSC," Chalice said, displaying the same set of credentials he had shown Jonas in Iraq.

McGurk was a large, burly fellow. Built like the college lineman he once was, he had a shaved head and closely trimmed beard of fading red hair. As Chalice knew, McGurk was a DIA case officer with the Defense HUMINT Service.

"First time in Korea?" McGurk asked.

"No. Did a tour up along the DMZ way back when I was on active duty."

"Okay. So, you're familiar with the situation in these parts."

"More or less... More so all the time."

"Right," McGurk said approvingly. "Let's go see my guy then."

McGurk led Chalice back to the transportation manager's office, which had been appropriated for the occasion. Sitting at a small round table in the office was a thin, reed-like Korean man. Gray and frail, he resembled a character from a medieval Chinese painting.

Chalice could only guess at his age, but he assumed the man could not possibly be as old as he looked.

"This is Min," McGurk intoned. "Min, this is Mr. Simmons. He's come all the way from Washington just to see you."

Min clambered to his feet and dipped his head in a respectful bow. "Honored to meet you, sir," he murmured.

"The honor is all mine," Chalice responded, taking Min's hand with both of his. "Please, Mr. Min. Sit."

When they had reassembled themselves about the cramped table, McGurk launched into the topic. "Okay, so we were tasked at Headquarters by our NSC liaison to insert one of our agents – Min here – into the North, coming in from China. He was to follow a given route, go to a specific place, make no contacts, and safely come out the other end."

"Yes."

"As you can see," McGurk said, gesturing proudly to Min. "He did it."

Min tilted his head and smiled thinly.

"You are a very brave man, Mr. Min," Chalice said. "We appreciate your undertaking of such a dangerous mission for us."

"It was of no consequence," Min said depreciatingly.

"I'm not so sure that it was of no consequence," Chalice replied. "It was of great importance to us."

Min nodded.

"Based on your experience, sir, could you tell me, how difficult is the internal travel in the North these days?" Chalice asked.

"Not so bad as before," Min said. "In the past years there were more controls. Tighter checks. More severe than now."

"And how is it now?"

"Still there are controls," Min said. "By law you even now require a permit to move about from town to town. Unless you are one of the approved travelers... But as all know, there is the official system of regulations, and then there is the *real system*."

"As in?"

"Life is hard in the North for officials and peasants alike. It is certainly better than in the time of starvation," he said, referring to the period of the mid to late 1990's. "But the people are still poor. Everyone there who controls the life of the common people is therefore open to bribery... A little money, or a small gift, will cause the officials to turn their eyes from you. Movement is very much possible – as you can see."

"Good to hear." It confirmed what Chalice had already been briefed from other sources. "You paid these bribes and they accepted them?"

"Of course," Min answered quickly. "I was not alone in doing it. Far from it."

Chalice pulled a large-scale military topographical map of the DPRK out of his attaché case and spread it open on the tabletop. It was a sizable chart, as North Korea occupied an area approximating the size of the American state of Pennsylvania.

He handed Min an orange colored, felt-tipped highlighter. "Can you walk me though your trip in detail?"

Min took a few moments to orient himself with the features of the map. Then, using the highlighter, he indicated a point along the China/North Korea border. "I crossed from here," he said, the marker squeaking softly against the surface of the paper.

"This point," he declared finally. "From China and into North Hamgyong province. It was late evening."

"Hard to do?" Chalice prompted.

Min shook his head. "Not so hard. Not if you are careful. As you may know, there is a lot of smuggling in this area. Chinese products are very popular among the Northern people. Some Japanese products too. This is how they come in. And how money goes out."

"How closely do the authorities monitor the local population in that area?" Chalice asked.

Min could not conceal a knowing smirk. "This province is the main drug production and commodities smuggling area in North Korea, Mr. Simmons," he said. "What do you think?"

"Point taken," Chalice admitted. "And then?"

Min paused and then applied the highlighter to the map once again. "From there, I took a train and a series of public buses from Onsong town southwards through these several places," he pushed the chiseled point of the pen repeatedly across the surface of the map, "until I reached the area of Nyongbyon."

"Okay."

"By law, travel passes are required for these types of travel," Min said. "But..."

"But bribes can smooth the way," Chalice guessed.

Min nodded, smiling.

"I was told Nyongbyon County was the regional area of interest for this mission," Min continued. He glanced over at McGurk, who nodded in agreement.

"I made my way by foot from the bus station to the town of Yongbyon. That is the location of the nuclear research site."

"Yes."

"I spent two days in Yongbyon. Of course, I was able only to see the perimeter area of the nuclear site," Min said. "But I made several sketches of the area in my notepad. I concealed these sketches in my baggage and later gave them to Mr. McGurk." Chalice nodded. He already had the drawings from the DIA officer. They had been satisfactorily matched to classified overhead satellite photography of the area.

"And, as ordered, I visited the park in the village that sits next to the nuclear site."

Min dabbed the point of the highlighter at the location of the park. "I was able to spend maybe an hour in the park, as Mr. McGurk requested. I did not see any government surveillance, any cameras, roving patrols or other such protective measures," he said. "The authorities seem to feel very secure in that area. I assume it is because the park is well beyond the gates of the nuclear site."

"Okay," Chalice said. "That is good."

Min returned his attention to the map. "And from there I moved by train. I went down through the Unam station to the Goeup station. At Goeup town I left the trains and made my way by foot further south overland. I did this until I reached the water inlet at, uh, this point."

Min circled the area with the squeaky tip of the orange highlighter.

"From there," McGurk said, taking up the thread of the tale, "Min was picked up by a man in a small fishing boat. He was taken offshore and met by a larger motorized boat operated by agents of the NIS, or South Korean Intelligence. The NIS boat then ran Min directly into Incheon... And here we are."

"Okay," Chalice said. "Sounds like a good mission. Anything further?"

"You have the rest of it in my written report," McGurk said.

Chalice again reached into his attaché case and withdrew an envelope containing a cash bonus – the amount previously agreed upon by McGurk and his superiors – and handed it to Min. "This," he said, "is for you. Please accept it as a token of our appreciation for your courage."

Min accepted the envelope and pocketed it without glancing at its contents. "Thank you, sir," he said softly.

After shaking Min's hand once again, Chalice was escorted back to the outer office by McGurk.

"Well there you have it," McGurk said. He hesitated, clearly straining at the limits of the need to know principle. "Obviously, your people are focused on that nuke site in Yongbyon. Whatever the reason, it must be pretty damn interesting."

"It is," Chalice admitted. "In fact, it's absolutely goddamn fascinating."

TWENTY-EIGHT: SANT'ANGELO

Rome, Italy
September 9, 2003

The afternoon sun was slowly disappearing over the jagged Roman horizon. Given the waning summer heat, it was the time of day when the majority of foreign tourists felt comfortable emerging from their air-conditioned surroundings. The refreshing evening air encouraged them to better absorb the outdoor atmosphere prior to dinner and whatever else the night might offer.

One of the many souls taking in the scenery that evening was the Bosnian national, Zlatko Piric. To the casual passer-by, he was nothing more than another wanderer who was simply dawdling on the ancient pedestrian bridge known as the Ponte Sant'Angelo.

The stone bridge on which he stood, surprisingly short in length, joined the south bank of the Tiber with the imposing circular edifice of the Castel Sant'Angelo on the northerly end. Originally built in 134 AD by the Emperor Hadrian as his intended tomb, it later became a fortress and safe-haven for many occupants of the papacy.

Perhaps most famously for an entire month in 1527, it protected the Medici Pope Clement VII from the marauding troops of the so-called Holy Roman Emperor, Charles V, during the horrific bloodbath known as the Sack of Rome.

Zlatko peered over the side into the muddy green waters of the Tiber River. Better known to the Italians themselves as the Tevere, the depths of the river had been the historical dumping ground for a countless variety of unfortunate souls – the innocent and guilty alike.

Quite often the Tiber received victims of murderous intrigue. The bodies dumped into its uncaring flow were an eclectic bunch. They ranged the gamut from pimps, common cutthroats, and politicos to members of the nobility and even popes.

In Zlatko's mind, the Ponte Sant'Angelo had that much in common with the so-called Latin Bridge in his native city of

Sarajevo. The latter was the site of the 1914 assassination of the Austrian Archduke, which culminated in the First World War.

Zlatko could easily recall seeing the bodies of his Serbian enemies - several of which he had himself dispatched – floating lifelessly downstream close to the bridge in Sarajevo, arms and legs loosely askew. For that, he had absolutely no regrets whatsoever.

On the contrary.

Continuing to wait, the Bosnian absently fingered a well-worn set of black Muslim prayer beads. The Vatican – the seat of Roman Catholicism - was just a few minutes' walk from his position. More than a little ironic, he thought.

For Zlatko, a nominal Muslim who was secular in the extreme, the beads had always been less a conduit with the divine than a habitual means of calming and centering himself. Such was still the case.

Behind Zlatko, across the narrow span and holding security, was his fellow Bosnian war veteran. The burly Escobar was leaning back against the stone railing and keeping a watchful eye on his partner. As before, he was playing the role of the emotionless criminal bodyguard. In his case, the role was not all that far from the reality of his true persona.

Ten more minutes passed uneventfully.

Zlatko glanced at his Seiko watch. The Korean bastard was late. Again.

The cell phone in Zlatko's pocket finally vibrated with an incoming text message. Checking the device, he saw the simple screen display: "On the way."

Pocketing the phone, he gave a quick glance to Escobar, who silently acknowledged the signal.

Glancing southwards, Zlatko saw the two Korean men stepping onto the bridge and coming toward his position. They were framed by the yellow and beige brick buildings behind them. The pair was immediately recognizable as Chol and Tae.

As they approached the center point of the bridge, Tae took the measure of Escobar waiting in the wings. It was nothing less than he had expected, given the paranoid security considerations of these European criminals. Yet they paid well, as he well knew from past interactions.

Taking his time, Zlatko turned to face the two Koreans. "My friend from Orvieto," he said at last, with Chol translating. "Very good to see you again. What have you brought for me this evening?"

Tae returned the greeting in his typically non-expressive fashion. Wordlessly, he produced a thick, letter-sized envelope from his jacket pocket and passed it into Zlatko's hands.

Taking care not to drop the envelope into the Tiber, Zlatko pried it open and briefly examined its contents. It was nearly a two-inch thick stack of $100 dollar US bills. Or so they appeared to be.

"Ah," Zlatko said admiringly. "The famous Supernotes, I take it?"

Hearing the translation, Tae nodded. His eyes continued to move suspiciously back and forth across the bridge.

Satisfied with the approximate count, Zlatko unsnapped the belt of the fanny pack he was wearing and passed it over to Tae. Then it was the North Korean's turn to assess the wad of bills – euros this time – buried within the fanny pack.

"You are happy?" Zlatko asked after a sufficient pause.

"Yes," Tae replied. "I am happy."

"Good... So, this is what happens next," Zlatko said. "We will return home with these notes. Once there, we will enter them into circulation. If we have problems with your dollars, you will not hear from us again.

"However, if we are successful, we will come back to you here in Rome and arrange for a major purchase of your product. In bulk."

Tae emitted what could have been construed as a smile. "Then I will be seeing you again," he said with confidence. "These notes are of the highest quality. Just as good as those made in Washington. No difference at all."

Zlatko flashed him a wide public relations smile. "I hope this is the case... If it is so, we look forward to doing business with you."

The mission at hand accomplished, Tae nodded his understanding and abruptly strode away. Zlatko and Escobar silently bade him farewell and watched as the North Korean disappeared into the dusky Roman night.

TWENTY-NINE: PROMETHEUS

Kadena Air Base
Okinawa, Japan
September 26, 2003

Lieutenant Colonel Sebastian Ephron was the senior US Air Force dentist at the Kadena Air Base Dental Clinic. He was justifiably proud of his award-winning facility. It was the largest of its kind on Okinawa, boasting over a hundred staff members in all.

Those hundred-plus staffers dealt with many thousands of teeth, in all their permutations, on a regular basis year in and year out. But none were quite like the ones he was expecting that September morning.

Earlier in that same week LTC Ephron had an unusual meeting with a special agent of the base's Air Force Office of Special Investigations detachment. The AFOSI agent, himself a senior non-commissioned officer, briefed him on the visitors he was soon to expect.

The patients would be three civilians, the AFOSI agent said. They were neither American family dependents nor Japanese civilians. Nevertheless, they would be appearing for a set of authorized routine procedures for which Ephron was more than qualified to administer.

As this was part of a classified project however, Ephron was asked – ordered actually – to sign a Non-Disclosure Agreement. The NDA would forever bind him to secrecy as to his involvement in what outwardly appeared to be a fairly normal day's work.

Mystified, Ephron obediently scratched his name onto the NDA form, dated it, and awaited whatever was to come.

And now, a few days later, it was here. In the general waiting room sat three young Asian adults, two men and a woman. A Caucasian male with strongly Mediterranean features and coloring accompanied them and guarded them watchfully.

At last leaving his charges behind, the American followed Ephron into his office. Once the door was closed, he produced a small gunmetal gray case from his bag.

"My name's Simmons," he said, producing a set of NSC credentials. "Thanks for your time today, Colonel. Much appreciated. We realize you are a busy man."

"Not too busy for, uh, whatever this is," Ephron said with a wave of a hand. "What is it, anyhow?"

"The installation of three temporary crowns," the American said. "One crown in the mouth of each of the folks sitting outside here now."

"Hmmm," Ephron said.

"Can do?" the man from the NSC prompted.

"Of course," Ephron said, a bit miffed at the unintended slight. "Three crowns? No problem at all."

"Great," Chalice said in a mollifying tone of voice. "All three crowns have to be sealed far more securely than you would do in the case with normal temporary crowns. We were told you are the best dentist in the region."

"Well..."

"Your Senior Master Sergeant, Ortiz, has already been briefed on this by the AFOSI det," Chalice continued. "He's prepped the office staff to be ready for the procedures."

"Three crowns," Ephron repeated. "Certainly. I can do two of them before lunch. One after."

Chalice sat the metal case on the desktop and snapped open the lid. Inside were the three off-white molar crowns, each cushioned within their foam rubber inserts. Each was sequentially labeled as either Male-One, Male-Two or Female-One.

Ephron pulled the Male-One crown from its artificial cavity and examined it more closely. It appeared to be very well prepared, he noted from a professional viewpoint.

Looking closer, Ephron saw it was somewhat larger in width and just a bit heavier than the normal temporary crown. He replaced it and turned his attention to Male-Two.

Although he was neither cleared for, nor had any possible way of knowing it, LTC Ephron was examining the Prometheus devices – the Org-issued vials of lethally fast acting poison. They would be the in-extremis way out for the three agents if, God forbid, they fell into the unforgiving hands of the Bowibu.

"And," Chalice added, "I'll need to be in the operatory while you do all three procedures."

"All of them?"

"All of them. Yes sir."

"You have a background in the dental sciences, Mr. Simmons?" Ephron asked, examining the Male-Two crown.

"No sir," Chalice said. "Just an observer."

What Chalice did not tell him was that he needed to be present to ensure the three agents were neither questioned nor were responsive to any issues regarding their upcoming mission.

"If you must," Ephron sighed.

* * *

LTC Ephron was as good a dental practitioner as had been advertised. As promised, all three procedures were conducted that same day.

Following several days of rest for the crowns to settle, Chalice took them back into the clinic for a follow-up appointment. Again, the verdict was success.

Their dental procedures at last completed, the remaining step was for Chol, Jina and Seok each to take separate flights into the Beijing International Airport, using South Korean passports.

And so they did.

THIRTY: LAUNCH

China/North Korean Border
October 7, 2003

Chalice energetically rubbed the palms of his hands together in a vain attempt to generate heat. The enclosed cargo holds of aging Chinese freight trucks were known more for their reliability than for their warmth or comfort. Bear, seated across from Chalice, nodded silently and tugged the edge of his knit watch cap closer down over his ears.

The truck was being driven by a wizened, Chinese man named Liu, himself an occasional Org asset.

Seok, Chol and Jina were propped up on the floor against their Japanese-made backpacks and tucked under woolen blankets. They were attempting to gain a few last minutes of sleep prior to hitting the border. Chalice noticed Chol and Jina were huddled closely together. He assumed it was not all in hopes of simply retaining body warmth.

Peering at the luminous dial of his watch, Chalice estimated they had to be nearing their destination – the outskirts of the rustic town of Yanji in China's Yanbian province. Situated directly west of the Russian city of Vladivostok and directly north-west of the nearest point along the DPRK border, Yanji was to be their meeting point with another Org agent who was called Lao Gao.

Gao was a *hwagyo*, or an ethnic Chinese resident of North Korea. As such, he was free to move back and forth across the border with relative impunity. His transnational status facilitated his primary occupation as a smuggler. All of this was more than acceptable to the profilers in the Org.

While ARGENT SUCCUBUS continued to ramp up, the people at Yongbyon had not been idle. Chalice knew from a briefing five days earlier – October 2nd – that the North Korean government announced it was reprocessing some 8,000 spent nuclear fuel rods. Although there were a number of innocent explanations for this activity, the primary concern involved the use of the recovered plutonium in the construction of nuclear weapons.

What Chalice could not have known was that, on the very same day as Pyongyang's announcement, a US official named David Kay was giving testimony to a closed session of the House and Senate Intelligence Committees in Washington.

Kay was Hector Jonas' Survey Group boss back in Iraq. Kay told Congress that Iraq's nuclear program was in a rudimentary condition and – while no chemical or biological weapons had been found – they had uncovered dozens of activities related to weapons of mass destruction. Even at that, he added, only ten percent of the 130 suspected Iraqi weapons depots had been searched so far.

From the perspective of the Org's overseers at the NSC, the impetus for penetrating the secrets of the North Korean nuclear weapons operations was increasing exponentially.

As the truck rumbled along, Chalice mentally reviewed the preparations for the mission at hand. Nothing was new. He and the team had repeatedly gone over the various contingency plans prior to departing the safe house in Shenyang for the launch site.

All three agents were carrying changes of worn-looking clothing and emergency foodstuffs, as well as sufficient quantities of cash. The money was both in terms of North Korean won as well as the more convertible Chinese yuan.

Each had also been supplied with North Korean identity cards, as well as internal travel passes to enable them to move from the northern border down to Yongbyon, and then to the southwest coastal region.

As the team leader, Chol had the small but highly powered covert radio transceiver secreted in his pack. Although he carried it, all three were trained in its operation.

The satellite uplink radio was known colloquially to the Org techs as a LRAC, or Long Range Agent Comms. It was designed for encrypted burst transmissions, the better to avoid interception and triangulation. Although the compact battery for the LRAC had more than enough power for the length of the intended mission, each of the Koreans carried a spare for emergency replacement.

Unlike the other two members of his team, Seok was armed. He was carrying a Type 68 semi-automatic pistol. The 7.62 mm handgun had a nine-round capacity, with one bullet in the chamber and eight more in the magazine. Similar in appearance to a Browning FN, the 68 was commonly used by the North Korean military and thus unlikely to stand out. Seok had several spare magazines of ammunition on his person and in his pack. He also had his counterfeit Bowibu credentials to justify his possession of the weapon.

All this gear was, of course, highly incriminating. On either side of the border.

And, toward that point, all three Korean agents had the Prometheus devices firmly embedded in their back teeth. Bear and Chalice did not.

After another twenty minutes, Chalice could feel the truck slowing, braking and then veering over to the right side of the roadway. Finally, it jostled to a stop and the engine was cut. Everyone in the cargo compartment was wide-eyed and alert now.

The door of cab squealed open noisily after a momentary delay. Someone, presumably Liu, eased himself out onto the road and slammed the door shut again behind him.

Bear nodded silently as he listened to two Chinese voices conversing outside. As always, the rapidly modulating high/low vocal tones of the language sounded like an argument to Bear's ears, no matter how amicable the interaction. This one was no different.

The two voices went silent, followed by the crunching of feet upon gravel as they approached the rear of the truck. There was another screech of metal as the latch of the double rear door was loosened.

Hoping he would not be next looking at a pair of Public Security officers, Chalice caught sight of Seok's fingers sliding toward the grip of his concealed pistol. "Christ no!" he willed soundlessly. "Don't do that!"

Weak daylight flooded in as the two doors were pulled open. Thankfully, as his eyes adjusted from the darkness, Chalice recognized the familiar smiling countenance of Lao Gao. Short and thin, Lao's lined face was framed by a crop of jet black hair.

Chalice assumed that the hair was regularly dyed for vanity's sake. The title *lao* was a respectful honorific to denote a man of relatively advanced age which, in Gao Chenglei's case, was approximately fifty-seven years.

"*Ni hao, Lao Gao,*" Chalice said, greeting him with a profound sense of relief. "*Hen gaoxing.*" Happy to see you.

"*Ni hao, laoban,*" Gao replied, referring to him as his boss. "*Haojiu bujian.*" Long time, no see.

Having come close to exhausting his fount of conversational Chinese, Chalice switched back to English. "Everything ready?"

"Yes," Gao said, wagging his head affirmatively. "All is ready. No problem. No worry."

"Police?"

"*Jingcha*?" Gao repeated. "*Meiyou*. No. All is good. But we must go now. No time here for talk-talk."

"*Tongyi*," Chalice said. Agreed. He reached over to pass several envelopes of cash to his cross-border agent. "Take care of them."

"*Dui, laoban*," Gao nodded. "Yes. But now we must go."

Bear peered out of the rear of the truck, his breath wispy in the cold evening air. It looked calm enough to him.

Chalice reached for Chol's hand and shook it slowly. "This is it, Chol," he said. "The launch point. Tim and I can't go any further. Gao will take you from here."

"I understand, Cody," Chol answered. "We'll see you on the other end. With our package."

"See you on the other end," Chalice affirmed. "With the package... Good luck and go with God."

"Yes."

Chalice shook hands with both Seok and Jina in turn and watched silently as they clambered out of the truck. Gao, he knew, would load them into his vehicle and transport them to, and then across, the border of the DPRK.

Unbidden, memories of the SOLO APEX operation hovered in his consciousness.

He nodded to Liu, who secured the door, climbed back into the cab, and took the two Americans back to Shenyang.

THIRTY-ONE: TUMEN

Onsong, North Korea
October 7, 2003

It was late in the afternoon when Lao Gao's battered sedan approached the narrow bridge over the Tumen River. The unremarkable span was one of several others like it that crossed the border from China into North Korea. The sun was already hanging low in the western sky, with the oncoming night promising to be increasingly frigid.

As Chalice and Gao both well knew, despite the popular misperceptions, the international border between the two Communist states was remarkably permeable – if one knew where to look. Purists, in fact, might debate whether either of the two states were technically 'Communist' by that point in history, in that one was embarking upon a form of controlled capitalism and the other was focused on a strict interpretation of family-run nationalism.

Regardless, the situation at the PRC/DPRK border was drastically different than the one on the southern boundary. There, the Demilitarized Zone (DMZ) between North and South Korea separated two countries that were still legally in a state of war with each other.

While a friendly wave to the familiar official on the Chinese end of the bridge sufficed, an expected packet of cash to the North Korean guard - a man Gao regularly did business with – was necessary to ease his uninspected return into the Democratic People's Republic.

Once across the Tumen, it was a short ride into the town of Onsong.

To those who were privy to such information, the Onsong area was known for its proximity to the former Prison Camp Number 12. Previously home to some 15,000 souls, Number 12 was notable in that it was the site of the DPRK's largest inmate uprising, which occurred in 1987. Needless to say, the revolt failed in dramatic fashion – to the detriment of the rebelling prisoners. The camp was closed in 1989.

Night had fallen by the time Gao and the team arrived at an isolated farm south of Onsong. All the surroundings were dark. That was not unusual, as street lighting was an unknown luxury in the rural areas. For operational purposes however, it was ideal.

The property was operated by Gao's brother-in-law who, thanks to new political developments, could legally prosper from the private sales of a portion of his rice and potato crops. Whatever the brother-in-law earned from his unofficial activities was another story.

Gao left his car next to his brother-in-law's small house. He then escorted his three charges to the barn – an enclosed shed really – behind the house.

The muddy, musky confines of the shed were cluttered with loose straw and a smattering of tools. Most of the interior, however, was taken up by the bulk of a small truck. It was a UAZ-469, a Russian-made light utility vehicle.

The blocky four-seater was a common sight in the DPRK, especially when employed in government service. This particular UAZ was painted a matte black and bore markings and license plates indicating it belonged to the State Security Department.

Now speaking to them in Korean, Gao gestured to the tight confines of the interior. "This is where you spend the night," he told them. "Tomorrow, you continue on to wherever you are going... I stay here."

"Thank you, Lao Gao," Chol said. "We appreciate all that you have done for us."

"I have done nothing," Gao said, self-depreciatingly. "But still, tomorrow you all must leave."

No sooner had Gao left them than his sister-in-law appeared. She delivered a small pot of rice and fish, with an accompanying container of tea, for their dinner. She smiled briefly but was clearly eager to exit the shed and leave her dangerous guests behind her.

The three ate their meal in a tense, wordless silence. The stillness was interrupted only by the muted slurping of tea and the soft scraping of chopsticks against their cracked ceramic bowls. They were fully aware of the reality that they were now behind enemy lines, in every hostile sense of the word.

To say they were at the mercy of the Kim regime would be a cruel interpretation of the term. If discovered on the territory of the DPRK, there would be no thought of mercy.

Finished eating, Seok wiped his mouth on a cloth and rose to his feet. "I'll take the first watch outside," he announced.

Chol and Jina looked up, nodding appreciatively.

The ex-ROK Marine acknowledged the unspoken message and stepped outside into the bracing night air.

* * *

Chol and Jina took advantage of the rare moment of privacy, spreading their blankets out on the ground next to the UAZ.

Facing each other on the cold earth, they made themselves as comfortable as possible in the packed straw. They were motionless for several long minutes, except for their hands which gently caressed each other in the dark. All was quiet but for their shallow breathing.

"And now finally, we are here," Jina said in hushed tones as she stroked the coarse strands of Chol's hair. "In the North."

"Yes," Chol agreed, well aware of her obvious concerns. "We are here, Jina. According to the plan."

Jina did not respond.

"You're afraid," Chol said. "I understand, but remember that Seok and I have done this before. And safely."

"I..." she hesitated. "I thought that..."

"That what?"

"That I would be ready for this," she said. "To come into the North. But I'm not... I'm frightened. This job is so..."

Chol kissed her softly on her forehead and then on both cheeks in the darkness. He was surprised to taste the saltiness of her tears.

"All of us are afraid," he confided in the same hushed tones that she was using. "This is a dangerous business, Jina... There are no heroes. Seok and I..."

Hearing Seok's soft cough outside the shed, Jina placed her fingers on Chol's lips. "Seok knows no fear."

"He's a little bit different," Chol admitted. "The mission is all there is to him."

"You and Seok both have the courage needed for this," she said, gently running her fingertips over the side of his face.

"No," Chol protested. "We..."

Jina shook her head, pressing her finger against Chol's lips. "No more talk," she breathed finally. "Not now."

Moving quietly, she undid the cords of her rough string trousers. Successful, she pushed them below her knees and kicked them aside.

"I need some of your courage," she murmured into his ear. She glanced over her shoulder toward the door of the shed. "And quickly!"

"*Sarang hae*, Jina," Chol whispered. I love you.

"*Na do sarang hae*," she replied. And you.

Moving as swiftly as possible, Chol unloosened his own clothing. He then pulled Jina's petite form atop of his and joined with her in the soft darkness.

THIRTY-TWO: CONTACT

Yongbyon, North Korea
October 10, 2003

Friday was of course a routine work day in Yongbyon. Fittingly enough, the afternoon was overcast and cold. While the weather was hardly unusual for the latitude, its chilled winds did not lend themselves to feelings of confidence on behalf of the contact team.

Jina was seated uncomfortably on a concrete bench at a public bus stop. It was about a block away from the Yongbyon park. She was wrapped in a quilted Chinese coat, not unlike the people surrounding her. While it did a good job of insulating her from the prevailing elements, it did nothing to displace her mounting apprehension.

A pair of peasant women were huddled together next to her on the bench. The two of them silently awaited the arrival of the public conveyance that would carry them back to the countryside.

While using them for cover, Jina well knew that she was doing no more than delaying the inevitable. After all of the training and preparations, she was now finally on target. As such, she was steeling herself for the approach into the park and the meeting with their objective – Hwa Nari.

Two days earlier the Org team departed the Onsong farm for their primary target area where they would meet the research scientist. Lao Gao and his brother-in-law were there to see them off. Given the circumstances, there was no pretense of reluctance to see them leave.

As for the team members, after all the months of detailed prepping, they were likewise eager to reach into the target area and get the job done.

Once in Onsong proper, equipped with forged domestic travel permits, Chol and Jina had separately boarded a public inter-city bus and settled in for the trip down country. The bus, sufficient for their needs but by no means a model of modern transport, eventually carried them south to the town of Kanggye.

Traveling alone and apart from the others, Seok took the ostensible Bowibu UAZ vehicle to parallel their journey southward.

It was terrain with which he was already familiar from previous operational forays. As expected, he arrived in Kanggye hours before they did.

The following morning, a Thursday, Seok again departed alone in the UAZ. For their part, Chol and Jina found seats on a Korean State Railways train that would take them relentlessly southward and into the Yongbyon area. Specifically, they were headed to North Pyongan province, which was the geographic home of the Yongbyon Nuclear Scientific Research Center.

The Org mission profile called for Seok to initially serve as an emergency backup for the contact team - if needed. In extremis, he was expected to perform as a solo operator in order to complete the operation. Chalice had earlier judged if any of the three could carry off that assignment, it would be the former ROK Marine.

After spending a sleepless night in the local inns, they were finally prepared to make contact and retrieve the defector.

By this time, as they knew, Ro should have made contact with his niece. He would have advised her that today was the day of her escape. They could only hope that the message was received without interception by the organs of North Korean security and counterintelligence.

Resolved for action, Jina fastened the buttons of her coat to the neck. Shutting her eyes, she consciously fought down the last-minute physical tremors of fear.

At last, she stood and began to make her way down the street and into the Yongbyon park.

Just prior to entering the gates, she caught sight of Chol, who was posted just a bit further down the street. According to plan, he would stay beyond the confines of the park, awaiting the successful target retrieval.

Crossing the street, Jina entered the area as casually as possible. While taking care to avoid presenting anything out of the ordinary, she was unobtrusively scrutinizing the area for any possibility of hostile surveillance. She found none.

She was relieved to see the layout of the park closely matched the satellite photography they were shown at the Kilo Site pre-deployment orientation. The Americans were on target, she thought. At least this far.

As Jina proceeded down the footpath, she saw the hulking, reassuring figure of Seok. He was lingering under a tree, focused on a book and ostensibly paying no attention to her whatsoever. Nevertheless, she knew that he was the final line of defense, prepared to provide whatever close cover he could.

As she neared his position, Seok produced a pair of cheap plastic sunglasses from a jacket pocket and absently placed them on the bridge of his nose. It was the expected final signal that Hwa Nari was in place and that Jina should proceed with the planned meet.

What was the American expression, Jina wondered?

Then she remembered. Game on.

* * *

Rounding a corner, Jina felt her throat catch despite her expectations. A young Korean woman, approximately her own age, was sitting alone on a wooden bench. Her arms were folded and she appeared to be resting comfortably.

That, unmistakably, was Hwa Nari. Niece of the Rome DCM Ro Jae-Ki. Member of a Nomenklatura family. And nuclear research scientist of the DPRK. Potential defector.

As she continued her approach, Jina's feelings of relief in recognition of her target were immediately tempered by what she saw resting at the other woman's knee – a small, but solidly packed, laundry bag.

Without breaking stride, Jina realized she was now entering a critical agent meeting with a far higher elevated state of concern. Certainly, Nari had been advised not to do anything that could alert security officials of her intentions. Such as leaving the facility with a sack-full of personal belongings. But there it was, right at her feet, and in plain view.

Too late for misgivings at that point.

Jina approached the bench and seated herself a socially respectful distance from her target. "Nari," she said after a few quiet moments. "My name is Jina."

Hwa Nari nodded mutely, her eyes downcast.

"I am privileged to know your family," Jina offered carefully.

"Yes?" Nari responded, not returning her gaze.

Jina swallowed tentatively. Feeding her the arranged clandestine protocol, she offered, "Your Uncle Sung sends his best and fondest regards."

Despite her obvious preparation, Nari glanced up suddenly. She looked as if she had been hit with an electrical shock.

"Uncle Sung sends his best and fondest regards?" she repeated with an odd hint of stupor.

"Yes."

Nari bit her lip and was silent for a moment. "I see... And now?" she asked finally.

Jina looked at her, ignoring the bag at her feet. "And now," she said. "Your new life begins."

Jina suppressed the desire to confront the defector over her decision to carry out a bagful of possessions, as it's very possession in the middle of the work day was itself possibly alerting behavior.

Nari rose to her feet unsteadily, reaching for the bag of possessions.

Jina rose with her. "Leave the bag here," she ordered, having come to an immediate decision. "We have supplies for you... Let's go. Now."

Resisting the urge to glance over her shoulder, Hwa Nari complied.

THIRTY-THREE: AURORA

McLean, Virginia
October 11, 2003

It was pushing four o'clock on an otherwise quiet Saturday morning when Meyer's hard-wired phone began to ring at his bedside.

"Ah for crap's sake," Meyer mumbled sleepily to himself, fumbling for the receiver in the darkness of the bedroom.

"Yes?" he answered, still in a bit of a fog.

"Mister Meyerhof?" the caller asked.

"The same," he replied, knowing what was surely coming next.

"Sir, this is the office."

"Tommy?" Meyer yawned, recognizing the voice, on the phone.

"Yes, sir."

Even in his sleep deprived state, he recognized that JICSA was on the other end of the line. He rubbed his eyes to clear them and groaned slightly.

"Okay, go ahead."

"Good morning, sir," the duty officer said. "Sorry to call this early but we have an incoming action message. You need to come into the office. Immediately, I'm afraid."

"Right." Kurt Meyerhof retrieved his wristwatch from the nightstand and peered at its luminous dial. "Got it. See you soon."

"Thank you, sir," the duty officer said, disconnecting the call.

"What is it this time?" Meyer's wife asked as he noisily replaced the receiver onto the cradle.

"What do you think?" he responded grumpily. "Got to get up and go into the office."

"Isn't this getting a little old? At your age?" she asked. The question was more rhetorical than practical.

"Maybe," he admitted, pausing to sit on the side of the bed and scratching his shanks sleepily.

"Drive safely," his wife muttered, turning her face back into the pillow.

"Back for breakfast," he said, padding toward the bathroom. "I hope."

* * *

Shortly after five a.m., yet well before the coming of the dawn aurora, an unwashed and unshaven Kurt Meyerhof pulled into the largely empty JICSA parking lot. The location was just off Route 123 in the Tyson's Corners area.

He quickly passed through the security procedures and made his way down into the duty officer's section, located in the nether regions of the building.

As he expected, Tommy was working the overnight shift. A wheelchair-bound former Army Ranger, Tommy had been critically injured in preparation for the now largely forgotten assault on the Cuban-held island of Grenada in 1983.

"Sorry to rouse you out of bed so early on a weekend, Mr. Meyerhof," Tommy said. He passed the JICSA deputy director a manila envelope and a mug of coffee. "Here you go, in any event."

"It's okay," Meyer said, accepting both. "Everybody has to be somewhere. I guess."

As Meyer propped himself up on the edge of a nearby table, Tommy returned his attention to his computer screen. Routine feeds from a variety of US and allied intelligence agencies were electronically coming in, demanding his practiced attention.

Meyer took an appreciative sip of the black coffee before he pulled the papers out of the manila envelope. From the headers, he immediately realized this was a report from a US military signals intercept unit.

Electronically sniffing the atmosphere, the military unit had recently caught an interesting series of fresh emanations coming out of North Korea. More specifically, the signals were from the SSD branch that managed the security of the Yongbyon Nuclear Scientific Research Center. The intercept had been immediately forwarded to the NSA at Fort Meade. From there it was flashed to JICSA in the middle of the night.

After nearly draining the mug of coffee, Meyer focused his attention on the report. As he quickly determined, it dealt with the ARGENT SUCCUBUS operation that was now into its most critical phase.

Meyer vaguely recalled the previous day had been the planned date for the SUCCUBUS agent team to make contact with the North Korean defector and extract her from the immediate area.

Per the internal JICSA report, the contact had indeed taken place. That was the good news.

The bad news was that, as feared, the local officials of the North Korean State Security Department noticed the defector – Hwa Nari – was found to be absent from her place of work. Her absence was longer than even someone with her elevated social status would be normally entitled. Following that development, as was SSD procedure, a silent alarm was immediately disseminated throughout the system.

What quickly came next was an agitated inspection of the facility and the surrounding physical area. Four hours after the sounding of the silent alarm, an intensive search located Nari's abandoned laundry bag in the park adjacent to the Nuclear Scientific Research Center. A national alert followed.

It was still in effect, as of the time/date stamp of the intercept.

Meyer was wide awake now. Unlike the majority of Org operations, he felt a high degree of ownership of this case. He had met with the three agents back at the Kilo Site. He had spoken with them directly and looked each of them in the eye. In his mind, they were his charges, just as much as they were Chalice's.

"What's the time difference between here and North Korea?" he asked.

Tommy tapped onto his keyboard. "They're twelve and a half hours ahead of us," he said. "Its late afternoon over there right now."

"Any need to notify the General?" Tommy asked.

"Not yet," Meyer said. "But I think I'll stick around for a bit. I'll be up in the office."

"Good deal," Tommy said. "I'll send out for some breakfast. Could be a long day."

"Yes," Meyer agreed glumly. "Could well be."

THIRTY-FOUR: OPTION CALL

South Pyongan Province, North Korea
October 12, 2003

Earlier that afternoon, Chalice and his crew were busily preparing to depart Sindo, an island outcropping of the Republic of Korea. Their destination was the Oejang-do area along the western coast of North Korea.

Simultaneously, the Org agent team was heading for the pick-up point from the other end of the geographic spectrum.

Ideally, the two elements would seamlessly meet in the cold, dark waters offshore in the Korea Bay.

Chol and Jina accompanied Nari on the journey toward the extraction point. The three of them had started the day by traveling via ramshackle local buses for the thirty-some mile trip from the Yongbyon area into the town of Anju – itself not that far from the coast of Korea Bay.

As before, Seok trailed their progress from a short distance behind in his camouflaged SUV.

By that point, Nari had been supplied with both a North Korean identity card and an official travel pass under an assumed name. The travel pass authorized her to move as far south as the capital city of Pyongyang. And no farther.

Both documents bore photographs that had been supplied by her Uncle Ro. And both had been produced on behalf of the Org by the skilled document forgers at CIA headquarters in McLean, Virginia.

After a meager dinner in Anju, for which none were truly hungry, the team began their final approach to the coast.

Twilight was falling by the time Chol, Jina and Nari departed Anju town. Based on information provided by Lao Gao, they located one of the area's rare taxi drivers, Hyuk by name, knowing he was fairly non-ideological and fully amenable to bribery.

Once contact was made, they arranged for Hyuk to take the three of them several more miles in a southwesterly direction to the coastal area of Sinanju. Armed with false assurances and a healthy tip, the driver quickly agreed to the proposal.

Seok waited silently in the distant background as the transaction was completed. He observed their departure, careful to ensure they were not under hostile surveillance. Satisfied, he gave them several more minutes to get away and then pulled out to follow in their trail.

The taxi carried the three passengers down the ill- prepared road toward the inland waterway that lay just north of Sinanju town. Moving forward, Hyuk kept his thoughts to himself. His wards did likewise as the bleak scenery rumbled past their windows.

The sun was finally down as they pulled abreast of the slow-moving waterway. Chol and Jina gingerly climbed out of the cab. They started pulling their belongings out of the trunk as Nari emerged and found her footing on the damp ground.

As was outlined in the exfiltration plan, a small boat was even then slowly making its way up the channel in their direction. This would be the fisherman who would carry them out of North Korea and into the waters of the larger Korea Bay. There they would link up with the case officer they knew as Cody. After boarding a larger craft at sea, they would be transported directly to South Korean territory and safety.

That was the plan.

Hyuk jerked about suddenly as the fisherman continued his steady approach. Chol then heard it as well. A vehicle was approaching them from the landside at a fairly high rate of speed.

"Bowibu," Hyuk muttered in a strained tone of voice.

As Chol turned to face the new development, a mustard colored sedan rattled into view. Breaking hard, it nearly skittered into the channel streaming a cloud of dust behind it, before the driver brought it to an inelegant stop.

Chol recognized neither of the hard faces of the men who exited the vehicle. These, he feared, were authentic, local SSD agents.

"Names," the senior of the pair, a sergeant, demanded. His fingers were already gripped on the butt of a holstered pistol. "Identity books."

The sergeant watched as his partner produced a flashlight to examine the identify documents first of Chol and next of the two women. He then turned to the taxi driver, whose nerve suddenly failed him.

Hyuk immediately stretched his hands up into the air, taking an involuntary step back toward the waterway. "Forgive me!" he blurted abruptly. "These are foreigners! ... I was threatened and forced to bring them here!"

Chol immediately realized Plan A was no longer a feasible option. He could see the senior of the pair had decided on taking an action of his own.

Chol dove at the sergeant as the pistol was coming out of the latter's holster. Latching onto the sergeant's gun hand, he began a frantic struggle for control of the weapon.

Startled, the junior of the pair reacted by drawing his own gun and letting go with two poorly aimed rounds in Chol's direction.

As the gunshots reverberated in the still air, a marked Bowibu UAZ vehicle came racing up into view. The SUV had barely stopped before Seok was out and on the ground, waving a set of credentials at them.

"Halt!" the new arrival commanded gruffly. "Orders of the senior sector captain! ... Lower your weapons! Now!" Notably, his own gun was now out of its holster and in his hand.

The two SSD officers, confused, rose awkwardly to their feet. Chol did not.

"Comrade Captain..." the senior officer began.

Seok acted immediately. Without hesitation, he raised his sound suppressed pistol and shot the sergeant once in the forehead.

Pivoting slightly, he shot the junior member of the pair, eliminating him as well with two muffled bangs.

Nari involuntarily cried out in response to the blur of unexpected violence. Unlike many of her far less privileged countrymen, she had never seen a dead body in person. And she had certainly never witnessed a killing up close.

Ignoring her display of panic, Seok stepped in tight with Hyuk and dispassionately killed him with yet another head shot.

"It is no longer good here," he declared as the taxi driver collapsed to the ground. "We need to go." He could see the "fisherman" was now back pedaling in the waterway. Having observed developments, their pick-up man was anxious to clear the scene.

Kneeling on the ground, Jina was transfixed on Chol. He remained on the muddy earth, wet blood slowly matting the front of his shirt. His mouth was open, painfully gasping for air.

Despite the tears blurring her vision in her eyes, Jina knew what must be done. As did Chol.

Moving swiftly, she withdrew a small pair of specialized pliers from her pocket. Sliding them into Chol's mouth, she caught hold of his prosthetic molar and twisted it, breaking it open. The action released the fluid of the Prometheus device, allowing it to trickle down his throat.

"*Sarang hae*," she whispered. I love you.

Chol silently fought for breath, his eyes rolling backwards. He convulsed once and was gone.

Seok was hustling Nari into the SUV and motioning for Jina to follow. While he waited, he reached for the LRAC radio on the front seat. He activated the set and hurriedly punched in the pre-set code to signal a failure at the primary extraction point. A failure with fatalities.

Satisfied that both women were safely aboard, he set a northerly course and departed the Sinanju coast in an orderly manner.

THIRTY-FIVE: OEJANG-DO

Korea Bay
Coastal North Korea
October 12, 2003

The sun was already well below the horizon, having disappeared aft of the boat. It had been so for the better part of an hour. Invisible in the dark distance ahead of them was the sparsely populated island of Oejang-do. Still further to the east was the coastline of North Korea itself.

They were silently riding the waters of the Korea Bay – just north of the Yellow Sea. It was definitely hostile territory, by any estimation.

It was a Sunday evening. Despite the close proximity of an atheistic coast, the Org case officer concluded it was probably an apt time for prayerful reflection.

The wind kicking up across the dark waters was becoming increasingly wet and cold. Unaccustomed to being regularly aboard watercraft, Chalice steadied himself against the portside railing as the boat gently pitched in the waves. A former Army warrant officer, he was not in his natural element and he knew it.

The craft that Chalice was riding was reminiscent of the Vietnam-era Swift boats. In those distant days, they were part of the so-called Brown Water Navy. Also known as PCF's – or "Patrol Coast Fast" vessels – the Swifts were employed to transport Navy SEALs and other irregular U.S. combatants through the rivers and coastal regions of Vietnam. The lithe little boats enabled U.S. elements to strike quickly and unexpectedly at enemy targets. And then withdraw without becoming decisively engaged.

This version however was technically upgraded, largely thanks to Israeli developers. It had quick engines and a low-profile hull. Strictly speaking, while it was not invisible to radar, it presented a minimal target to hostile searchers and was capable of high speed evasive maneuvers.

"Low observable" was the current catch phrase. And so it was.

Over seventy feet long, the boat was called the SEALION, or SEAL Insertion, Observation and Neutralization craft. Also known as the "Alligator", thanks to its low-profile appearance, it was painted in a flat matte black coloring.

The crew, a handful of Americans in their early to mid-thirties, were all dressed in casual civilian clothing. Despite their thin cover tales to the contrary, Chalice knew they were all Naval Special Warfare personnel, through and through.

In fact, each of the crewmen aboard the Alligator were members of an operational platoon out of SEAL Team Five. Five was one of the west coast teams, based out of Coronado, California. Among Five's area responsibilities was the Korean peninsula. That being the case, there had been no shortage of volunteers for this particular deployment.

Assuming all went as planned, they would shortly be meeting up with a small local fisherman's skiff. Aboard that skiff would be the members of the ARGENT SUCCUBUS team and their long sought-after prize – the nuclear research scientist Hwa Nari.

Glancing at his wristwatch, Chalice saw they were more than forty-five minutes past the time of the planned contact with the party on shore. Not good, but still not panic time.

Not yet anyhow. Contingencies on the mainland hardly lent themselves to precise timing. He would give them another hour before gaffing it.

Just as he was processing that thought, the secure comms device aboard the Alligator beeped three times. It was the indicator of an in-coming transmission. "Inbound message, sir," the senior NCO announced.

Nodding with some degree of apprehension, Chalice stepped over to tap his user name and password into the classified system. The thirty-plus seconds it took to load felt like an inexcusably painful expanse of time.

At last the text of the encrypted communication was glowing in green font on the blackened screen:

FLASH MESSAGE//FLASH MESSAGE
*STAND BY FOR ARGENT SUCCUBUS OPERATIONAL
MESSAGE*
MESSAGE IN SEVEN PARTS
MESSAGE FOLLOWS NOW
PART ONE – SIGNAL EMERGENCY//SIGNAL EMERGENCY

*PART TWO – SUCCUBUS TEAM REPORTS HOSTILE CONTACT
AT POINT ALPHA*
*PART THREE – TEAM CASUALTY//FATALITY REPORTED AT
POINT ALPHA*
PART FOUR – TARGET PACKAGE INTACT//INTACT
PART FIVE – POINT BRAVO NOW DEEMED INOPERABLE
PART SIX – TEAM NOW EVADING TO POINT CHARLIE
*PART SEVEN – REQUIRE EXTRACT AT POINT
CHARLIE//WILL ADVISE TIMING*
ACKNOWLEDGE RECEIPT
MESSAGE ENDS

Chalice felt his heart catch as he absorbed the content of the message. Things on the ground had suddenly gone to hell, as they always might have done.

It was clearly apparent the mission was no longer nominal. On the down side, one or more of his three agents was lost. On the up side, their defector – the target package - was still alive and well. So far.

Chalice reluctantly typed in his acknowledgment and hit the send tab.

"Okay, Chief," he said quietly. "Looks like we're done here. No pick up tonight. Let's go ahead and clear the area."

Nodding, the senior NCO slapped the helmsman on the shoulder. "You heard the man, Robby. This mission just shit the bed. Haul ass out of here. But carefully... Hear me?"

"Aye Chief," the helmsman responded, hitting the ignition button. As he did so, his team-mates began to relax their hold on their individual weapons.

"Careful as she goes," the senior NCO repeated.

The Alligator's twin engines immediately burbled up. In so doing, they quietly pulled them away from the North Korean coast – and, simultaneously, pulled them away from the remainder of the ARGENT SUCCUBUS team.

As he felt the SEALION begin to ease back from the coastal islands, Chalice silently prayed he would not suffer the return of the SOLO APEX nightmares. But he was not confident that such would be the case.

THIRTY-SIX: DAGGER

Rome, Italy
October 13, 2003

The *Sette Colli* are the fabled seven hills of ancient Rome. The Quirinal is one of them.

In these days, however the northernmost cropping of the Sette is less associated with the trappings of empire than in times past. The Quirinal is currently better known for its proximity to the residence of the Italian President and several governmental departments.

Dominating the center of the Quirinal is the wide and open piazza named for the medieval Barberini family.

The majority of tourists and locals who seek out the Piazza Barberini likely do so for the view of the sculptor Bernini's nearly four-hundred-year-old Fontana del Tritone, or the Triton Fountain. The classic work had been commissioned by Pope Urban VIII, himself a Jesuit member of the Barberini family.

Others – including those perhaps less artistically inclined – are just as happy to make their way into the busy interior of the welcoming place called Pepy's Bar. The bustling establishment was perched on the southern cusp of the wide piazza.

It was shortly after eight in the evening. The threatening late afternoon drizzle had progressed into a full-fledged rainstorm.

Nardo Puccio, having just visited the necessaries room on the second floor of Pepy's, was making his way back down the narrow steps as a wind-driven sheet of rain dramatically splashed across the plate glass windows that protected them from the street.

Glancing pointedly at his watch, Puccio wove his way through the crowd to join Zlatko Piric at one of the small metal tables near the bar. Zlatko, the nominal Muslim, was just receiving an uncorked bottle of red wine from the young waitress.

"Our friend is late," Puccio complained, dropping into his chair. He latched onto the bottle and poured a stream of dark wine into his glass. Puccio was feeling edgy. He was concerned for his pending late-evening dinner appointment with a local female acquaintance.

"Bad weather," Zlatko muttered. "He will be here."

No sooner had Puccio raised the glass to his lips than the door to the street blasted opened, allowing another unwanted gust of wet air to chill the inhabitants. A newcomer quickly stepped inside. He closed the door behind him and paused to scan the interior for familiar faces.

He was built like one of those American football linemen Puccio had seen on television. His darting eyes had a noticeable Slavic cast to them. His pale complexion was accentuated by a trim, ginger-colored beard.

Zlatko caught the newcomer's attention. He nodded and raised a hand in greeting. Responding in kind, the man made his way over to their table and wedged himself into an available chair.

Having met the newcomer previously, Zlatko handled the introductions. "Pooch," he said in his accented English. "This is our associate, Andrei... Andrei, this Italian gentleman to your right is Nardo Puccio. You can call him Pooch."

"Pooch," Andrei repeated, shaking the Italian's hand as Zlatko extended a glass in his direction.

"Welcome to Rome," Puccio said. "This is your first time here?"

"No," Andrei said.

"You've been here on business before?"

"Yes."

"You enjoy the city?"

"Yes."

"And I understand you speak some Korean?"

"Spent a little time there."

Puccio frowned. "You don't talk so much."

"No."

Zlatko chuckled softly as he filled Andrei's glass with Sangiovese. "Our friend is not here to give speeches," he observed.

That much was certainly true. Andrei, a recently retired Delta Force trooper, was not known for the lubricity of his social interactions. There had never been much need for it during the course of his military career.

Andrei was better known to his colleagues by his former Delta call-sign of *Dagger*. The son of Ukrainian emigrants, he was a native of Cleveland. Following one unhappy semester at OSU in the late 1970's, the Ohio teenager enlisted in the US Army. For the next twenty-plus years, he was all professional Army with no looking back.

In retrospect, his career path appeared to be pre-determined. Finishing basic infantry training, he volunteered to become a paratrooper. After five years in the 82nd Airborne Division, he earned a slot in the elite 75th Ranger Regiment. Then, at the ripe age of thirty-two, after an earlier failed try-out, he finally passed the grueling Selection and Assessment course conducted at Camp Dawson and Fort Bragg and was accepted into the 1st Special Forces Operational Detachment – Delta.

And there he remained, on the forward edge of military operations across the far reaches of the globe, for the remainder of his years in the Army. Admittedly, it gave him a certain perspective on life.

Andrei's - or Dagger's - time in Delta involved him in many of the unit's more significant actions. Early on, in 1993, he was sent to Somalia as part of Operation Gothic Serpent. His visit to Mogadishu culminated in the chaotic Black Hawk Down affair. It was there, during the so-called Battle of the Black Sea, that he won his first Purple Heart as the result of RPG fragmentation.

The Somali experience left him with a two-inch slash to his right cheek. Now, enjoying the more relaxed grooming standards of a civilian, the beard served to cover the scar.

Christmas Eve of 2001 found him arriving in Afghanistan as part of Operation Enduring Freedom. Hot on the heels of the 9/11 attacks, Andrei was more than willing to forego holidays in the States for an opportunity to exact what he saw as personal vengeance on the hated enemy.

As the first of many deployments into that theater, he was involved in the killing and capture of numerous HVTs, or High Value Targets, among the insurgent population. The pace of their lethal work, conducted primarily by night, was endless. Andrei unabashedly enjoyed it.

By the Spring of 2003 Andrei was an E-7, a senior NCO. He was in the midst of processing his retirement papers when the word came down that his squadron was to be part of the upcoming assault on Mesopotamia. This one was to be called Operation Iraqi Freedom.

Unwilling to let the long-awaited assault on the Saddam Hussein regime get away from him, Andrei called in favors from all quarters to get himself a piece of the game. His efforts proved out. He successfully snagged an available billet, and experienced a final, brief bit of trigger time in a hostile country.

And then it was over for him.

Or so he thought.

Unknown to Dagger, one of his former Delta commanders, JD Tucker, was now the director of JICSA. When Tucker caught word of Dagger's impending retirement through the grapevine, he reached out and invited him into the Org. Andrei accepted at once.

This was his second Org deployment overseas.

"You are aware of your role in the scenario?" Zlatko asked.

"Yes."

"Any issues?"

"No."

Nodding, Zlatko passed him a thin, pocket-sized notebook. "This contains the action plan from the Boss. Study it and see if you have any questions."

Dagger briefly thumbed through the notebook and pocketed it without any further comment. "Okay. That's it for now?" he asked.

"Yes," Zlatko said.

"We'll be in touch then," he said.

Dagger took another drink of the red wine. He nodded to each of his tablemates and disappeared out into the driving rain once again.

"Well," Puccio said, watching the now empty doorway drift closed against the wind. "I guess I can go and enjoy my dinner after all."

"And go with God," Zlatko told him, reaching for the bottle to refill his glass.

THIRTY-SEVEN: EXERCISING THE OPTION

Chongsong, North Korea
October 16, 2003

It was an uneventful final Thursday evening in North Korea. At least, so far.

Darkness was quickly enveloping the frosty border area that divided the Democratic People's Republic of Korea from the People's Republic of China.

From his vantage point in the Korean tree line, Seok dropped to a prone position and peered through his night vision lenses. He took several long minutes to carefully scope out the dimming landscape before him.

The terrain consisted of two slices of unexceptional land, separated by the thin strip of the north-south waterway that was the Tumen River. A thin crust of fresh snow blanketed the area. Hopefully, he prayed, the path to salvation was waiting for them on the far shore of the river.

If salvation awaited them there, it would only be taking the form of the American that he knew as Tim (aka Bear) and the *hwagyo* they knew as Lao Gao.

In the expanse behind him was the shoddy North Korean border town of Chongsong. Had the place been notable to the outside world for anything, it would have been for its location as a horrific prisoner of war camp during the Korean War.

Nothing further from salvation was waiting for them in Chongsong. That much he knew for sure.

Further back in the woods, safely concealed under the cover of the trees, Jina was outfitting Nari for what would surely be a frigid river crossing in the best of circumstances. Using supplies that had been secreted under the seats of the UAZ vehicle, all three of them were now wearing thermal wetsuits under their clothing. Jina was in the process of affixing Nari with a floatation vest, despite the fact that this point of the river was specifically chosen for its narrow and shallow features.

Three days earlier, the initial and preferred extraction attempt on the southwest coast had dramatically failed, thanks to the coastal shootout resulting in the death of Chol and the subsequent execution of the taxi driver and the North Korean security agents. As per the contingency plan, Seok had taken control of the mission and diverted their path of travel away from the coast and the DMZ.

This was to be the attempt at the Org's least preferred exit route: Option C, i.e., traveling in a north-easterly direction and crossing back into China from whence they had originally come.

Check that, he thought. The *least preferred* option would have been the proverbial 'go to hell' plan that involved hiking over to the east coast and awaiting an unspecified maritime pick-up.

Pushing forward along the roadways, the team hit a number of expected security checkpoints. At each, the police were appropriately respectful both at the sight of the UAZ vehicle markings and Seok's imposing State Security credentials.

Also at every checkpoint, Seok conveyed the cover story that he was transporting the two young women in his vehicle northward with the intent they be sold as brides across the border to wealthy Chinese merchants. This was not an unheard-of transaction by any means. North Korean women were highly sought after in China as wives for a variety of reasons - above board and otherwise.

In many cases the Korean women were volunteers for a hoped-for better life. In other instances, they were little better than indentured servants in a foreign land.

To ensure the compliance of the check-point police, Seok handed over a small wad of currency to bolster their meager salaries. In every case the bribe was gratefully received as they passed him along the road.

Upon reaching the outskirts of Chongsong, Seok once again linked up with Lao Gao and his North Korean brother-in-law. The latter was unhappy in the extreme to see the return of the agent team, keenly aware of the danger they presented. But by now he was irretrievably locked into the process.

As Lao Gao had previously ascertained, while there were normally two guards of the Border Security Command working in the area, only one of them regularly covered the desired crossing point. Not unusually, both were susceptible to financial incentives that would enable them to turn a blind eye to illegal activities.

The Org had foreseen this contingency and budgeted for it. Upon reaching the outskirts of Chongsong, Seok provided Lao Gao with the North Korean won equivalent of $1,200 USD for bribery purposes. It amounted to some $400 per head for each of the intended border crossers. It was more than enough.

The former ROK Marine tugged a pair of infrared goggles down over his eyes. That done, he opened his mouth wide to enhance his sense of hearing. He was straining to acquire the unwelcome sounds of a motorized patrol. If that development should befall them...

Seok peered at the face of his wristwatch. It was, he saw, past the agreed-upon time. They were now at least fifteen minutes behind schedule. Behind him, Jina knew it as well. Her preparations with Nari were complete and she was only awaiting the signal to move.

From across the river came a pair of triple infrared flashes, indicating the signal standing by.

For her part, Nari well knew she was on the verge of committing two serious crimes: illegally exiting the confines of the DPRK with the aim of defecting to the West, and illegally crossing the border of the PRC. If captured on either side of the river, her ultimate fate would not be pleasant.

Once again, her thoughts returned unbidden to the fate of her family members. Certainly, some form of revenge would be taken on them for her decision to quit the Yongbyon Center, even if they did not know she was in the company of American agents. Perhaps it already had.

She forced her mind back to the current dangers that she was facing. They were oddly less distressing.

Seok felt his stomach muscles tightening. The local area Border Security man was well and truly bribed. The question was – for how long?

Several more agonizing minutes passed without action.

At that moment, a muffled crump reverberated dully far to the south of their position. That was the work of Gao's reluctant brother-in-law. It was the noise of a small, delayed action explosive, designed to serve as a distraction.

Moving as one, all three of them rose to their feet and started loping forward to the edge of the Tumen River. Splashing into the shallows of the river, Seok and Jina each took hold of one of Nari's arms and began moving forward into the rushing waters.

They continued sloshing toward the darkness of the Chinese far shore till the water of the Tumen reached above their waists. At that point, Seok and Jina dove forward and began to swim, tugging Nari along between them – just as they had trained for at the Kilo Site.

With the frigid water burning at their exposed flesh, all were grateful for the wet suits fitting snugly under their external clothing.

Struggling against the water currents, Seok and Jina remained tense, each awaiting the feared echoes of sirens or sharp cracks of rifle shots. Neither came.

* * *

Seeing the team enter the river unobstructed, Bear lifted his infrared penlight and flashed the all-clear signal toward the river. Satisfied that Seok had received it, he then sent another burst transmission signal to the driver Liu, who with Lao Gao, was manning the transport truck. That done, he gathered up his belongings and headed down to the riverbank to briskly welcome the Org team back into China.

Next stop – the safe house in Shenyang.

THIRTY-EIGHT: ITALIAN EXTRACT

Rome, Italy
October 17, 2003

Deputy Chief of Mission Ro Jae-Ki summoned Tae to his office in the DPRK embassy shortly after lunch that Friday afternoon. At the time, the DCM was dealing with a matter of mundane importance. On the other end of the internal line was the embassy's tiresome Consul General.

The CG was carrying on about his favorite matter of complaint: the perceived lack of reciprocity on visa issues. That few Westerners ever sought a visa to enter the DPRK was lost on the dullard CG, who was himself another well-placed relative of the ruling regime back home.

Tae waited respectfully until the DCM uttered a series of sharp words for his administrative underling and slammed the phone down on its receiver.

"Sit," Ro said, glancing up with a look of irritation on his face.

"There is a problem?" Tae ventured cautiously, obediently taking a seat.

"With that idiot and his visa complaints, yes," Ro said with exasperation. "With you, no."

Tae nodded, relieved. While he waited for the DCM to jot some private notes, ostensibly composing himself, Tae rested his eyes on the familiar large portrait hanging behind Ro's desk. It was the stock image of the Dear Leader Kim Jong-Il, Marshal of the Democratic People's Republic of Korea. As with all diligent DPRK officials, Tae was wearing a small lapel pin bearing a likeness of the Dear Leader.

Tae wondered if his summons to the front office was somehow related to the sensitive matter of Kim Jong Nam, the Dear Leader's eldest son. Until recently Jong Nam had been presumably next in line to assume ultimate power in Pyongyang.

At least that was the case until Jong Nam was caught foolishly trying to enter Japan on a false Dominican passport. And of all things, he was there to visit Tokyo Disneyland. Sorely embarrassed, the senior Kim shunted him aside in favor of a younger son.

The word now was that Jong Nam had recently taken up residence in Macau - the source of much of the Supernote laundering.

"Do you have any assigned collateral duties for the rest of the day?" Ro asked at last.

"I am assisting Ky with the inventory and destruction of outdated sensitive documents this afternoon. That will take maybe two hours," Tae responded. "After that sir, nothing."

"Good."

Ro nodded in the direction of the door leading to the balcony outside of his office and motioned for him to follow. "Let's smoke," he said.

They stepped out onto the small balcony, closing the door behind them. Better than the majority of the embassy staff, they were aware of the possibility that even the DCM's office might be planted with listening devices that were beyond even their purview.

That week Ro was serving as the Charge d'Affaires, or the acting ambassador. The actual ambassador had been recalled to Pyongyang for consultations on technical issues, or so they said. In terms of the more critical matter at hand, it was so much for the better.

Once outside of the executive office and into the sunlight, Ro produced a packet of thin Italian cigars. He offered one of them to his co-conspirator and took another for himself.

The calm pond waters of the Lago dell'Eur were displayed before them. After lighting their cigars, they paused to meditate on the deceptively placid view.

"I have received important news," Ro muttered, just slightly above a whisper.

"Yes?" Tae prompted.

"The East European friends are prepared to meet with us again... They are ready to exchange for the special papers," he said. "They are meeting our terms in full."

By special papers, Ro was referring to the counterfeit Supernote bills. That the exchange would be for genuine euro notes was understood.

"When is this to happen?" Tae asked. He had already calculated his potential cut of the profits at the high end of the deal. They were substantial.

"This evening," Ro said. "You will be ready."

"Yes sir."

"Good," Ro said dismissively. "I will contact you."

Bobbing his head compliantly, Tae found his way off the balcony and back into the DCM's office. Ro stayed behind to linger in his thoughts.

Once again alone, the DCM narrowed his eyes and leaned his elbows against the railing of his balcony. He puffed contentedly on his cigar, steadying his nerves, until it was finally time to go back inside to his office.

He would miss Rome, he reflected a bit nostalgically.

* * *

What Tae had, of course, not been told was that Nardo Puccio had executed a classic brush pass with Ro Jae-Ki earlier that very morning. The pass occurred while Ro was out taking the air near the embassy grounds. The solo morning walks, establishing a new behavioral pattern, was a practice La Bella Savina had urged upon him months ago during their clandestine meetings for just such a purpose.

The DCM had recognized Puccio from their initial encounter at the *caffe bar*. As they passed each other on the sidewalk, the Italian deftly slipped a tightly folded note from his hand to the Korean's without breaking stride.

Ro expressionlessly accepted the delivery. Pocketing it unobtrusively, he casually continued along his way. Had there been any onlookers, he would have been the image of innocence itself.

When Ro had time to privately examine the note that had been palmed to him, he saw that his niece had been safely taken out of North Korea by the Americans. Consequently, it was now his time to move. Quickly.

He carefully destroyed the note.

* * *

Shortly after 2000 hours, Ro and Tae pulled out of the DPRK compound and headed southward. Their destination was known as the Catacombs of Saint Callixtus. It was situated along the ancient *Appia Antica*, or the Appian Way. The Catacombs formed the burial site of a number of martyrs and more than a dozen popes.

More to the point, it was to be the ostensible transfer point between their valise full of counterfeit $100.00 Supernotes and the East Europeans' satchel of genuine euro bills. As far as Tae knew, this was to be but the first of an ongoing series of profitable cash transfers with these new contacts. He was eagerly looking forward to the exchange.

The Catacombs, themselves a lesser-known tourist attraction, were closed for the day. Zlatko and Escobar were however already on site, awaiting the arrival of the Koreans.

Thanks to the intercession of Nardo Puccio, the Bosnians had purloined keys to the facility. These allowed them access to both the front gate as well as the primary building with its macabre underground passages. Once inside the grounds, Escobar took up his normal glowering security position at the gate while Zlatko waited deeper within the walls of the compound.

After pacing the darkened grounds for thirty minutes, Zlatko's cellphone quietly began to buzz.

"Yes?" he answered.

"They are close," said the voice on the phone. It was Puccio. "Coming to you now."

"Yes," Zlatko repeated, ending the call. He whistled to alert Escobar at the gate and dialed another quick number to pass the message along.

Within five minutes the DPRK embassy sedan appeared along the quiet roadway. It slowed briefly for passing traffic and then glided through the gate Escobar was holding open for them. Escobar tugged the gate closed behind the sedan as it entered.

Zlatko waited patiently as the sedan slowly rolled to a stop. After a pause, the doors on both sides opened and the two North Koreans exited the vehicle.

"Welcome, sir," Zlatko said to Ro. "I am happy to have the opportunity to meet you at last."

"And I you as well," Ro added, smiling amiably.

Meanwhile Tae stood in the semi-darkness absorbing his surroundings while the two exchanged pleasantries. The former commando officer did not like the vibes of the unusual circumstances.

Feeling a pang of nerves with the uncontrolled environment, he uncharacteristically blurted out a muted phrase in staccato Korean.

Escobar alerted at the unexpected outburst. Although his arms were complacently folded across his chest, his right hand was already on the butt of his shoulder-holstered revolver under his jacket.

Ro smiled understandingly, raising a hand to calm his subordinate. "He is asking – where is the money?"

Zlatko nodded with understanding. Aware of the fact that Tae had a smattering of English language ability, he said, "I might then ask - where are the Notes?"

"Right here," Ro said, gesturing. "On the back seat of our car."

"Very well," Zlatko said. "Our money is inside the building – along with the interpreter. We felt it would be even more secure in there."

Zlatko pointed a finger to the sky. "These new drone machines," he said, if by way of apology.

Ro accepted the cover story and instructed Tae to go into the building and conduct the exchange.

In response, Tae reached back into the sedan and extracted a locked valise that was packed with Supernotes. Escobar watched carefully to ensure the game did not suddenly reverse itself in its final moments.

The valise secured, Tae quietly followed Zlatko into the dank structure of the Catacombs.

Once inside the building however, Tae found not the absent interpreter Chol but the looming figure of Andrei, the Org operator who was also known as Dagger.

"You are?" Tae demanded impatiently.

"Good evening, Captain Tae," Dagger replied in heavily accented Korean. "Or it is *Major* Tae now?"

Tae stopped dead in his tracks. "You are the new contact?" he asked warily.

"I am your fate," Dagger replied flatly.

Reacting on instinct, Tae dropped the valise, preparing himself for action. As he did so, a gravity blade knife appeared in his right hand. With a flick of his wrist, a keenly honed four-inch blade snapped into the open position.

At once lurching forward, Tae slashed at his opponent from right to left, aiming for the throat.

Dagger juked backward in response. While deflecting a more serious injury, he did not escape the opening of a narrow gash across his upper chest.

Tae quickly recovered from the near miss and advanced on the American once again, this time with a thrust aimed directly toward his target's heart in a killing blow.

Relying on his past Aikido training, Dagger sidestepped the second attack while latching onto the wrist of Tae's knife hand. Simultaneously applying his free hand against the attacker's elbow, Dagger quickly spun Tae in a disorienting circular motion downward and to the right.

The North Korean, taken off balance, was slammed face-forward to the floor. Upon impact, the knife clattered away harmlessly on the ancient stones of the catacombs.

Ignoring the knife, Dagger threw himself onto Tae's back and immediately clamped both arms about the North Korean's neck and throat. The stranglehold abruptly shut off both blood and air passages – a move designed to rapidly bring about unconsciousness.

Rolling over onto his back, Dagger pulled Tae atop of him and clasped his legs over Tae's lower torso, further restricting his freedom of motion.

As expected, Tae violently resisted the effort. Fighting for air, the Korean initially attempted to slam his elbows back into Dagger's ribs. That having no effect, he weakly pounded his feet to the ground to gain leverage.

Also to no avail.

Maintaining control, Dagger closed his eyes and held onto Tae's trapped neck for several moments longer until his victim went limp. Dagger then repositioned his hands and violently snapped the bones in the North Korean's neck.

The former Reconnaissance Brigade officer was dead.

Zlatko policed up the fallen valise of Supernotes while Dagger pushed Tae's lifeless form away from him.

"My friend, you very nearly came in second this time," Zlatko observed curtly.

Dagger nodded, mopping blood from his chest wound with the loose tails of his shirt.

Outside, Escobar opened the gate to permit another vehicle to roll into the compound. This one, an Alfa Romeo SUV, was driven by Puccio. Savina was in the passenger's seat holding a short-range radio in her lap.

While the Bosnians and Dagger busied themselves with Tae's body, Puccio hustled Ro out of his sedan and into the back seat of the Alfa Romeo. Without another word, he reversed out of the compound and headed back down the road to the southeast.

Their destination was Ciampino Airport. It was just outside of the ring road autostrada that encompassed Rome. With no lack of irony, they were aware that Ciampino's international airport code was "*CIA*".

* * *

They were met in the executive parking lot of Ciampino by a local expediter. He escorted the three passengers thru the formalities in the terminal, which included the examination of a South Korean passport identifying Ro Jae-Ki as a frequent business traveler under an assumed name.

After the authorities satisfied themselves with the documents, the expediter led them out onto the tarmac where a sleek Gulfstream executive jet awaited them.

The South African co-pilot welcomed the three of them aboard. He secured the door while motioning them to their seats. Already the plane was in motion, taxiing out toward the central runway.

Their pilot, a Canadian national, already had the course dialed in. Minus refueling stops, their final destination was IAD - Dulles International Airport in Fairfax County Virginia.

THIRTY-NINE: ERBAN

Beijing, China
October 22, 2003

It was an unusually bright day in Beijing. The sky was sunny and blue, as opposed to the frequently smoggy gray overcast conditions. Nari squinted her eyes as she continued to put one foot in front of the other, propelling herself toward the inevitable. Outwardly, it was a seemingly simple task.

Nevertheless, to say she was feeling anxious would be putting it mildly. To say she was struggling to maintain control of her inner terror would have been far more accurate.

For the first time in this deadly escapade, Nari would be completely alone and directly confronting an official of the Chinese Government. This would be someone who could initiate the process of returning her back to North Korea and whatever panoply of horrors that might await her there.

Nari was walking down the sidewalk of the busy Guanghua Road at what she hoped was a normal, non-attention gathering, pace. It was mid-morning - a regular time for Consulate business at the American Embassy in Beijing.

Chalice and Lao Gao had just driven her to the eastern outskirts of Ritan Park, several blocks from the American Embassy. There they released her.

"Okay. You know what to do?" Chalice asked one last time before opening the door.

"Yes."

"Good," he smiled confidently, gently touching her hand with his fingertips. "See you in America."

"Yes. Okay."

Her destination was called *ErBan* - literally the Second Compound of the American Embassy. It held the busy Consulate and a variety of administrative support offices.

Across a narrow street from ErBan was *SanBan*, or the Third Compound. That was the nerve center of the Embassy, containing the Ambassador's office and all the sections involved with Political, Economic, Military, Security and other sensitive activities.

The final section, several blocks away to the east, was *YiBan*, or the First Compound. On YiBan was found the Ambassador's official residence, the medical unit and the public affairs section.

Nari kept walking. Not far ahead of her, at the intersection of Guanghua Road and Xiushui East Street, she was guaranteed to come face to face with one of the green uniformed members of the PAP - the People's Armed Police.

The PAP was a Chinese paramilitary organization. It was charged with widely diverse duties ranging from riot control, to border protection and the security of forests and gold mines. More to the point, they also maintained physical control of the external perimeters of foreign embassies and consulates throughout China.

Despite their ostensible protective mission, they were on site primarily to monitor those entering and exiting the grounds of the US Embassy.

And there at the far corner, as predicted, was the lone, stolid figure of the PAP soldier. For all his power, he looked so young, she thought. And so thin. Almost like a North Korean himself.

"Let your nerves work for you," Chalice had advised while preparing her for this pivotal step.

"It wouldn't be unusual for even a totally innocent Chinese national to display some uneasiness when confronting an authority figure like the PAP," he said. "Just go with it."

Swallowing her fear, she stepped forward to address the sentry.

* * *

Although it felt like ages, it had been less than a week since Nari's rescuers had spirited her out of the Democratic Peoples' Republic of Korea. The journey had been the most traumatic experience of her life to date. She vividly recalled anticipating the wail of sirens or the impact of bullets in her back as they pulled her across the frigid river waters. Thankfully, none came.

Once on the other side of the river, a large blond American man met the team and spirited them back into the concealment of the tree line. He was known to the Korean team as Tim. A minimum of words was spoken, and even those few were expressed in hushed, hurried tones.

As soon as they were out of sight of the river, the American - Bear - draped a woolen blanket around Nari's sopping wet shoulders. "Welcome to China," he whispered. "This is your first step into freedom."

At that point, the fact that Chol was missing became a reality to Bear. It confirmed the identity of the lost agent as the Org already suspected. For Bear, it also dredged up old memories of lost teammates from other conflicts.

Nodding to Seok and Jina, Bear had led them on a short and slippery jaunt down the reverse slope of the hill until they reached a concealed holding area where a panel truck was awaiting them. In the rear of the vehicle they found dry coats and changes of clothing. Once again, the truck was manned by Lao Gao and the able Mr. Liu.

Bear accompanied the Koreans in the cargo compartment of the truck as it cautiously made its way away from the border area and back to the city of Shenyang, the capital of Liaoning Province. The journey, though fraught with worry, was uneventful.

Chalice had been waiting in the safe house to greet them. By the time Nari set eyes upon this new Westerner, she was too exhausted to react with any additional fear or politeness. There was little left to do but sleep. And sleep heavily she did.

* * *

The next day, the four core members of the Org team, the two Americans and the two South Koreans - along with their prized defector - gathered to partake in a late morning breakfast that was jointly prepared in the safe house. The meal was consumed with very little conversation.

After eating, the dishes were cleared, washed and stored away, purposefully establishing some sense of normality in their highly abnormal surroundings. Those mundane tasks completed, Chalice gathered them around a small table to discuss the remainder of the exfiltration plan.

A map of the Shenyang municipality was spread out on the table top. Cups of hot tea were distributed all around.

"So here we are," Chalice quietly intoned, once all were settled back down again. "We've made good progress, but we're not out of the woods yet."

"Not out of the woods," Jina repeated softly, savoring the American phrase.

"Yes. But first, let me say how sorry we are for the loss of Chol," Chalice said. "He..."

"He knew the risks," Seok interrupted calmly. "We all know the risks."

Bear and Chalice exchanged glances.

"Chol was a brave man. And now he is gone. We can't change that," Bear observed. "But there are still more risks to get past. For everyone involved."

Jina kept her eyes downcast and said nothing.

Nodding agreement, Chalice turned his attention to Nari. "I know you are wondering what comes next," he said.

Nari sat mute.

"You are now out of North Korea," Chalice told her. "But we still need to get you out of China and back to America. Only then will you be safe."

"I thank you for all of this," Nari ventured. "And I am sorry for the death of the man at the coast..."

"Not your fault," Chalice assured her.

"Thank you all again," she said. "But from here...?"

Chalice sipped at his tea. "There are several possible ways out," he began. "One would be a lengthy trek from right here to leave from the coast of the Sea of Japan. But that would be fairly difficult at this point. Not the least of which would be the need to cross Russian territory in order to hit the coast...

"Or going down to Liaodong Bay," he placed the point of a pen on the blue portion of the map to their southwest. "And we have no assets in either place to assist."

"Another proven route," Bear chimed in, "would be overland. Either traveling up north and into Mongolia or going all the way down south to the Burmese border."

"But that would entail a lot of across the road exposure for all of us," Chalice added shaking his head. "Too risky."

Chalice again pointed at the Shenyang map on the table before them. "The most obvious choice would be to try and smuggle you into the American Consulate right here in Shenyang.

"That is located there," he said, tapping at a point on the map. "Just north of the waterway. It's situated next to the South Korean and Japanese Consulates as well."

Picking up on the thread, Bear added, "Close, but also a problem," he sighed. "The Chinese have intensified their surveillance on all three Consulates. Especially on the South Koreans, which is almost right in the backyard of ours. Apparently, the word is out that something has happened."

Nari studied the map glumly. "Then what can be done?"

Chalice paused and then gave her a half smile. "The most secure option at this point?... Let's go right to the heart of it," he said. "Beijing."

* * *

The PAP soldier's name was Xing. He was a model of correctness in his trim and tight olive drab uniform. Born in Wuhan, he was of genuine worker class parentage. Unlike some of the others.

Xing's parents were justifiably proud of their only son. Their pride was based not only of his position in the People's Armed Police, but the fact that, after only five years of service, he was trusted enough to be posted at the prestigious American Embassy in the capital.

The twenty-four-year-old Xing watched impassively as the attractive young woman approached him.

"Hello," she greeted him in acceptable Mandarin Chinese.

"Hello," he replied tightly. "Your business here today?"

Nari fumbled with the documents in the shoulder bag she was carrying. "I have an appointment here," she explained. "For a visa. A student visa. To attend graduate school in America."

Xing's teeth tightened involuntarily. This was a personal issue with him. University training in America was usually reserved for the children of the rich. Or for the children of Party nobility. Not much difference between the two, he reminded himself. But it was beyond his control.

If he were in charge however...

Nari handed the PAP a sheaf of papers that outlined her proposed applications to colleges in Virginia and North Carolina. Forged acceptance letters were included.

Xing glanced at them absently and pushed them back toward her. "Appointment slip?" he demanded.

"Oh yes," Nari, murmured. She pulled the slip out of her purse and passed it along to Xing. It documented the fact that the Org had, in fact, made a consular appointment for her days earlier.

Xing briefly scrutinized the familiar form. "Identity card?"

As if an afterthought, she dug out a forged resident identity card. Complete with photo, it described her as Xu Li, a Chinese citizen from Liaoning Province. That supposed northeastern origin also explained the Korean accented Chinese.

Xing examined the card briefly before returning it to her along with the appointment slip. "Go on," he said dismissively.

Nari's heart resumed its steady beating as Xing turned his attention to the next visa applicant. She turned the corner and started down toward the final checkpoint.

Once there she found yet another security force member. As she had been briefed however, this blue uniformed figure was a Chinese employee of the Embassy's own Local Guard Force. Knowing that Nari had already passed the external PAP screening, the LGF guard ran her and her personal belongings though the metal detector and explosives sniffer. Satisfied she presented no physical threat to the installation, he admitted her into the Consulate building.

Stepping into the busy yet orderly Consular hall, Nari finally breathed a sigh of relief. For the moment, she was technically on the soil of the United States of America.

"*Ni hao*," a seated female clerk greeted her. "Your appointment slip?"

"Yes," Nari replied in Mandarin, passing the appointment slip to her. "I am Xu Li. I also have some transcripts that must notarized for American colleges."

Hearing that, the ears of a nearby American officer perked up. Coming over the appointment desk, he took the slip from the clerk's hands. "I can take care of Miss Xu," he said. "Thanks."

"Kevin," the American said to her by way of introduction, briefly shaking Nari's hand.

In reality, a reclusive member of the Other Government Agency, Kevin had been forewarned of Nari's arrival and was given a single, simple mission. He accompanied her past the visa windows and down a short hallway by the Consular administrative offices.

Pausing at the door at the end of the hall, Kevin punched a series of numbers into a Simplex lock and opened the door.

"Up the stairs and down the hall," he told her, quietly admitting her into the American side of the building and closing the door behind her.

Nari carefully made her way up the winding staircase to the second floor. She then wandered past the financial cashier's window, finally coming to a stop before the open door of an American officer.

Inside the office, the Embassy's Senior Human Resource Officer was working at her desk. The papers in front of her dealt with applications for NSDD-38's or additions to the compliment of official Americans in the China mission.

Sensing the figure paused at her doorway the officer glanced up over the edge of her reading glasses. "Can I help you?" she asked.

The visitor hesitated nervously.

"Yes," she said. "I am a North Korean... Asylum?"

FORTY: OUTFLOW

Beijing, China
October 2003

Nari's appearance on the grounds of the US Embassy suddenly caused a great deal of commotion. The issue rapidly escalated from an Administrative and Consular issue to the level of Political and Security concerns.

Security personnel quickly determined that she posed no physical threat to the Embassy or its personnel. The international complications she did pose, however, was another matter altogether.

The US Mission quickly recognized it had a tar baby on their hands. It was not the first incident of North Korean refugees seeking asylum at western diplomatic facilities. But it was a first for the Americans.

While sympathetic to the plight of refugees, the Embassy's first inclination was, of course, to keep intruders out. Once they were in - if North Korean - however...

The Managerial, Security and Political wings of the Embassy were immediately called into action. A seldom used side room in the Bruce Building (housing the Admin offices) was cleared out and supplied with spare furniture, a small TV set and bedding from the GSO warehouse. That was to be Nari's home for the time being. Her few personal effects were taken away from her for safekeeping.

Simultaneously, the word went out that in fact no word was to go any further as to the presence of their surprise guest - who would heretofore be referred to only as the *Guest*. And no photos were to be taken of her.

A roster of available cleared Americans was drawn up who could babysit the Guest day and night, allowing her a degree of privacy so long as she remained in her assigned room. She would be escorted for the use of bathing and toilet facilities but would otherwise remain static.

The next morning an Emergency Action Committee was convened in one of the secure areas of the SanBan chancery. It was chaired by the Deputy Chief of Mission, or DCM. The management of this crisis was assigned to him by the Ambassador.

The Chinese Ministry of Foreign Affairs (MFA) had already contacted the Political office that morning to inquire into the situation with the Guest. Unsurprisingly, the cat was no longer in the bag.

* * *

Events began to follow an unexplored version of an essentially time-worn path.

On the Security side, a senior police official of the Beijing Public Security Bureau (PSB) requested a meeting with his counterpart, the Embassy's Regional Security Officer, or RSO. The RSO was a twenty-year plus veteran of the Diplomatic Security Service and was well-practiced in sparring with host country law enforcement representatives.

At lunch in the restaurant of a local hotel, the PSB official said, "You should really just turn her over to us. That would be the best solution. She will be well cared for. She will be back with her family. Then everything would go back to normal."

To which the RSO replied, "It's not quite so easy for us... We understand if we did, she would then be sent back to North Korea. And imprisoned. And maybe killed."

"Oh no," the PSB official quickly assured him with a smile. "No. That never happens. We see the same people crossing the border all the time. We arrest the same people and send them back quite often. They are very safe."

The PSB official's deputy nodded in solemn agreement.

"With all respect," the RSO responded, sipping his iced tea. "That's not what we hear."

* * *

The following day, the US Embassy's Minister Counselor for Political Affairs (or POLOFF) found himself in a familiar, well-appointed conference room at the Ministry of Foreign Affairs on *Chaoyangmen Nandajie*. His counterpart, the Director General (DG) from the MFA's America Desk was seated across the table from him. Both were accompanied by junior officers who served as note takers.

"Thank you for making the time to gather with us so quickly," the DG opened.

"It is always my pleasure to visit your beautiful Ministry building," the POLOFF replied, crossing his legs. "The tapestry and artwork are always impressive."

"Oh, it is sufficient for our needs," the DG countered, raising a hand politely. "Nothing more."

The POLOFF cleared his throat. "Your message said you had urgent business," he said, deciding to cut to the chase in a most un-Chinese fashion.

"Yes. Yes, we do," the DG said, also seemingly happy to be able to get straight to the point. "While our government, unofficially, understands the situation you are in with this, uh, visitor on your premises," the DG said, "we have other serious concerns as well."

"And those are?" the POLOFF asked, knowing the answer.

"Our colleagues from the mission of the Democratic People's Republic of Korea," the DG said. "Clearly, they want their national returned to them. At the earliest practicable time."

"I see," the POLOFF said. "But, as I'm sure you understand, she does not want to go back there. Not at all."

The DG smiled understandingly. "But she must," he said. "She simply must... It is where she belongs. And, with my apologies, that is all there is to it."

"Certainly, you must appreciate the humanitarian aspects of this situation," the POLOFF countered. "The situation for people in the DPRK is by no means as good as it is here in the PRC."

"She must go back," the DG reiterated.

Suspecting this tact, the POLOFF paused, making a show of producing a small notebook from his coat pocket. He opened the notebook and appeared to examine its contents in great detail.

The POLOFF exchanged mumbled remarks back and forth with his note taker. Finally, he returned his attention to the DG. "As you well know, we are working on a full Presidential visit to China in roughly three months' time. Beijing and Shanghai. Yes?"

"Of course, yes," the DG replied.

Of course. And the POLOFF knew the prestige of the Chinese government was highly invested in the success of this well-publicized visit.

"This guest of ours is a minor issue," the POLOFF said with a sigh of exasperation and a wave of his fingertips. "Really of no concern to either party... Certainly not to me.

"But now," he continued in a more serious tone, "as you see, the honor of the United States has been involuntarily caught up in this matter."

"We understand," the DG replied. "Completely."

The POLOFF closed his notebook and slipped it back into his suit jacket pocket. "We realize the problem is presented by Pyongyang, not you. But if Beijing amplifies the issue, I am told the Presidential visit may have to be postponed... Indefinitely."

There was a moment of silence in the room as the implications of this statement were digested on the Chinese side.

"I do see," the DG replied, frowning. "That would be... Unfortunate. Let me discuss this with my colleagues on the DPRK side and we will consult again."

"Of course," the POLOFF assured him.

* * *

Four days later the POLOFF and the DG met again at the MFA headquarters.

"I have very good news," the DG brightly announced as tea and cakes were being served. "Our DPRK colleagues are willing to consider the matter further."

"I am very glad to hear that," the POLOFF said. "Thank you for your efforts on our behalf."

"But," the DG said, "they must first assure themselves that she is doing this of her own free will. And not that she is being held by the Americans by force."

The DG waved that thought away dismissively. "Not that *we* believe this to be the case. But you understand their concerns."

"Of course." The POLOFF said. "What are the details?"

"The DPRK side," he said, "would like to interview her in two days' time. At their embassy. As you of course know, it is not very far from your own. Very easy to do."

The POLOFF maintained a practiced, unexpressive countenance.

Out. Of. Their. Fucking. Minds.

That is what the POLOFF was thinking. But what he said was, "That would be inconvenient. From our side.... The young lady is under the protection of the United States Government. You understand this."

The DG's smile faded away in clear, or feigned, disappointment. "But then how to resolve this?" he asked. "The situation cannot be allowed to persist forever."

"Let them come to our embassy," the POLOFF said. "The DPRK side can speak with her there. If she chooses to leave with them, we will not stand in the way."

The DG pretended to ponder this new proposal deeply.

"Very well," he said at last. "A delegation of DPRK officers may be able to come to your embassy to interview her. I will have to present this to them."

"Not a delegation," the POLOFF countered. "One officer. Of any rank. With an aide, if they wish. At our embassy at a time and date of their choosing."

The DG was downcast. "You are being difficult my old friend, but *hao de* - good. We will try to arrange this with our DPRK colleagues."

"Thank you, my good friend," the POLOFF smiled. "You have our confidence."

* * *

Three days later a black sedan with North Korean diplomatic plates appeared at the American Embassy. It was waived through the usual security screening protocol as a show of respect. It slowly cruised down XiuShui Street, past SanBan, and turned left though an open gate and onto the grounds of the ErBan complex.

Nothing happened for nearly a full minute after the vehicle came to a full stop. At last, the right rear door was opened and a grim-faced First Secretary of the DPRK mission exited the car with a massive show of offended dignity. An interpreter/note taker exited via the left rear door of the sedan.

They were met by a mid-level Foreign Service Officer from the Political Section named Levy and escorted into a conference room in the Bruce Building.

The three men settled on opposite sides of a plain wooden table in the bare room. There was no tea, no cakes, no water. Only Nari, aka "Xu Li", was waiting for them.

But she no longer resembled Hwa Nari. Kevin, the OGA officer who first met her in the Consulate, had arranged for a disguise artist to be flown in from Tokyo. The technician was able to outfit her in such a manner that her appearance was subtly, but definitively, altered.

The pivotal meeting was brief and unpleasant. It established that Nari was (falsely) who she claimed to be, that she fled North Korea for want of a better life, and that she did not wish to go back. She wished to go to the United States.

The meeting continued for thirty combative minutes until the First Secretary declared himself to be unsatisfied and stormed back out to his sedan.

Despite the expected unhappiness of the North Koreans, the decision of their senior partner, the Peoples Republic of China, was that Xu Li was permitted to leave the country. Her departure was premised on the understanding that she would travel to the United States only, and not to the puppet regime of South Korea. The American side readily agreed.

Within the week, Nari (still in her OGA disguise) was escorted to Beijing Capital Airport by the RSO, the DCM, an expediter and FSO Mark Levy. Levy was to accompany her on the flight to the United States.

Despite time allowed for a last-minute arrival at the gate, the flight was briefly postponed for mechanical reasons. Following an anxious forty-five minutes of waiting in a departure lounge, Nari and Levy boarded the plane without complications and went wheels-up.

FORTY-ONE: NAME OF THAT TUNE

San Francisco International Airport
San Mateo County, California
November 2003

Special Agent Zeigler waited at the gate as patiently as possible. This was one of three VIP meet and assist taskings he had to conduct that very afternoon. And this particular flight had already been twenty minutes late in arriving. He anxiously glanced at his wristwatch for the third time in two minutes.

The flight from Beijing had just pulled up to the gate. Even from inside the busy terminal, one could hear the engines of the massive airplane wearily winding down from their non-stop flight across the Pacific Ocean.

A uniformed officer from the Airport Bureau of the San Francisco Police was standing next to Zeigler, thumbs tucked absently into his gun-belt. He did not share the other's impatience. He really had nowhere else to be for the next few hours.

After another handful of minutes, there was a flurry of commotion at the VIP exit. "Here we go," Zeigler told his uniformed partner.

"Okay."

A gate agent from the airlines emerged from the jet-way carrying a sheaf of paperwork. Behind her was a disheveled, tired looking Caucasian man with rimless glasses and whispy blond beard. Right beside him was a young Asian woman who appeared to be equally exhausted.

Zeigler approached the man directly. "Mr. Levy?" he asked.

"I'm Mark Levy," the other answered. "State Department."

Zeigler displayed a set of leather-bound credentials with a gold badge. "My name's Zeigler," he said. "I'm an agent with the DS San Francisco Field Office."

"Good to see you," Levy replied, offering his hand. "You have someone for us to meet?"

"That I do, sir," Zeigler said. "Follow us please."

With the uniformed officer leading the way, Zeigler escorted Levy and Nari to a nearby first-class club lounge.

Inside the lounge a party of four awaited to receive the new arrivals: Chalice, Bear, Jina and Seok. Recognizing the familiar faces, Nari was immediately energized. She embraced to two Koreans gratefully and exchanged a quick patter of greetings with them.

Next, she shook hands with Chalice and Bear with a bit more reservation.

"Welcome to America," Chalice said.

"Yes!" Nari gushed in relief. "Thank you. Thank you all for getting me to this place."

"Everything good here?" Zeigler asked.

"I think we're good," Chalice said. "Mr. Levy?"

The FSO gave Nari a brief, brotherly hug and patted her on the shoulder. "We're good," he said to Chalice.

Turning back to Nari, Levy added, "You are home now. And I have some calls to make to people in Washington. Take care."

Nari smiled, tears unexpectedly springing from her eyes.

As Zeigler, Levy and the police officer departed, Nari made a few more moments of small talk with her rescue team. It was her first time in the United States and, clearly, she was struggling to adapt to the new circumstances.

"Take it slowly," Chalice advised her. "All of this is very new to you. But you're safe now. You'll get used to these surroundings."

Another trio of Americans, two men and a woman, then arose from the corner couches and approached them. It was the team of her new CIA handlers.

"Nari," Chalice said quietly. "These people will accompany you from here. They will take care of you and see to your safety and welfare."

More tears flowed uncontrollably down Nari's cheeks. "Will I see any of you again?" she asked, clinging to the final scraps of familiarity that remained in her life.

"Possibly," Chalice said, knowing he was lying to her. "Time will tell."

"Thank you again," she repeated, once more shaking hands with all four of them. She paused to embrace Jina one last time. "I am very sorry for your lost friend," she whispered.

Chol.

Jina nodded silently, tears now welling up in her own eyes. Seok looked on impassively.

The Org personnel watched silently as the CIA people led Nari to a private exit from the lounge. From there she would go down to a set of vehicles secured on the tarmac and then on to her new life.

After she left, Chalice had the two Korean agents sign and date the usual post-operational non-disclosure agreements. Bear had signed a similar document earlier that morning.

And then it was over.

Jina planned to spend a few days with relatives in Los Angeles, while Seok was going to catch the next flight back to Seoul. They bid their farewells and exited the lounge together.

Chalice and Bear remained at the door of the lounge until their two agents split apart in the concourse to go their separate ways.

Bear sighed heavily. He was relieved the operation ended well, but reluctant to let go. "And that's the name of that tune," he finally observed, quoting a line from an old TV cop show.

"Indeed," Chalice agreed. "Indeed it is."

FORTY-TWO: RETROSPECT

Leesburg
Loudoun County, Virginia
November 26, 2003

Erik easily weaved through the thin Leesburg traffic. As usual, he was making good progress. This time of the morning was never a problem.

It was less than a half-hour from home to office. Just another reason why he enjoyed living and working in the area. He could not imagine suffering the congested commute around the McLean headquarters. Never mind DC itself.

He pulled into an available parking slot behind the Kovach Group Insurance Brokerage building. He locked the door of the silver Volvo and stepped back to admire it. The XC90 was Volvo's first SUV model and he loved it. Best of all, it still had that fabulous new-car smell.

Tomorrow was Thanksgiving and with it the promise of a long weekend. It would be the first holiday dinner with his new in-laws. That could be good or bad. Probably good, he hoped.

All had gone well with that date he had planned last year in Georgetown. In fact, they were married just the past September. She was a great catch. Smart, pretty, well-educated, and from a rich, horse-country family as well!

Life was good.

Erik approached the rear employee entrance door, punched in his code and entered the building. He greeted the actual insurance workers on the first floor and scampered up the stairs to the second floor. There he keyed his way into the workspaces where the real activity was done.

He dropped into his chair and fired up the computer, thereby accessing a variety of classified CIA work feeds. As they churned to life, he set about the business of opening his coffee cup and breakfast bag.

His new wife was already insisting on a low carb diet for both of them. Could be worse, he guessed.

Erik suppressed a frown, catching sight of Theo approaching his own opposite work station. His former office-mate, Patty, had finally retired after reluctantly putting off the decision for several months. This was her replacement.

While Patty was never really the life of the party, Theo was the stereotypical grumpy introvert who gave intel analysts a bad name across the board.

Theo reminded Erik of the old joke: How can you tell an introverted analyst from an extroverted analyst? Answer: the extroverted analyst looks at *your* shoes when he talks to you.

Funny.

"Morning Theo," he panned in a dull monotone.

"Yeah," came the response.

Yeah.

As Erik began to sip at his sweetened coffee, he immediately caught sight of a message that was specifically directed to him from the Directorate of Intelligence (DI) central repository. It included the DI version of an apology that he had been dropped from this feed for more than a month.

An apology from Headquarters? Highly unusual. But whatever.

He put down the coffee and dialed open his two-drawer Mosler safe. Consulting a worn green notebook, he saw that DI's message referenced the old Romeo/Thirty-Five/Lima virtual walk-in case. That was, he noted, last seen more than a year ago.

Coincidentally, it was around the same time he met the lady who was now his wife.

At last, Erik was able to open the DI folder. It held a number of foreign news articles, all helpfully translated into workable English. The majority were from Italian publications.

The tenor of the articles ranged from the forthright, 'just-the-facts ma'am' pieces, to the purple hues of outraged scandal. But the essence of all were of a general theme.

<u>One</u>: An international political drama was brewing in Rome. It was developing in the shadows of the Vatican itself.

<u>Two</u>: The deteriorating body of a North Korean diplomat had been fished out of the Tiber River. He had been identified as Tae Soon, a member of the DPRK Defense Attaché's office. Given the unspecified injuries found on the body, suicide on the part of Signore Tae had been definitively ruled out by Italian forensic authorities.

<u>Three</u>: A high-ranking DPRK diplomat, Ro Jae-Ki by name, was now missing. It was unknown as to whether he was complicit in the presumed murder of Signore Tae or was himself a victim of foul play.

<u>Four</u>: Allegations of drug smuggling activities via DPRK diplomatic pouches have surfaced in the news from several anonymous sources.

<u>Five</u>: Pyongyang vehemently denounced any allegations of malfeasance on the part of their diplomatic staff. They are protesting the criminal action and attributing it to "*black matters*" on behalf of Western special services.

<u>Six</u>: The DPRK ambassador to Rome has been replaced due to ill health.

<u>Seven</u>: The Commanding General of the Italian Carabinieri announced that no stone will be left unturned until the truth of this sordid matter has been revealed to the public.

<u>Eight</u>: A coalition of Italian atheists has declared they have incontrovertible proof that the Vatican Curia is itself behind this crime.

<u>Nine</u>: The United States Embassy (Rome) had no comment.

"Wow!" Erik exclaimed, causing Theo to peer at his cubicle wall irritably. "I imagine the Boss will want to see this."

He punched the print button and went to fetch it.

FORTY-THREE: THE 'BURGH

Market Square
Pittsburgh, Pennsylvania
January 28, 2004

Chalice doffed his blue woolen watch cap, shrugged out of his jacket and eased into the confines of a wooden booth across from his two hosts. He was there to join them for supper. They were in a popular eatery on Market Square in the Downtown district.

"Just in time," Bear announced. "Here come the drinks." He leaned back to allow the server to deposit two frosty mugs of beer and a chilled glass of white wine on the tabletop between them.

"Timing is everything," Chalice said.

"That's what I hear."

"You must be Kelly," he offered, shaking the hand of the diminutive blonde woman at Bear's side.

"I am," she smiled.

"She is," Bear affirmed socially. He clinked his glass against the other two. "We're all friends here and I'm thirsty... Here's at 'ya."

Kelly took a tentative sip of her wine and nodded agreeably.

"Not too bad," Chalice observed, sampling the beer. "This is the local brew that you keep talking about?"

"You got it... Iron City Beer." Coming from Bear though, it sounded more like '*Ourn City*' Beer.

"Good to finally meet you, Mister ah..." Kelly began.

"Chalice," he said. "Just that. Good to meet you as well. Thanks for putting up with the Big Guy's absences from home. It was a great help to us."

Bear had told her they would be having dinner with an old Army buddy and occasional business partner. That was truthful enough, as far as it went.

"Wish I could have gone along on one of the trips," Kelly sighed. "I've always wanted to see Italy. And, despite what Bear says, I'm sure you guys had enough free time between all of that bodyguard training to see some of the sights."

"Well, you know," Chalice demurred. "Business..."

"Speaking of business," Bear quickly interjected. "How are the clients doing these days? Everyone happy?"

"Yes. Happy. All satisfied customers."

Chalice knew Nari was now out in California. She was beginning an intensive technical debriefing program. Her American team of interlocutors was largely comprised of the people with the fifty-pound brains from the Lawrence Livermore Labs. They were reinforced with a few of the Agency's own Science and Technology types.

Her uncle, Ro Jae-Ki, was on the other side of the country. At least temporarily sheltered amidst the Korean community in Annandale, Virginia, he was embarking on his own series of lengthy political and intelligence debriefings. At some unspecified future date, he would be relocated elsewhere in the country with a new identity and a fresh background.

As to the fate of their families left behind in the DPRK, Chalice had no knowledge, but it could not be good. The likelihood of what befell them nagged at Chalice in the quiet moments. He consoled himself with the fact that the protection of the relatives in North Korea - an impossibility in any case - was never part of the mission profile.

Bear had no need to know any of these specifics. Nor would he ever presume to ask.

"You ever get a chance to visit the Fort Pitt Blockhouse today at last?" the former SOG soldier asked, changing the subject.

"Yeah, I did," Chalice said. "Went into that museum they have there at the Point as well." He paused for another mouthful of beer. "Interesting. Had no idea that the French and Indian War was such a factor around these parts."

"I guess there's nowhere really peaceful - if you dig into the past far enough," Bear mused.

Chalice took a moment to admire the bright, multi-colored Murano Glass medallion Kelly was wearing over her sweater. "That's a very attractive design," he said, as if seeing it for the first time. "It really brings out your natural coloring."

"Well thank you," she beamed. "Aren't you a sweetheart... Bear found it for me in Italy."

"Good eye, Bear!" Chalice enthused. In reality, he knew that the piece had been procured for her by one Nardo Puccio, along with a few other keepsakes, on Bear's behalf. That commission was accomplished while the former narc was arranging the reception team for the Koreans in faraway China.

Chalice noted a modest diamond ring on Kelly's finger as well. Puccio had nothing to do with that.

The waiter came back, quickly took their orders, and wafted away again.

"You catch that news on Iraq today?" Bear asked.

Chalice had. By coincidence, that very morning David Kay, head of the Iraq Survey Group, appeared in front of a US Senate committee in Washington. Kay's message was that the epic hunt for weapons of mass destruction in Iraq had been based on faulty intelligence. Despite their best efforts, no WMD had been found.

Nevertheless, Kay assured the Senators the failure did not mean Saddam had not been a dangerous foe – not the least exemplified by his willingness to gas his own citizenry when the need presented itself.

"All that effort," Bear reflected flatly. "That's just some amazing, uh...," he paused to cast a sidelong glance at Kelly, "stuff."

Forty-some days earlier, American troops had unceremoniously pulled President Saddam Hussein out of his hidey hole. He had been found on a farm in Ad-Dawr, not far from his hometown of Tikrit.

Chalice shrugged. He had nothing uplifting to add. He knew the classified traffic coming out of Baghdad was not good. No point in sharing that dour news tonight.

At last the waiter returned carrying a platter loaded with three huge sandwiches. He spread them out on the table and ensured their drinks were in order. Satisfied, he moved on to the next group of customers.

Chalice peered into his sandwich with a shred of disbelief. "French fried potatoes *inside* the sandwich?" he murmured. "Really?"

"Anyone visiting the 'Burgh has to have a Primanti's sandwich," Bear declared, latching onto his own with both hands. "City ordinance. Or should be."

At that, the three of them invested themselves in their dinners. Kelly was the more delicate in devouring her meal. Bear and Chalice were much less so.

As the dinner finished, the main point of the meeting was at hand - from the perspective of the Org.

"Bear. I was wondering. Any likelihood of accepting future consultancies with us?" Chalice explored in a casual tone of voice. "Just asking."

Bear paused, and then shook his head. "No," he reluctantly admitted. "I'm over it... My little security business here is going pretty well. And more to the point, Kelly and I have decided to get married."

"I see that," Chalice said, gesturing at the diamond ring. "Congratulations to you both."

"Thanks. We're not getting any younger," Kelly observed. "None of us."

"Besides," Bear continued, "I think I've used up all of my Nine Lives."

"At the very least," Chalice agreed. "Maybe ten or eleven lives by now."

In fact, Bear had once nearly lost one of them less than two blocks from where they were sitting. It occurred late one humid summer night in the early days of his undercover career with the County Police. He was in the midst of an open-air buy/bust deal when the edgy suspect abruptly pushed a gun into his face and pulled the trigger.

Luckily the weapon, a cheap Saturday night special, misfired. Bear's covering team quickly moved in and, along with him, administered an immediate dose of street justice on the would-be cop killer. After that, the suspect was arrested and transported to the ER at Mercy Hospital where the staff attended to his injuries.

That was then.

Dinner over, Chalice reached for the check but Bear was faster. "My treat, brother," he said with a smile. "Came into a little extra money lately."

Nodding, Chalice clambered to his feet and slipped into his jacket. "Thanks," he said, gripping Bear's hand tightly. "Thank you for *everything*."

"My pleasure," Bear replied, lightly punching him on the arm. "Always has been."

Chalice stepped back outside alone, pulling on his cap. As he zipped his jacket and turned up his collar against the cold air, he caught sight of the lights of Grandview Avenue twinkling across the river on Mount Washington.

Beneath the lights, the sturdy little Duquesne Incline was continuing its never-ending slog up the hill. He paused for another moment to appreciate the view. The 'Burgh, he reflected.

He figured he would get a nightcap at the hotel bar and then turn in. He had an early flight to catch tomorrow.

As he started walking, the cellphone in his pocket began to thrum quietly. He stopped and flipped it open.

It was a text message from the 412 area code. Had to be Bear.

Squinting at the illuminated screen he read:

DON'T LOSE MY # BRO
JUST N CASE
-B-

Chalice smiled knowingly to himself, pocketed the phone, and continued on into the darkness.

-The End-

POSTSCRIPT

As of the moment (Winter of 2018), North Korea is existing under the third generation of Kim Family rulers. The founder, Kim Il Sung, was selected and emplaced by the Soviet Union in 1948 following the close of WWII. His installation was replete with an elaborately contrived version of his alleged heroic war-time escapades.

It was he who developed the Juche theory of nationalist self-sufficiency which essentially supplanted traditional Communist theory. It remains the prevailing ideology today.

His eldest son, Kim Jong Il, assumed power in 1994 following the Great Leader's death. He became known for his high living and elaborate spending habits in the face of deprivations and starvation.

The supposed product of a mythological mountaintop birth (but in reality, delivered in a Soviet village), Jong Il also proved to be interested in such diverse topics as expensive cognac, foreign films and the acquisition of nuclear weapons.

Seventeen years later he was succeeded by his son, Kim Jong Un. The latter quickly gained a reputation for his willingness to execute numerous members of DPRK officialdom, to include several of his own relatives. His methods of execution varied from the more prosaic poisonings and firing squads to the more exotic, such as death by an exploding mortar round, a flamethrower and anti-aircraft gun. There was even a report that a pack of hungry dogs was employed to dispatch a troublesome uncle. More likely, the uncle was just shot.

What is known is that Kim Jong Nam, his older half-sibling - and one-time potential heir to the DPRK throne - was murdered in the Kuala Lumpur airport while awaiting a return flight to his home in Macau. He was assassinated via direct application of the nerve agent VX. Though as yet unproven, investigators are looking at Jong Un as the likely perpetrator.

Meanwhile the North Korean nuclear capacity is growing. So far, they have succeeded with six detonations taking place between October 2006 and September 2017. Their current focus is on long range missile and submarine borne warheads. They show no indication of losing interest in the project. Like it or not, they are now a member of the Nuclear Club.

Recognizing the plight of the people of North Korea, the US Congress passed the North Korean Human Rights Act (NKHRA). The Act provided for human rights and democracy support, radio broadcasts into North Korea, assistance to external groups, and a Special Envoy for North Korean human rights.

From the purview of American diplomatic establishments abroad however, the most significant feature of the Act was that it obliged them to admit any North Korean refugees who made it to their doorsteps in much the same way as Cuban refugees were treated upon arriving on Miami Beach.

Although this story is largely set in 2003, the NKHRA was actually passed into law in 2004. It was reauthorized in 2008 and again in 2012 - extending it to 2017.

The North Korean regime is now facing increasing resistance from the governments of the United States, Japan and South Korea - coupled with possibly decreased enthusiasm on behalf of the Chinese.

Whether the Kim Family Business will progress into a fourth iteration remains to be seen. The continuation of the regime is by no means a certainly.

Printed in the USA
CPSIA information can be obtained
at www.ICGtesting.com
LVHW092046270923
759264LV00002B/199

9 781506 900377